NETWORK+ CERTIFICATION STUDY SYSTEM

NETWORK+ CERTIFICATION STUDY SYSTEM

Joseph J. Byrne

® IDG Books Worldwide, Inc
An International Data Group Company
Foster City, CA • Chicago, IL • Indianapolis, IN • New York, NY

**IDG
BOOKS**
WORLDWIDE

Network+ Certification Study System

Published by

IDG Books Worldwide, Inc.

An International Data Group Company

919 E. Hillsdale Blvd., Suite 400

Foster City, CA 94404

www.idgbooks.com (IDG Books Worldwide Web site)

Library of Congress Catalog Card No.: 99-63695

ISBN: 0-7645-3344-4

Printed in the United States of America

10 9 8 7 6 5 4 3 2 1

1B/RX/QW/ZZ/FC

Distributed in the United States by IDG Books Worldwide, Inc.

Distributed by CDG Books Canada Inc. for Canada; by Transworld Publishers Limited in the United Kingdom; by IDG Norge Books for Norway; by IDG Sweden Books for Sweden; by IDG Books Australia Publishing Corporation Pty. Ltd. for Australia and New Zealand; by TransQuest Publishers Pte Ltd. for Singapore, Malaysia, Thailand, Indonesia, and Hong Kong; by Gotop Information Inc. for Taiwan; by ICG Muse, Inc. for Japan; by Norma Comunicaciones S.A. for Colombia; by Intersoft for South Africa; by Le Monde en Tique for France; by International Thomson Publishing for Germany, Austria and Switzerland; by Distribuidora Cuspide for Argentina; by Livraria Cultura for Brazil; by Ediciones ZETA S.C.R. Ltda. for Peru; by WS Computer Publishing Corporation, Inc., for the Philippines; by Contemporanea de Ediciones for Venezuela; by Express Computer Distributors for the Caribbean and West Indies; by Micronesia Media Distributor, Inc. for Micronesia; by Grupo Editorial Norma S.A. for Guatemala; by Chips Computadoras S.A. de C.V. for Mexico; by Editorial Norma de Panama S.A. for Panama; by American Bookshops for Finland. Authorized Sales Agent: Anthony Rudkin Associates for the Middle East and North Africa.

For general information on IDG Books Worldwide's books in the U.S., please call our Consumer Customer Service department at 800-762-2974. For reseller information, including discounts and premium sales, please call our Reseller Customer Service department at 800-434-3422.

For information on where to purchase IDG Books Worldwide's books outside the U.S., please contact our International Sales department at 317-596-5530 or fax 317-596-5692.

For consumer information on foreign language translations, please contact our Customer Service department at 800-434-3422, fax 317-596-5692, or e-mail rights@idgbooks.com.

For information on licensing foreign or domestic rights, please phone +1-650-655-3109.

For sales inquiries and special prices for bulk quantities, please contact our Sales department at 650-655-3200 or write to the address above.

For information on using IDG Books Worldwide's books in the classroom or for ordering examination copies, please contact our Educational Sales department at 800-434-2086 or fax 317-596-5499.

For press review copies, author interviews, or other publicity information, please contact our Public Relations department at 650-655-3000 or fax 650-655-3299.

For authorization to photocopy items for corporate, personal, or educational use, please contact Copyright Clearance Center, 222 Rosewood Drive, Danvers, MA 01923, or fax 978-750-4470.

 is a registered trademark or trademark under exclusive license to IDG Books Worldwide, Inc. from International Data Group, Inc. in the United States and/or other countries.

ABOUT IDG BOOKS WORLDWIDE

Welcome to the world of IDG Books Worldwide.

IDG Books Worldwide, Inc., is a subsidiary of International Data Group, the world's largest publisher of computer-related information and the leading global provider of information services on information technology. IDG was founded more than 30 years ago by Patrick J. McGovern and now employs more than 9,000 people worldwide. IDG publishes more than 290 computer publications in over 75 countries. More than 90 million people read one or more IDG publications each month.

Launched in 1990, IDG Books Worldwide is today the #1 publisher of best-selling computer books in the United States. We are proud to have received eight awards from the Computer Press Association in recognition of editorial excellence and three from Computer Currents' First Annual Readers' Choice Awards. Our best-selling ...For Dummies® series has more than 50 million copies in print with translations in 31 languages. IDG Books Worldwide, through a joint venture with IDG's Hi-Tech Beijing, became the first U.S. publisher to publish a computer book in the People's Republic of China. In record time, IDG Books Worldwide has become the first choice for millions of readers around the world who want to learn how to better manage their businesses.

Our mission is simple: Every one of our books is designed to bring extra value and skill-building instructions to the reader. Our books are written by experts who understand and care about our readers. The knowledge base of our editorial staff comes from years of experience in publishing, education, and journalism — experience we use to produce books to carry us into the new millennium. In short, we care about books, so we attract the best people. We devote special attention to details such as audience, interior design, use of icons, and illustrations. And because we use an efficient process of authoring, editing, and desktop publishing our books electronically, we can spend more time ensuring superior content and less time on the technicalities of making books.

You can count on our commitment to deliver high-quality books at competitive prices on topics you want to read about. At IDG Books Worldwide, we continue in the IDG tradition of delivering quality for more than 30 years. You'll find no better book on a subject than one from IDG Books Worldwide.

John Kilcullen
Chairman and CEO
IDG Books Worldwide, Inc.

Steven Berkowitz
President and Publisher
IDG Books Worldwide, Inc.

Eighth Annual Computer Press Awards 1992

WINNER
Ninth Annual Computer Press Awards 1993

WINNER
Tenth Annual Computer Press Awards 1994

WINNER
Eleventh Annual Computer Press Awards 1995

CREDITS

ACQUISITIONS EDITOR
Jim Sumser

DEVELOPMENT EDITOR
Diane Puri, MCSE, MCT

TECHNICAL EDITOR
David Schueller, A+, MCP

COPY EDITOR
Lauren Kennedy

PRODUCTION
IDG Books Worldwide Production

PROOFREADING AND INDEXING
York Production Services

ABOUT THE AUTHOR

Joseph J. Byrne lives in St. Cloud, Minnesota with his wife, Debra; daughter, Danielle; and son, Steven. Mr. Byrne was born in Chicago, Illinois in 1958, and became fascinated with computers at the time of the personal computer's genesis. In 1979, soon after starting his career as a software developer, Mr. Byrne realized the importance of the personal computer and began learning about computer networking. In 1985, Mr. Byrne founded his first company, which provided PC-based network services and support, in Riverside, California. In 1995, he sold the business and took a position as a senior systems engineer with Marco Business Products, Inc. in Minnesota. During his 20 years in the Information Technology field, Mr. Byrne has achieved many industry-respected certifications. At the engineer level, Mr. Byrne has obtained Microsoft's Certified Systems Engineer (MCSE), Novell's Master Certified NetWare Engineer (MCNE), Compaq's Accredited Systems Engineer (ASE), and the Certified Network Professional (CNP) certification. He is a member of the Institute of Electricians and Electrical Engineers (IEEE) and the Institute of Network Professionals (INP). Currently he is working on his UNIX certification, and is exploring both Microsoft's and Novell's certified trainer credentials.

To my family for supporting me on this project and unselfishly sacrificing our time together so that I might realize a long-held dream

FOREWORD

If your service organization is focused on providing better customer satisfaction and improved productivity because technicians are able to troubleshoot problems more quickly, then the *Network+ Certification Study System* is an excellent practical resource for you.

Just as A+ certification reduces training costs, Network+ certification saves training time by determining technician competence in a broad range of network tasks and customer practices.

Joe Byrne's 20 years of technical experience and network expertise are captured in this book. This nonvendor, training tool assesses a technician's knowledge in configuring, installing, and troubleshooting basic PC network components.

Whether you endorse a formalized training needs/skills assessment process for technical education, or an informal self-study approach, the marketplace rewards certified and measurable technical competency. *If you can't measure it (knowledge), how can you manage it?*

Technical knowledge management is critical to your company's success. Remember that anyone whom ceases getting better, ceases being good. *Network+ Certification Study System* is your commitment to continued learning and improvement.

Gary Marsden
President, Marco Business Products, Inc.

PREFACE

Network+ Certification Study System is designed to teach entry-level PC technicians about basic computer networking components, concepts, and theories. The target audience is technicians with 12 to 18 months of PC repair experience who have obtained A+ Certification, or have the equivalent skills. *Network+ Certification Study System* takes the reader through the entire Network+ objectives blueprint with exceptional clarity, encompassing not only the core requirements, but also providing the reader with real-world applications of the skills necessary for a career in this fast-paced field. The author is a member of the Network+ exam objectives team, and presents material entirely relevant to the subject matter. The Network+ Certification program has been well received by the industry as a whole, and is sure to set minimum standards for technical people entering the PC networking field. This study system is an excellent learning and reference tool for anyone pursuing Network+ certification.

HOW THIS BOOK IS ORGANIZED

Each chapter in the book is designed to build on the previous one. At the end of each chapter, you'll find a series of multiple-choice, true/false, and fill-in-the-blank questions. If you read the chapters and answer the questions, you should be able to pass the Network+ Certification exam.

The book is divided into two parts:

Part I: Knowledge of Networking Technology

The first part of the study system defines what networking is and how it is useful in business. It covers the theories and concepts behind moving data between computers, the standards on which network designs conform, fundamental devices used to connect various components, the language PC networks speak, and how all of these items interrelate to form a working PC network. This section focuses on practical knowledge; it is the how and why portion. As any builder knows, a good structure begins with a solid foundation, and Part I gives you the tools you need to lay a strong career foundation in PC networking.

Part II: Knowledge of Networking Practices

The second part of the study system covers 33 percent of the Network+ exam material. It focuses on the *soft skills*, your ability to actually *use* the knowledge you have learned. It covers practical, hands-on material in order to prepare you for the scenario type of questions on the exam. The soft skills are just as important, if not more so, than the technical knowledge covered in Part I. A network engineer needs to know how and when to apply technology as much as he or she needs to understand the technology itself.

HOW TO USE THIS BOOK

This book can be used by individuals or as part of a classroom experience. Most important, I recommend you develop a plan of attack to complete the book and pass the exam.

First, read the "Exam Preparation Summary" section at the end of each chapter. Then go back and quickly read the chapter itself, scanning for information that helps you understand the material more completely. Go back and review the "Exam Preparation Summary" section again. Answer the Instant Assessment questions and check your answers. Review, in the chapter, the answers for each question. This may sound repetitive, but you will retain almost all of the material if you do this.

Progress through each chapter in this manner until you have completed the entire book. After you have done this, get a spiral-bound notebook, start at the beginning of the book, and write down the key points from each chapter. This reinforces your learning.

Five days before you are scheduled to take the exam, go through the notebook and quickly review everything you wrote. If you are unclear about a point, go back into the book and quickly review that section.

The day before you take the exam, review all of the material one last time before you go to bed. Don't try to cram right before you take the exam.

CD-ROM

The accompanying CD-ROM contains the following materials:

- An electronic version of this book in Adobe Acrobat format
- Adobe Acrobat Reader
- BeachFront Quizzer test simulation software
- Microsoft Internet Explorer 5.0

PREREQUISITES

Network+ Certification Study System is designed to teach the entry-level PC technician the basic components, concepts, and theories of computer networking. This book assumes that you have the following knowledge or abilities:

- You are a PC technician with 12 to 18 months of PC repair experience.
- You have obtained A+ Certification, or have equivalent skills.
- You desire to become Network+ certified. (The book can provide you the knowledge, but only you can provide the desire to learn.)

HARDWARE AND SOFTWARE YOU'LL NEED

You will need access to a variety of hardware and software to complete many of the examples presented in this book. While it is not mandatory that you set up a home network, history shows that hands-on experience is almost essential in mastering the knowledge required to pass the exam. If you don't have the specific hardware listed, feel free to substitute where appropriate.

Hardware Requirements

The minimum hardware requirements are as follows:

- A minimum of two Intel-based computers with 486/66 processors or higher, 16MB RAM, 100MB of available hard disk space on one PC, and 500MB available on the other so it may act as the server
- A Network Interface Card in each PC
- A four-port Ethernet hub
- Two, five-foot Category 5 STP patch cables
- A VGA monitor and a graphics card

   Optional hardware includes the following:

- An additional computer
- A printer
- A modem and an Internet connection

Software Requirements

Appendix B lists Internet sites where you can download trial versions of the network operating systems. The minimum software requirements are as follows:

- Microsoft Windows 95 on one PC
- Microsoft Windows NT Server for the second PC
- Novell NetWare Version 4.11 or higher

ICONS USED IN THIS BOOK

Several different icons used throughout this book draw your attention to matters that deserve a closer look:

 caution

Be careful here! This icon points out information that can save you a lot of grief. It's often easier to prevent tragedy than to fix it afterward.

This icon directs you to another place in this book (or to another resource) for more coverage on a given topic.

 This icon identifies important advice in relation to the Network+ Certification exam.

 This icon draws your attention to the author's real-world experience, and shares information intended to help you on the job and on the Network+ exam.

 This icon points out an interesting or helpful fact, or another comment that deserves emphasis.

 This icons offers a little piece of friendly advice, a shortcut, or a bit of personal experience that may be of use to you.

ACKNOWLEDGMENTS

Putting together a book is a huge undertaking that requires many individuals, working many long and hard hours. Several very important people were essential to the completion of this book. I'd like to take a minute and recognize some of these people personally for their help.

To David Schueller for your work and diligence as my technical editor, and for adding many excellent points and examples, as well as verifying many of the detailed facts. To Mike Welling, Wayne Gamradt, Terri Gill, Dick Deal-Hanson and the many talented engineers who work with me at Marco Business Products, you have all contributed ideas and technical details for this book in one way or another.

The IDG Books Worldwide team has been super to work with, especially acquisitions editor, Jim Sumser; development editor, Diane Puri; and copy editor, Lauren Kennedy. I thank you for countless hours spent reviewing chapters and helping me through the publishing process. All of these people helped make the final product a well-polished one. And thanks to the production team for their efforts.

CONTENTS AT A GLANCE

CONTENTS

Knowledge of Networking Technology

Welcome to *Network+ Certification Study System*. Based on the tremendous success of the A+ Certification program, CompTIA (the Computing Technology Industry Association) has introduced the Network+ Certification program. This non-vendor specific certification is targeted at PC technicians with 18 to 24 months of experience who are either A+ certified or have the equivalent knowledge.

This book is designed to give you the knowledge you need to successfully enter the networking field and to pass the Network+ exam. As a subject matter expert (SME) participant in the development of the Network+ program objectives, I am able to bring you valuable insight into the exam topics and help you achieve certification.

This book is divided into two distinct parts followed by the Network+ exam blueprint. The first section covers the necessary aspect of basic PC network technologies and corresponds directly to the Network+ Knowledge of Networking Technology section of the exam. In this part, I define networking and how it is useful in business. I discuss the theories and concepts of moving data between computers, the standards on which network designs conform, fundamental devices used to connect various components, the languages PC networks use, and how all of this interrelates to form a working PC network. You can think of this section as the practical knowledge, the how and why, portion. As any builder knows, a good structure begins with a solid foundation, and Part I gives you the tools you need to lay a strong career foundation in PC networking.

N+

The Basics of Networking Technologies

About Chapter 1

This chapter introduces the fundamental concepts of PC networking and some of the vocabulary commonly used in this field. I begin by defining some common terms used in the industry, and then take a look at the basic components used to connect PCs into a network. I discuss both hardware devices, and the network operating system (NOS) software. Once I've covered essential concepts, I present an overview of how data is transmitted and shared between the connected computers using the most common forms of network *languages*: Ethernet and Token Ring. Because the Network+ program assumes that you have experience with basic PC hardware, I focus on the components unique to networked PCs, such as network interface cards (NICs), hubs, routers, and special disk storage systems that provide added security. Later chapters cover many of these components and concepts in greater detail; however, it's important to have a strong grasp of these basics before diving in further.

THE INFORMATION TECHNOLOGY FIELD

Personally, I can't think of a more exciting career choice than the *Information Technology* (IT) field. Not only is it an ever changing, constantly evolving industry, but there are so many aspects to the field that just about anyone can find his or her *technology niche*. If you're artistic, you can design colorful, interactive Web pages. If your creative outlet has more of a musical bend, you can use the power of the PC to create a complete symphony! And, of course, those with the temperament to write hundreds and thousands of computer instructions, or programs, all day long (known as *programmers*) will always be in big demand. From my point of view, however, the most fascinating and rewarding side of the IT business is PC networking.

As powerful as the PC is, it's true potential can't be realized until it's connected to other computers, and it shares resources. Probably the best example of networked PCs is the Internet, and although most business networks consist of two hundred or less connected computers, the functions of these networks are much the same. People need and want fast access to all sorts of information, and there simply isn't enough computing power available on a single PC to hold all the data that everyone needs to access. Due to its relatively low cost and ease of growth, PC networks have all but eliminated large-scale mainframe networks in most businesses. Keeping these networks running, and managing the services they provide, is a never-ending and stimulating challenge.

NETWORKING CAREERS

The primary goal of networking is to facilitate communications between computer users and to set up shared resources such as printers, modems, and disk space. This is accomplished by connecting computers together with cables, telephones, and even satellites. Networking seems commonplace nowadays, but in reality, as little as ten years ago, only a handful of companies used PC networks. Today, however, companies of all sizes, from those with only a few employees to those that are Fortune 500s, consider PC networks to be their most valuable business tool. It is estimated that the number of PCs connected to corporate networks is doubling each year, with little or no slowdown in sight!

Within the network field (or networking), there are two distinctively different job paths: internal support or network integrator. Most large companies need internal support staff, such as help-desk persons, service technicians, and network administrators. Such positions concentrate on a single system and the particular habits of the network and its end users. On the other side, there is a need for network integrators who service many customers and work with teams of networking professionals. This work requires that you are highly flexible and knowledgeable about many different systems; it is quite possible that you may be working on an NT network in the morning and a Novell system in the afternoon.

No matter which career path you choose, continuing education is a must. Most employers and customers expect you to stay abreast of new technology. One way the networking industry differentiates among trained network professionals is through certification. Most network vendors have implemented certification processes for their products. These programs are intended to provide formal proof that a person has expertise with the vendor's products. Because many networks involve more than one vendor's products, multiple certifications are not uncommon among network professionals. Likewise, many certification programs offer varying levels of certification. For example, network operating system vendors usually offer a range of programs, from those for certified administrators, which deal only with the administration of the network, to programs for full system engineers that certify the individual is capable of installing, implementing, administering, and

troubleshooting the operating system. Novell was the pioneer in professional certification for the networking field; the Certified NetWare Engineer (CNE) program
was created in the late 1980s for individuals who wanted a formal method to prove
their abilities with Novell networks. Microsoft, Banyan Vines, Cisco, and other
software companies have all since followed suit. In July of 1993, the Computing
Technology Industry Association (CompTIA) introduced the A+ certification program. It was one of the first non-vendor specific programs available to certify the
competency of entry-level service technicians. A+ certification is obtained by passing a series of computer based exams. In 1999, CompTIA will introduce the
Network+ program, which is the logical next step for an A+ technician or someone
with equivalent skills. As with A+, this is an entry-level certification program, and
is not tied to a particular vendor or manufacturer. While A+ is designed to certify
that an individual has the skills to install and repair standalone, non-networked
computers, the Network+ program certifies that an individual has the knowledge
to configure, install, and troubleshoot basic PC network components. An entry-
level position in the network field requires that the individual is responsible for basic administration functions, for diagnosing network connection problems, and
for assisting experienced engineers in designing and installing PC networks. To
pass the Network+ skills test, you need to understand TCP/IP (explained in detail
later in this book), be conversant with local area network (LAN) technologies, and
be familiar with wide area networks (WANs) and Internet connectivity. Once you
successfully complete the Network+ program, you will have a proven, measurable
skill that will assist you in obtaining your first job in this rapidly expanding field.

Basic Vocabulary 101

I will argue that you can spend a lifetime simply trying to learn half of the
acronyms used in computer circles. So, here's a bit of advice: do not concern yourself with the multitude of acronyms; instead, concentrate on networking concepts
and practical applications. You'll pick-up the jargon quickly enough. However,
there are some terms that are so common you do need to understand them. I have
listed a few below. Do not become overly concerned if they don't make sense right
away; we will discuss the terms in greater depth as we go along.

- **LAN** (local area network): A LAN is a communications system much like a
  telephone system except that data, not voices, is usually shared. In recent
  years, the term *network* is often substituted when describing a LAN.

- **WAN** (wide area network): A WAN is a communications network that connects two or more sites over a wide geographic area such as a state or country. Most WANs are either connected point-to-point (a dedicated connection between two LANs) via a physical line that is owned or leased by a private company, or by switched technology where data is broken into *frames* and transported over the public telephone network. Increasingly, the Internet is being used as a WAN connection.

- **Login/Logout**: The act of supplying a unique user name and optional password to gain access to a network (login), and to disconnect from a network (logout).

- **Authenticate**: The process a server uses in order to assure the user name and/or password supplied to log in to the network is valid.

- **Protocol**: A set of rules that is established for communications between computers. Protocols govern all aspects of how data is formatted and transported between devices. IEEE committees set standards for protocols.

- **IEEE** (The Institute of Electricians and Electrical Engineers): One of the largest professional organizations. IEEE is responsible for defining and publishing many of the PC and networking standards. Project 802, discussed in Chapter 2, is one example of their work.

- **Client/Server**: A typical network has a primary *server* PC with a large amount of RAM and disk storage and a number of *client* PCs with less RAM and disk storage. The clients connect to the server in order to share data, printers, and other peripherals, and the server provides services such as file access, print spooling, or remote execution of programs. In a true client/server network, applications run on the network server opposed to being transferred to client PCs for execution.

- **Peer-to-Peer**: This type of network consists of two or more *equal* computers. Any PC on a peer-to-peer network can share its resources (disk space, printers, modems, and so on) with other computers on the network, and likewise any PC on a peer-to-peer network may request resources from any other connected PC. However, there is no centralization in administration.

- **Workstation**: A PC that participates in a network is often called a workstation. The term distinguishes a *network connected* PC from a non-connected (or standalone) PC.

o **WorkGroup**: A set of workstations or users that share computer resources, normally on a peer-to-peer level.

o **NIC** (Network Interface Card): Typically, an add-on board that plugs into an ISA (Industry Standard Architecture) or PCI (Peripheral Component Interconnect) slot of the PC, although newer PCs and *network-ready* PCs have NICs built into the system board. A network cable attaches to the NIC at the PC end and into the network on the other end.

o **Hub**: A device that serves as the central location for attaching wires from workstations. Typically, the hub is a nonintelligent box that adopts the star-like shape of the physical cabling system.

o **Topology**: How devices in a network are configured. For example, a *ring* topology describes PCs that are connected (conceptually, not physically) in a circular fashion.

o **Full Duplex**: The capability to transmit and receive simultaneously. In a digital network, with supporting hardware and software, workstations and servers that send and receive data at the same time have a dramatic increase in performance.

o **Half Duplex**: The capability to only transmit or receive data at any given time.

o **Baseband**: A communications technique where digital signals are transmitted across the physical medium (wire) without a change in modulation. The transmissions are generally limited to a few miles and do not require complex modems or other devices. Baseband techniques are commonly found in Ethernet and Token Ring LAN topologies; baseband transmissions use the full bandwidth of a channel by interleaving the electronic pulses with time division multiplexing (TDM).

o **Broadband**: A communications technique, much like cable television, used for data, voice, and video using frequency division multiplexing (FDM). The entire media bandwidth may be divided into multiple channels, and modems are required because the digital data has to be modulated onto the line.

o **Modulation**: the method of *blending* a data signal onto a physical medium for transmission. For example, modems *modulate* digital computer data on one end over a voice connection to a modem on the other which *demodulates* the voice signal back to digital.

COMPONENTS OF THE NETWORK

Every LAN is composed of basic components that are required for communications to take place. Although these components will vary somewhat from LAN to LAN, depending on individual needs, the basic devices perform similar functions.

Network Interface Cards

All PCs on the network, both the workstations and the server(s) need a Network Interface Card (NIC). If the PC does not have a NIC built in, you need to plug one into a free slot on the system board. Generally the manufacturer supplies the software driver for the NIC. Client operating systems such as Windows 95 often supply generic drivers, but I recommend you use the manufacturer's drivers whenever possible. Not only will the vendor's drivers most likely be current, but the vendor will usually not provide troubleshooting support unless you have installed their drivers. On older, non-Plug and Play NICs, you will need to configure the NIC to use a free IRQ (interrupt request) and possibly an I/O (input/output) address and a DMA (direct memory access) channel. The most common reason a workstation is unable to connect to the network is due to a misconfigured NIC, and most of the NIC problems result from IRQ conflicts. Even with Plug and Play systems, you need to make sure you have an available IRQ for your NIC. Normally you can use IRQ 10 or 11, but you may need to rearrange or completely remove some other boards in order to free up an IRQ. On non-Plug and Play systems, boot into your CMOS (complementary metal-oxide semiconductor) setup and verify that the IRQ you need for your NIC is available.

Often times, if you are using an ISA (Industry Standard Architecture) card, you will have to define the ISA setting for the required IRQ on your motherboard's setup screen. Some older 8- and 16-bit ISA Token Ring cards will only operate on IRQ 2, but for all other situations these interrupts should be avoided. Because these two IRQ are shared, a device set to IRQ 9 may cause the NIC on IRQ 2 to miss an interrupt. And because the NIC is your communication lifeline in the PC, you don't want other devices to cause it to fail.

NICs also require *drivers*, software that enables the NIC to operate properly when sending and receiving data on the network. When you install the drivers, always check the manufacturer's World Wide Web site to see if newer drivers have been released since your NIC was shipped. But if you end up having problems with the latest drivers and the ones that shipped with the NIC are older, reinstall them. If neither of these work, try using generic drivers if the drivers are supported. Most Ethernet cards support the standard NE2000 driver available with versions of Windows 3.11 and higher. For DOS installations you will need to contact the NIC vendor to obtain the proper generic driver.

You should familiarize yourself with the diagnostic LEDs (light-emitting diodes) of the NICs you use. When you troubleshoot workstation connection problems, the NIC should, at least, have a *link* light to indicate whether it is receiving a signal from the hub. Likewise, if the physical connection between the NIC and hub is working, you should see a corresponding link light on the hub.

Network Cabling and Topologies

Once you have the NICs configured, you need to connect them with some form of wire. The basic wire types, or network cables, are coaxial (coax), shielded twisted-pair (STP), unshielded twisted-pair (UTP), and fiber-optic.

Coax

Coax, similar to cable-TV cable, is an older technology and is rarely used for new installations. This type of cabling, also referred to as 10Base2, uses barrel (BNC) connectors (refer to Figure 1-1 for commonly used cable connectors) and is usually laid out as one long continuous run, referred to as a bus topology. (See Figure 1-2.) A *T* connector attaches to the NIC and taps into the cable. On the T connector of the last workstation, on each end of the cable, a 50 ohm terminator, or end-cap, is attached to close the circuit. (See Figure 1-3.) Coax is inexpensive, relatively easy to install, and is not as susceptible to outside electromagnetic interference as twisted pair cable. The downside to the coax bus is it has a speed limitation of 10Mbps (megabits per second), and if the cable is disconnected at any point, or a NIC failure occurs, all PCs on that cable will lose the network connection. This happens because the bus is not properly terminated at the break. Without termination, frames bounce back to the transmitting computer causing collisions that prevent the network from functioning.

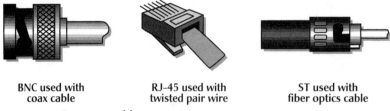

| BNC used with | RJ–45 used with | ST used with |
| coax cable | twisted pair wire | fiber optics cable |

FIGURE 1-1   Common cable connectors

exam
preparation
pointer

The Network+ exam expects you to be able to visually identify BNC and twisted pair network connectors. It gives you a visual representation of a connector and asks you to identify it from a list of choices.

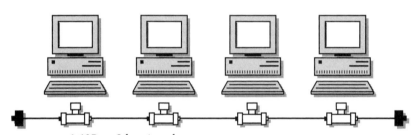

FIGURE 1-2   A 10Base2 bus topology

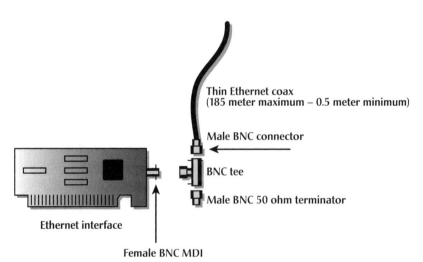

Thin Ethernet coax
(185 meter maximum – 0.5 meter minimum)

Male BNC connector

BNC tee

Male BNC 50 ohm terminator

Ethernet interface

Female BNC MDI

FIGURE 1-3   10Base2 NIC connection and termination

Unshielded twisted-pair

UTP resembles standard telephone wire. The wires within the sheathing are twisted in pairs (hence the name) and are crimped down on RJ-45 connectors (again resembling telephone wire ends, only larger). The wires are twisted around each other to minimize interference, also known as *crosstalk*, from other twisted pairs in the cable and electromagnetic radiation outside the cable. Two types of UTP wire are commonly used: Category 3 and Category 5 (Cat3 and Cat5, respectively). The categories are based on their transmission capacity; the higher the level, the more capacity it can handle. Cat5 is the selection of choice for new installations, and is quickly replacing Cat3 in existing networks. Although UTP is much more susceptible to electromagnetic interference (in spite of the twist) than coax, and has a shorter distance limitation than coax, it is the minimum requirement for transfer speeds greater than 10Mbps.

Shielded twisted-pair

STP is nearly identical to UTP except that the wire pairs are wrapped in a metal sheath for added protection against external electromagnetic interference. STP is primarily used in Token Ring networks (discussed later in this chapter).

With the exception of bus topologies, the network cables connect from the NICs to a hub, a switch, or an MAU (Medium-Attachment Unit), depending on your network topology. (I will discuss these devices in greater detail in Chapter 2.) UTP is usually described as being in a *star* configuration. The wiring is run from each workstation back to a hub or switch in the center point. (See Figure 1-4.)

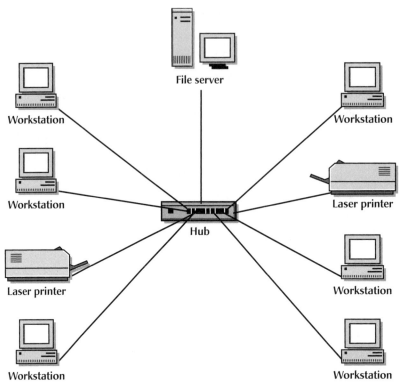

File server
Workstation
Workstation
Laser printer
Laser printer
Hub
Workstation
Workstation
Workstation
Workstation

FIGURE 1-4 A 10BaseT star topology

There are numerous network protocols in use today, but by far the most popular are Ethernet and Token Ring. Of these two, 10Mbps Ethernet, commonly
known as 10BaseT, is the most popular due to its low cost and ease of installation.
Fast Ethernet, or 100BaseT, however, is quickly becoming a replacement. Both of
these Ethernet standards run over UTP cable in a star topology (see Figure 1-4).
Cabling for Fast Ethernet comes in three types: 100BaseTX, the most common,
uses two pairs of Category 5 UTP, 100BaseT4 uses four pairs of Category 3 (rarely
used), and 100BaseFX uses Multimode Fiber-optic cable. In order to run at
100Mbps, the NICs, hubs, and switches must all support the faster standard.

Data grading categories

Higher level, or category, cables have better conductors, better insulation, and more twists per foot. The levels and what they are used for are as follows:

Level 1: Used for up to 1 megabit per second (Mbps)

Level 2: Used for up to 4Mbps

Level 3: Used for up to 10Mbps

Level 4: Used for up to 16Mbps

Level 5: Used for 150-ohm data grade applications. Required for true 100Mbps.

Wiring considerations

The RJ-45 is the key to the whole system. The NIC and hub must have the cables done in a certain way in order to work. The punch blocks, patch panels, and so on, really don't matter as long as the wire continues correctly from end to end. *However*, do yourself an enormous favor and do your wiring consistent with industry standards.

Four-pair wire is the standard with pair 1 as blue, pair 2 as orange, pair 3 as green, and pair 4 as brown. Colors are always shown with the base color first, then the stripe color. The RJ-45 is wired as outlined in Table 1-1:

TABLE 1-1 RJ–45 WIRING DEFINITIONS		
PIN #	*COLOR CODE*	*FUNCTION*
Pin 1	White/Orange	Transmit +
Pin 2	Orange/White	Transmit –
Pin 3	White/Green	Receive +
Pin 5	White/Blue	
Pin 6	Green/White	Receive –
Pin 7	White/Brown	
Pin 8	Brown/White	

If you refer to the RJ-45 connector in Figure 1-1, pin 1 is on the left-hand side. A cross-over patch cable can be used to connect two hubs together, or to connect two PCs directly to each other without a hub. The cross-over cable simply *crosses over* the transmit pins to the received pins. This is normally done internally by the hub or switch. To make a cross-over patch cable, wire one end of the cable as outlined in Table 1-2:

TABLE 1-2 RJ–45 WIRING DEFINITIONS OR A CROSS–OVER CABLE			
ONE END		**THE OTHER END**	
Pin 1	White/Orange	Pin 1	White/Green
Pin 2	Orange/White	Pin 2	Green/White
Pin 3	White/Green	Pin 3	White/Orange
Pin 6	Green/White	Pin 6	Orange/White

The point is that the transmit pins have *crossed over* to the receive pins — a function normally done by the hub or switch.

Many NIC vendors provide diagnostic software to test the functionality of the network card. These tests require a *loopback* cable to correctly operate. To make a RJ-45 loopback tester, wire one single connector to itself as outlined in Table 1-3:

TABLE 1-3 RJ–45 WIRING DEFINITIONS FOR A LOOPBACK PLUG	
PIN #	**COLOR CODE**
Pin 1	White/Orange
Pin 2	Orange/White
Pin 3	White/Orange
Pin 6	Orange/White

All cabling systems have defined limitations on the maximum transmission speed of the data and the distance from end devices. On a bus topology, the limitation is imposed between the devices on each end of the cable segment. In a star topology, the distance is measured from the end device to the hub or switch. (See Table 1-4.) It is imperative that these distances are respected. While exceeding the limitations may not appear to cause problems right away, as more and more of the cable is used, traffic problems will begin to have catastrophic effects on the LAN. (I will discuss these problems in greater detail when I explain the nature of Ethernet communications.)

TABLE 1-4 MAXIMUM CABLE LENGTH AND TRANSMISSION SPEEDS FOR COMMON CABLES		
TOPOLOGY	MAXIMUM LENGTH	MAXIMUM SPEED
10Base2(thinnet)	200m	10Mbps
10Base5(thicknet)	500m	10Mbps
10BaseT	100m	10Mbps
100BaseTX	150m	100Mbps
100VG–AnyLAN	100m	100Mbps (Cat3) 150Mbps (Cat5)

Token Ring   Token Ring was originally designed by IBM and has a strong following although it is not as popular as Ethernet. Like its name implies, Token Ring uses a *token* passed from PC to PC in a ring configuration (see Figure 1-5). Only when a PC has the token is it able to transmit data on the wire. This technique ensures that each user has a regular turn at transmitting data. All PCs (up to a maximum of 255) connect to a central wiring hub called a Multistation Access Unit (MAU). There are two types of Token Ring networks: type 1 permits up to 255 nodes per network and uses shielded twisted-pair (STP) wires with IBM type 1 connectors, type 3 Token Ring permits up to 72 devices per network and uses unshielded twisted-pair wires (Category 3, 4 or 5) with RJ-45 connectors. Although fast Token Ring is being deployed, typically Token Ring runs at 4Mbps or 16Mbps.

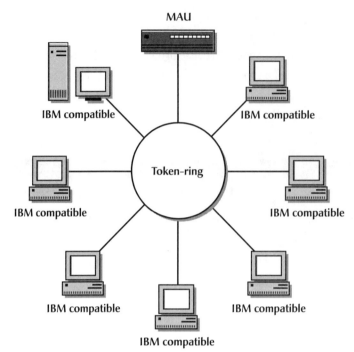

FIGURE 1-5 Example of a ring topology

IBM type designations

The IBM type designations are as follows:

o **Type 1**: Two pair of 22-gauge wire. Each pairs' foil is wrapped inside another foil sheath that has a wire braid ground. This is usually what most people think of as shielded twisted-pair.

o **Type 2**: A type 1 with four telephone pair sheathed to the outside to permit one cable to an office for both voice and data.

o **Type 3**: Four pair of unshielded 22- or 24-gauge wire. Each pair is wrapped at least twice per foot. This is what most people think of as unshielded twisted-pair.

o **Type 5**: Fiber optic.

o **Type 6**: Two pair of stranded, shielded 26-gauge wire to be used for patch cables.

o **Type 7**: One pair of stranded, 26-gauge wire.

○ **Type 8**: Two parallel pairs (flat wires with no twist) of 26-gauge wire used for under carpet installation.

○ **Type 9**: Two pair of shielded 26-gauge wire used for data. Type 9 doesn't carry data as well as type 1 due to smaller conductors.

Network Operating Systems

The software that makes all of this hardware useful is called the *network operating system*, or NOS. The NOS oversees all of the services a network provides. Some examples of NOS services include file and print sharing, security, hardware sharing (such as modems), and internetwork access (such as connecting to file servers at remote offices, or the Internet). There are basically two types of NOSs: Peer-to-peer, and client/server.

Peer-to-peer networks

This type of network consists of two or more *equal* computers. Any PC on a peer-to-peer network can share its resources (disk space, printers, modems, and so on) with other computers on the network, and may likewise request resources from any other PC connected to the network. All Windows products developed after Windows for Workgroups offer peer-to-peer networking functions (such as shared files and printers), while other NOS specific products, such as Lantastic, are more robust; they offer more network-like features including tighter security policies and the ability to handle a larger number of users. Peer-to-peer networks are fine for networks with only a few PCs because you only need basic file and print sharing, and security is not a major issue. In most cases, the performance of most of these NOSs is acceptable. One major drawback, however, to a peer-to-peer network is that computers which have resources to share must be powered on in order to be accessed. This can be inconvenient, and possibly create unacceptable security problems

Client/server networks

The client/server concept is based around one or more dedicated computers (the *servers*), which provide all network functions to end-user computers (the *clients*). This type of network is very scaleable from two to thousands of users. The servers can perform very advanced authentication for security purposes; track file usage and changes; provide centralized, automated backups of critical data; and overall, perform better than peer-to-peer systems. This is why, generally, businesses invest heavily in server hardware and less on desktop systems to leverage the benefits of the client/server environment.

There are many NOS products on the market, but the three most common, and the three that you will be expected to know about on the test include:

o Unix

o Microsoft Windows NT

o Novell NetWare

 All references to 32-bit Windows software include Windows 95/98 NT Workstation and NT Server.

UNIX

I use UNIX here more as a generic name because there are many flavors of UNIX available through a number of different vendors. Also, as this book is being written, a *freeware* derivative of UNIX called Linux is quickly becoming a serious contender in the networking world. For the most part, UNIX is quite different from the Microsoft and Novell platforms that are both based more on traditional *DOS* concepts. UNIX is predominately a character-based system (although a graphical interface called x-Windows is popular) and typically runs over serial connections to dumb terminals. The strength of UNIX lies in its portability across multiple vendor hardware platforms, its vendor independent networking, and the strength of its application programming interface. Very little of UNIX is written in assembly language, thus it is relatively easy for computer vendors to get UNIX running on their systems.

Vendor-independent networking enables users to easily network multiple UNIX systems from various vendors. An excellent reference for UNIX fundamentals can be found at the official UNIX homepage on the World Wide Web at: http://www.ugu.com/.

Microsoft NT

NT is Microsoft's high-end, 32-bit NOS. In the past few years, it has become very popular because it provides an easy software development platform for programmers to write for. NT offers file and print sharing, and because of its multi-threading architecture, it is well suited as an application server. For example, a company with heavy database needs might deploy an NT server specifically for database services, and use other servers for file and print services. NT also offers cost effective Internet-related services such as Web publishing and e-mail. Prior to NT, most of these Internet services were done with more expensive UNIX systems.

NT is sold in two flavors: Workstation and Server. They are nearly identical in most cases. Workstation is intended for high-end client users, and the Server provides multi-user server services. The current version of NT is based on a *domain* concept. In this environment, clients belong to a *domain*, or *specified group*, of network users centered around a main server called a *Primary Domain Controller*, or *PDC*, that provides the authentication of users within the group. Multiple domains may exist within an NT network, but unless users are specifically defined in multiple domains, they are unable to access domains outside of their primary group. This method enables a single network topology to consist of many smaller groups of LANs, each managed by a different network administrator, or if properly configured, each managed by a single administrator.

In order for multiple domains to be accessed, a *trust* must be established between domains. A trust is simply a method of enabling users access to one domain's resources when they are *authenticated* by another domain. Take for example a situation where two domains exist, one for sales, and one for financial. The sales manager needs access to financial documents stored in the financial domain, but because the manager is only a member of the sales domain, these documents are not accessible. A network administrator, with network rights on both domains, can setup a trust between the sales and financial domains so that the sales manager is *trusted* by the financial domain as a valid network user. The manager does not need to specifically authenticate into the financial primary domain controller because it *trusts* that the sale domain PDC has already validated this user. It is important to know that NT trusts are unidirectional. For example, if the financial domain trusts the sales domain, the sales domain *does not* automatically trust the financial domain. A trust will have to be established in each direction for this situation to occur. In networks where there are many domains, and central administration is desired, a *full trust model* can be established where all domains trust all other domains. NT2000 (Version 5) will completely redefine the domain concept with the introduction of the *Active Directory,* which will be more closely related to Novell's Directory Service.

Novell NetWare

NetWare is the granddaddy of PC based NOSs. Novell created NetWare in the 1980s and it has dominated the market until recently, when NT gained in popularity. NetWare's base service has always been file and print sharing, and a very robust security model.

Until the recent release of NetWare Version 5.0, NetWare's native protocol was IPX, which is extremely well-suited for LANs, but not as efficient as IP is for WANs and Internet access. Many Internet-related services found in NT have been added to NetWare, starting with Version 4. Version 5 continued in this direction by adding support for true IP as the core protocol. In addition, Novell developed a directory service unparalleled in the industry today. *Novell Directory Services* (NDS), gives NetWare the ability to manage and maintain any network object (hardware, software, or users, for example) quickly and easily. It is also the foundation for providing users' their own *network persona* so that no matter where they enter the network, all of their personal settings are available to them.

NDS is a distributed database, based on the international X.500 standard, that stores information about hardware and software resources available within a given network. It provides network users and administrators global access to all network resources through a single login and a single point of network administration. All network resources are represented as objects that are maintained in a hierarchical directory tree and accessed through a 32-bit Windows program called *NWAdmin*. With NDS, administrators can maintain the entire network regardless of where they are located. Unlike the domain concept, in a Directory Service model, users are part of the whole network or *enterprise*, and obtain access to any service or resource in the network simply by having rights granted to them by an administrator. The directory simplifies administration, and increases security by creating a single point of login and administration for the entire network no matter how large or dispersed it may be. Currently, this is the single biggest advantage of NetWare over other competitive NOSs.

exam preparation pointer

The Network+ exam expects you to know that NT and UNIX primarily run TCP/IP, and NetWare runs IPX by default.

You should know that the advantage of a directory service-based network over a domain-based network is its simplicity of administration, its ability to distribute the database across multiple servers for security and redundancy, and its added security with the single login process.

NOS Client Software

Each workstation that needs to connect to the network also needs *client* software. These are the software components that enable the NIC to communicate over the network. Typically, each NOS supplies the client side software, but desktop operating systems such as Windows 95 and NT Workstation provide generic client software for the most popular NOSs as well. For DOS-based workstations, you must use the software supplied with the NOS.

Because most workstations are now Windows-based, the Network+ exam concentrates only on the 32-bit Windows client software for NT and NetWare.

NetWare Client32

Novell's NetWare provides a set of client drivers called *Client32*. When you install a workstation into a NetWare environment, it is recommended that you use this software component. It is always wise to check Novell's Web site for newer versions because this client software has a history of changing frequently. Client32 provides full access to NetWare's Directory Services, and takes full advantage of the NetWare product line. You do have the option, however, to use the generic Client for NetWare Networks that is included within the 32-bit Windows operating system. There are, in fact, many application programs that still require this more basic software to operate correctly. When in doubt, check with the software manufacturer to see if their application is supported under Novell's Client32.

To install Client32, you simply run the SETUP program provided with the software. You need a copy of the original Windows operating software to complete the setup, so make sure you have that available *before* you begin. When the installation is complete, and you've rebooted your PC, you will see the NetWare login screen as shown in Figure 1-6.

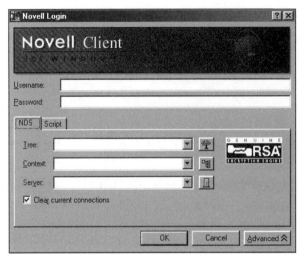

FIGURE 1-6   The NetWare Client32 login screen for Windows 9*x*

At this point, you will need to provide your user name, password, and may need to provide a directory context, or a tree, or a server name, or a combination thereof, to log in. On subsequent logins, you will only need your password because the data for the other fields will be remembered.

Client32 has over 30 fine-tuning options that you can set to further customize its behavior in your environment. These properties can be viewed and modified within the Windows 9*x* Network Properties Dialog box. The fastest way to display this screen is to *right-click* the *Network Neighborhood* icon, and then select *Properties* from the drop-down menu. Once the main Network components box is displayed, you can click on Client32 for NetWare Networks, and then click on Properties.

 in the real world **Most of the time you will not need to make any changes to the client, but you should know the options that exist, and where to find them.**

Client for Microsoft Networks

If your network consists of all or mostly NT, and you use an NT server to authenticate to, or you wish to use the peer-to-peer features of the 32-bit Windows operating system, then you must use Microsoft's Client for Microsoft Networks. This software is installed by default during the Windows installation if a network card is detected. You can manually install this client from the Windows Control Panel ⇒ Networks ⇒ Add ⇒ Client ⇒ Microsoft. When the client is installed, the network Properties box will look similar to the one in Figure 1-7.

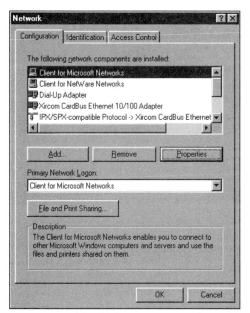

FIGURE 1-7 The Windows 9x Network Properties box displays which network clients are installed

Within the Network properties, there are a number of settings that you should be aware of. (See Figure 1-8.) First, under the *Identification* tab, you need to make sure that you supply a *unique* computer name. This name must be unique within the network you are connected to. Also, you should have a Workgroup name and an optional description. The Workgroup name identifies the members of a peer-to-peer network, and is necessary if you wish to share your printers and/or data with other users on a peer level. If you'll be logging into an NT domain (a client/server network), then you should put the *Domain Name* in the Workgroup Name box. The Domain Name is assigned to the network when the first server (the *Primary Domain Controller*) is installed. The computer description field is optional but it helps identify the workstation more clearly.

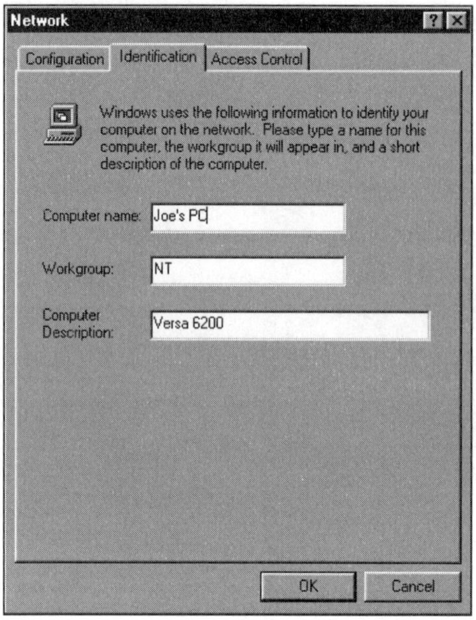

FIGURE 1-8 The Network identification screen
for Windows 9x workstations

If the workstation PC is to be part of an NT domain, then you also need to tell the client software that you wish to log in to the NT domain. You do this in the *Client for Microsoft Network Properties* for the client software. Figure 1-9 shows this property box. In order to access Client for Microsoft Networks Properties, use the main Network dialog box. Highlight the Client for Microsoft Networks by clicking once on it, and then click the Properties button. You have three areas to fill in on this screen. First, place a check mark in the box labeled Log on to Windows NT domain. Second, enter the *exact* name of the domain in the box labeled Windows NT Domain. And third, under Network logon options, choose if the operating system should wait to reconnect the shares established on network drives until you need them, or reconnect them when you first log on. The first option enables you to log on more quickly, but each time you access a shared resource, the network will need to reestablish the drives are ready for use. The second option may cause a slight delay during the login process, but will work more quickly when you access shared resources later. The choice between options lies in where your resources are located. If all of your shares are local, then reconnecting them at login may be your best choice. However, if most of your shares are on the other side of a WAN link, especially if the WAN connection is slow (such as with a modem dial-up), then you probably do not want the operating system to reestablish those connections until you absolutely need to.

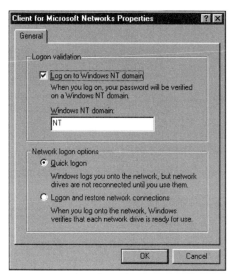

FIGURE 1-9 The Client for Microsoft Networks
Properties box

BASIC ETHERNET CONCEPTS

As I stated earlier, Ethernet is by far the most popular networking protocol in use today. Ethernet is fast, with speeds from 10Mbps to 1Gbps (gigabits per second). When you install an Ethernet based LAN, you can choose your components from hundreds of vendors with a wide range of prices. Ethernet is easy to configure, easy to work with, and it is supported by all of the major network operating systems (NOS). Ethernet is an IEEE 802.2 and 802.3 standard.

Ethernet transmits data in *frames*, or small *packets*. The size and length of each packet is determined by many factors, but most importantly the minimum size is 72 bytes, and the maximum length is 1518 bytes. When tuning a LAN for performance, you should pay special attention to the size of your Ethernet packets. The larger the size, the more efficient the bandwidth is, and the increased speed due to larger frame size can be quite noticeable to the workstation user. Each data packet contains a header of information that includes, among other things, the source and destination addresses. In other words, each packet has the address of the PC the data is intended for, and a *return* address to identify the PC that sent the data. Also, every Ethernet packet contains a trailer that holds error correction data that is used by other protocols to assure data in the middle of the packet was not corrupted someplace during the transmission.

Ethernet uses a transmission method known as *Carrier Sense Multiple Access/Collision Detection* (CSMA/CD) that occurs in two stages. First, only one device on an Ethernet segment can place data on the cable at a time. Therefore, when a PC wants to transmit data, the Ethernet protocol states that the cable must be free of any other traffic. This is the Carrier Sense portion of the CSMA technology. Because you must have more than one PC in order to be a LAN, the Multiple Access portion of the equation means that Ethernet understands each device on the network is *sharing* the common media or cable. As you may guess, timing is critical to this protocol. It is very likely that two or more devices will *listen* on the wire at the exact same time and, thus, not hear any other traffic. Each will assume the cable is free and begin transmitting data. Because only one device can *talk* on the wire at any given time, such activity breaks the rules of the protocol. When it happens, the data bits collide with one another and basically make a real mess of things. Ethernet, therefore, must be able to *detect* these collisions and do something about it; hence, the second part of the CSMA/CD technology, Collision Detection.

When a collision is detected, each device is programmed to back off and wait a random amount of time before trying the process over again. This back-off algorithm is built into the Ethernet devices to assure different timing states between attempts to retransmit. (It certainly wouldn't work if each device waited the exact same amount of time to start sending their data again. The collisions would simply reoccur and data would never get through!) When a packet is sent out on the wire, the sending device waits a predetermined time and listens for a collision before sending the next packet of information.

Obviously, a number of potential problems exist with this protocol. First, an Ethernet backbone will collapse completely if too many devices are trying to share the same cable. In fact, the utilization of any single cable segment should never exceed 30 percent. (Peaks and spikes in use over 30 percent is normally acceptable, but sustained use should always remain below the 30 percent mark.) The term *Collision Domain* is commonly used to describe a group of devices that share a single cable segment and, therefore, contend for time on the same wire, and CSMA/CD is known as a contention-based cable-access method. As soon as a

Collision Domain exceeds the 30 percent threshold, you need to do something to break-up or *segment* the domain in order to reduce the total number of devices sharing the cable. Typically this is done with devices known as *routers*, *bridges*, or *switches*. (I cover these later in this chapter.) Also, if most of the devices within the Collision Domain are communicating with a server, another option is to put two NICs in the server, and attach them to different hubs. The workstations can then be balanced between the two hubs and effectively cut the Collision Domain in half.

Another problem with this access method occurs when the length of the cable segment is too long. If you recall, the protocol requires the transmitting device listen for collisions for a specific amount of time. Thus, it is possible a collision can occur far away from the transmitting device, and the device fails to detect the collision before beginning to send more data. In the real world, this happens frequently, and it is a mistake that often leads to excessive diagnostic time. Fortunately, there are a number of cable testers available on the market to identify segments that exceed specifications.

Ethernet is considered a *broadcast* form of protocol. Broadcasts are packets sent out on the cable topology without a specific destination address. Each device on the wire picks up a broadcast packet to determine if it has any reason to respond. This is evident in the Novell NetWare world. When a PC first comes on line, it performs a broadcast known as *Get Nearest Server*. Basically, the PC tells each device on the cable that it is looking for a server so that it can log in to the network. All devices see this data packet, but only file servers respond. This can result in the common network problem, called a *broadcast storm,* when a misbehaving network card floods the network with broadcast packets. All devices are busy looking at the broadcast to determine if they need to answer, and no real data packets are capable of getting through.

A *multicast* is similar to a broadcast. But instead of not including destination addresses, the multicast packet contains a specific set of destination addresses. Each device on the list of addresses receives the same packet, but any device not listed will not. If you use any form of automatic news-gathering software on the Internet, such as PointCast or BackWeb, then you are subjected to a multicast process. Services such as these *push* predetermined news items to a member list of PCs via the Internet.

In most real world situations, you should consider Ethernet first when designing a new LAN. Faster Ethernet technologies are developed more than any other protocol and if you watch your specifications, Ethernet is quite simple to configure and maintain.

BASIC TOKEN RING CONCEPTS

Token Ring networks are defined by the IEEE 802.5 specification and were primarily developed by IBM. As its name implies, this type of network is designed in a ring topology and uses a *token* to control the transmission of data on the network. The token is a special purpose frame that is passed from station to station around the ring. When a station needs to send data (assuming it has control of the token), it first modifies the token's *start-of-frame* header, identifying that this station is circulating data. The data is then put out on the wire. Stations, in turn, look at the token to see if the data is addressed to them; if data is not addressed to a particular station, the token is regenerated on to the next station in the ring. When the proper station acknowledges the token is addressed to it, the token's message is copied, and the token is recirculated back on the cable with a reception confirmation message for the transmitting station. When the transmitting station gets the token back, it removes the message from the network and transmits a new *blank* token for the next station that needs to transmit data. A process called *token holding timer* is implemented by the protocol to regulate the maximum time a workstation can transmit data so that no single station can monopolize the network. Thus, there is no contention to access the cable.

The biggest drawbacks to Token Ring are the near-proprietary nature of IBM's influence, the high price of the basic equipment, and its maximum speed limitation of 16Mbps. The speed limitation, however, may well be dwindling because Fast Token Ring networks with speeds up to 1Gbps are beginning to make headway.

It's important to note that Token Ring does have some major advantages over Ethernet. The maximum frame size for Token Ring is 4K; it is much more efficient than the small Ethernet maximum. Token Ring has longer distance capabilities and is more *deterministic* than Ethernet. Every station in the ring is guaranteed access to the token at some point to transmit data. Error detection and recovery techniques are also enhanced in a Token Ring environment through a monitor function that would be otherwise controlled by a server. For example, if a token is lost or corrupted, the protocol provides a mechanism to generate a new token after a specified time interval has elapsed.

HUBS, BRIDGES, SWITCHING HUBS, AND ROUTERS

Now that I have covered installing network cards in PCs, and cable topology, it is important to discuss the devices that tie it all together. For a 10Base2 network, each device is simply attached to the cable segment in order. Star and ring topologies include other devices that centralize the wiring system. Later on in the book I'll explain in more detail how to select the proper device, but for now I take a look at the options available and describe their basic functions.

Hubs

The most common device is a hub. (See Figure 1-10) Hubs are normally found in the logical center of an Ethernet LAN and act as the collecting point for all of the cable runs. There are two types of hubs: *passive* and *active*. A passive hub, the most common, does nothing with the data, whereas an active hub regenerates packets in order to maintain a stronger signal.

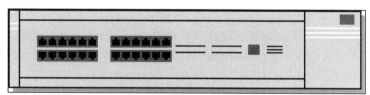

FIGURE 1-10 **A view of a generic Ethernet HUB**

As you add PCs or other devices to the LAN, you may soon run out of ports at your hub to plug into. In this situation, you can *daisy-chain* multiple hubs together by inserting a special patch cable, known as a *crossover* cable between ports on the hub. The difference between a normal patch cable and a crossover cable is that the transmit and receive lines are crossed (this is a function normally done by the hub). Some hubs require you use a specific port when daisy-chaining devices, and others provide a push-button that internally crosses receive and transmit lines, thus enabling you to use a normal patch cable. While hubs are generally inexpensive and easy to install, you have to keep in mind that a hub does not segment the cabling system. In other words, a hub is simply another part of the collision domain. If you add more hubs, you extend the size of the collision domain.

Bridges

A bridge is used to connect two or more similar segments together (for example, Token Ring to Token Ring or Ethernet to Ethernet). It has two purposes: The first is to extend the length and number of stations that a segment can support. The second is to reduce overall traffic flow by only passing data packets that are not destined for a hardware address on a local segment. All broadcast traffic crosses a bridge because no specific destination point is known. Because broadcasts are destined for all devices, the bridge forwards broadcast traffic to all connected segments. Similarly, a bridge forwards multicast packets that have destination addresses beyond the local segment. I'll discuss bridging concepts in much greater detail in Chapter 2.

 For the Network+ exam, you should know that bridges are used to *segment* a single collision domain into multiple collision domains.

Switching Hubs

While bridges do a good job breaking up collision domains, segments can still become over-burdened as they require more and more bridge devices. This not only becomes expensive, but it also introduces many more points of failure on the LAN. A newer technology, known as *switching*, has been developed to address this shortcoming. A switching hub, or more commonly called a *switch*, creates a point-to-point channel between two devices. If you have a workstation connected to one port on a switch, and a file server connected to another port on the same switch, the switch creates a dedicated connection between these two computers without having to share the path with any other device. As you see, this eliminates the collision domain concept completely! Because only two devices are on the cable, they take advantage of the speed capabilities of the media.

Typically, switches are more expensive than hubs, so often times the switched ports are used more like a bridge. Rather than placing computers out at the end of the switched ports, hubs are connected to the switch instead. This enables you to create many smaller collision domains because the switch directs the hub traffic to its destination. Typically, the file servers are connected directly to the switch on one side, and hubs with PCs are connected on the other side. (See Figure 11.)

While switching seems like the perfect solution to shared media access problems, be aware that it can also introduce problems. For example, a small LAN with twenty-five workstations and one file server are all connected directly into a switch. Each PC has its own segment so it can transfer data at near wire speeds. However, since all of the twenty-five workstations are connected to the file server, each one has direct, unrestricted access. The file server may not be able to process all of the service requests pouring into it. When you look at performance issues, its important to examine the entire structure to make sure you're not simply moving the performance bottleneck from one subsystem to another. Figure 1-11 shows how a switch can be placed into the LAN with both hubs and PCs connected.

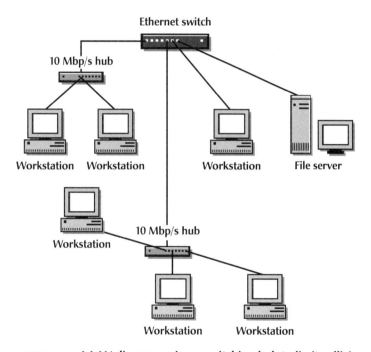

FIGURE 1-11   A LAN diagram using a switching hub to limit collision domains

Routers

Routers are complex devices that use a number of different techniques to move data from one place to another depending on the situation the router is called for. For example, a router is required when you combine LANs of different topologies. If you have both an Ethernet and Token Ring network, and you need the ability to pass data between the two, a router can be used to convert the frame from one format to the other.

Wide area networks (WANs) require a router to bridge the various LANs together. When a packet on the local network needs to get to a remote PC, the router is the device responsible for locating and transporting the data. Routers (sometimes referred to as *gateways*) are commonly used on corporate LANs to connect to the Internet.

DISK SUBSYSTEMS AND DATA PROTECTION

The last overview I provide in this chapter covers physical hardware as it relates to data storage and protection. Typically, file servers hold the bulk of the data stored on a LAN. This includes the networking software, system data, application software, and user files. A simple LAN may have a single server doing all of the data storage. Larger systems may have multiple servers, separate dedicated storage devices, or a combination of these configurations. Because recovery from a disaster is a critical component to networking, it pays to think ahead and implement features to protect the data in the first place. Daily, verified backups are essential, but moreover, there are a number of disk storage options that minimize the time a network is down after a hard drive failure occurs. As with death and taxes, catastrophic disk crashes are certainties.

RAID Level 0 (Volumes)

RAIDs (Redundant Array of Independent Disks) are organized in levels ranging from 0 to 10. All levels of RAID, with the exception of level 0, offer an amount of data redundancy. RAID 0 splits data evenly among multiple drives, arranging the data on the disks through a process called *data striping*; the data is interleaved by groups of several bytes or sectors. The result is a single file stored on multiple disks. Because a file can be written or retrieved using multiple, simultaneous writes or read operations, RAID 0 usually offers the highest performance. However, if one disk fails, all data in the array is lost, and all disks must be reformatted.

RAID Level 1 (Mirroring)

At the bottom of the fault tolerance techniques is RAID 1, also known as *disk mirroring*. With RAID 1, two disk drives of *equal* size and type are installed. When data is written to the primary drive, it is duplicated exactly (mirrored) to the secondary drive. This mirroring can be done by special hardware controllers, or by software implemented by the network operating system. If the primary disk crashes, the system can quickly be reconfigured to use the secondary drive to get the network back up and running. However, this level of protection is only good in the event there are problems to the primary hard disk.

RAID Level 2 (Duplexing)

RAID 2 takes mirroring one step further, and protects you in the event of a disk *controller* failure. To implement RAID 2, you simply add a second controller and run one drive on each controller. Because hard drive technology has improved so much over the years, and the extra cost of a controller is minimal in comparison to the overall cost of the server, RAID 2 should always be used instead of RAID 1.

RAID Level 3 (Data Guarding with Parity)

The previous levels of RAID have two inherent problems: First, half of the actual drive space goes unused until the first drive or controller fails. Second, in both cases, you will suffer some network downtime while you switch over to the secondary drive. While this is faster than having to restore the whole system from a backup, your network is still unavailable for a period of time, users lose their connections, and users possibly lose data depending on what they were doing when the hard drive/controller failed.

This leads us to the next level of protection: RAID 3. This level requires a *minimum* of three hard drives. One of the drives is used to store parity information about the data written to the other drives. This parity information can be used to reconstruct the data from the failed drive. For example, if drive 1 of a RAID 3 system dies, the data that was stored on that drive will still be available to users because the data is re-built from the information stored on the parity drive. In a number of server-level drive cages, these drives are *hot swappable,* meaning that the server or drive box does not need to be powered off in order to replace a failed drive.

RAID 3 is beneficial in situations where data fault tolerance and system up time are critical, and drive space needs to be maximized. On the downside, because the parity drive is constantly being written to, performance can be degraded, especially in environments where a high percentage of disk operations are writes rather than reads. Also, if the parity drive fails, the fault tolerance of the array is lost.

RAID Level 4

RAID 4 is very similar to level 3, except for the fact that disks are managed independently rather than in unison. It is for this reason that RAID 4 is not often used.

RAID Level 5

RAID 5 solves the dedicated parity drive problem of RAID 3 and RAID 4, and it is almost always the best choice. Like RAID 3 and RAID 4, RAID 5 requires a minimum of three drives, but the parity data is distributed across all drives in the array instead of a single, dedicated drive. If one disk fails, the data that was stored on that disk is recreated from the parity information stored across the other drives. For any number of disks in the array, the equivalent of one drive is given up for this parity. RAID 5 also improves I/O performance over RAID 3 or RAID 4 because write operations often occur in unison with other disk access operations. Also, I/O degradation decreases as more drives are added to the array. Some high-level server equipment is capable of implementing a *stand-by* disk that remains idle until a drive fails. When a failure occurs, the stand-by drive is rebuilt from the stripped parity data with minimal loss of time or performance to the end user.

RAID Level 10

RAID 10, or more appropriately, RAID 1,0 combines the concepts of RAID 0 and RAID 1. Data is written across multiple drives without parity for maximum performance, but the entire array is also mirrored (and sometimes duplexed) to another array of drives for fault tolerance. Given the high quality and low failure rate of current drive and controller technologies today, this method provides the highest level of I/O performance with enough fault tolerance to keep downtime at an acceptable minimum.

Regardless of which method you select, always keep in mind your objectives. The major issue you have is balancing maximizing useable drive space, performance, and network downtime. As with most components in a network, no single technology is *right* for every situation.

EXAM PREPARATION SUMMARY

This chapter introduced you to some of the fundamental concepts associated with PC networking. We discussed some key terms used in the industry, some wiring standards, the basic concepts of how Ethernet and Token Ring networks operate, and the fundamental design considerations of fault-tolerant disk storage. I discuss many of these concepts in more detail in later chapters, but, before moving ahead, you should review the key concepts below to make sure you understand the material you just read.

- The basic vocabulary associated with PC networking, include:
  - Full- and half-duplexing
  - Server and workstation
  - Cables and NICs
  - WAN and LAN
  - Client/server and peer-to-peer
  - Broadband and baseband
- The basic characteristics of network structure, including segments and backbones
- The characteristics of star, bus, and ring topologies, and the advantages and disadvantages to each
- The major network operating systems including Netware, NT, and UNIX
- The client components of the major network operating systems, client component resource requirements, and where they are best suited
- The concept of Directory Services and what services are offered by the major operating systems
- The default protocols of IPX and IP with their NOS

- The following terms and how each relates to fault tolerance or high availability:
  - Mirroring (RAID 1)
  - Duplexing (RAID 2)
  - Stripping (with and without parity (RAID 3, 4, 5 and 10))
  - Volumes (RAID 0)
- The following characteristics of networking media and connectors:
  - The advantages and disadvantages of coax, Cat 3, Cat 5, fiber optics, UTP, STP, and the appropriate conditions to use each
  - The length and speed of 10Base2, 10BaseT, 100BaseT, 10Base5
  - The visual appearance of RJ-45 and BNC connectors and how they are crimped

APPLYING WHAT YOU'VE LEARNED

The following review questions give you an opportunity to test your knowledge of the information presented in this chapter. The answers to the assessment questions are in Appendix A. If you miss questions, review the sections in this chapter that cover those topics before going further.

1. Define a LAN:

2. Define a WAN:

3. What type of network is composed of a number of computers that connect to a central computer for file storage, printing, and shared applications?

4. What type of network topology is depicted by a single cable where devices connect using *T* connectors?

    A. Star

    B. Bus

    C. Ring

5. What type of network topology is usually depicted when a hub is used with Ethernet?

A. Star

B. Bus

C. Ring

6. Name the three most popular network operating systems used today:

7. Which operating system uses IPX as its default protocol?

8. Which operating systems use TCP/IP as their default protocols?

9. Why is disk redundancy important, and what characteristics are common to all RAID levels?

10. What level of RAID is defined by using three or more disk drives where the data is stripped across all drives in the array?

11. What RAID level offers the greatest performance?

12. What RAID level offers the least fault tolerance?

13. What happens when a device is disconnected from the middle of a BUS network?

14. What type of cable is used on a 100BaseT network?

15. Name the maximum distances of 10Base2, 100BaseTx, and 10Base5:

16. What is a crossover cable typically used for?

17. If your Ethernet LAN contains a large number of devices and performance is poor, what type of device can you install to create more collision domains?

18. What kind of device might you need if you wanted to connect your corporate LAN to the Internet?

19. A modem would be normally used in:

A. Baseband communications

B. Broadband communications

20. What are some advantages of a client/server network over a peer-to-peer network?

The OSI Model and Network Devices

About Chapter 2

This chapter introduces the industry-accepted standards on which networks are built. I look at the OSI (Open Systems Interconnection) and the IEEE (Institute of Electrical and Electronic Engineers) standards, and explain how they help multiple network devices communicate. Next I examine the fundamental components of a network and discuss how data is passed between devices and disperse local area networks (LANs).

This chapter examines the OSI model in detail. Make sure that you read these sections carefully, and that you fully understand the principles the OSI model defines. They are fundamental building blocks of PC networks. As you progress through your career, knowing how various devices fit within the OSI standard will be critical. The OSI model is also required knowledge for all other vendor certification programs.

In addition to these OSI and IEEE standards, this chapter delves into networking devices such as NICs (Network Interface Cards), hubs, switches, bridges, and routers. I explain how these devices are used in a real network, how to configure some of their hardware components, and which devices are best suited for particular situations.

NETWORKING STANDARDS

A near blunder by IBM in the earliest days of the Personal Computer may have been the biggest boon to the industry, and to the consumer. By the time IBM realized that companies such as Radio Shack, Commodore, Apple, and others were making real headway with their small computers, IBM, in order to compete in the market, had less than a year to introduce their product. There was no time to develop proprietary components, and IBM had to use readily available parts. Perhaps the successful companies foresaw that standardization would be crucial to future success! In years past, many companies with proprietary system platforms have gone by the wayside.

When computer networking began to take shape, it was clear that standards had to be created in order to reap the maximum benefits of this new technology. The need for standards was also evident because in the early years, companies purchased products from many different vendors with a multitude of proprietary designs. The industry had to assure customers that these various products could all coexist. Two organizations stepped up to lead the standardization charge: the Institute of Electrical and Electronic Engineers (IEEE), and the International Standards Organization (ISO). The ISO developed a model for network communications called the *Open Systems Interconnection* model, or OSI, and by adhering to the OSI definition, multi-vendor, multi-protocol devices can communicate.

The OSI Reference Model

The OSI reference model is not a protocol in itself, but rather a conceptual architecture with which to build communication systems around. It does not promote any one vendor's product or technology. The model divides the communication process into seven interdependent layers (see Table 2-1). Each layer is responsible for a specific function, and when combined with other layers, enables data communications to take place. The grouping of these programs in the OSI model is called the *protocol stack*. It is extremely important to understand what each layer defines, and how the layers relate to other layers, and to the model as a whole.

exam preparation pointer

Concepts of the OSI model are covered specifically in the Network+ exam as well in as all of the vendor certification tests. Before going further with your studies, make sure you fully understand the OSI model and the functions of the seven layers.

tip

One method of recalling the names of the seven layers is to remember the first letters in the phase: All People Seem To Need Data Processing (APSTNDP). Another mnemonic device is Please Do Not Throw Sausage Pizza Away (PDNTSPA).

TABLE 1-1 THE OSI REFERENCE MODEL	
OSI LAYER	*SERVICE DESCRIPTION*
7. Application	Services such as file transport, e-mail, and terminal emulation (FTP, Telnet, SMTP/POP3)
6. Presentation	
5. Session	
4. Transport	Reliable end-to-end data transportation using protocols such as IP, UDP, TCP
3. Network	
2. Data–Link	Physical connections responsible for moving data over the network media
1. Physical	

Layer 1: Physical

As would appear logical, the Physical Layer describes the functions of the *physical connection* between a PC and other network devices. Most commonly, this layer describes the network cabling, but it also defines the electrical characteristics of the physical components as well. The network's *topology* (physical layout) is defined by Layer 1 as is the cable's *bandwidth*, or speed. For example, with Ethernet 10BaseT, the OSI's physical layer definition describes it as twisted-pair wire with a maximum bandwidth (speed) of 10Mbps. The physical layer is responsible for placing and receiving data bits to and from onto the connecting medium. Layer 1 does not understand the bits' meanings, and simply deals with the electrical and mechanical characteristics (current, voltage, connectors, and NIC) of the signals and signaling technologies.

Layer 2: Data-Link

The Link Layer, or in formal terms, the Data-Link Layer, handles the point-to-point transfer *and* validity of data across the physical media link (network cable). A link is a direct communication path between two network devices. The transmitted bits are divided into small chunks, or *frames*. This layer is responsible for sending the frames down the channel with the proper error control, flow control, and synchronization. Layers 1 and 2 are required for every type of network communication. There are two sublayers within the Data-Link Layer: the top layer, called the *Logical Link Control* (LLC), and the bottom layer, called the *Media Access Control* (MAC).

The LLC sublayer establishes the communication links, handles frame error correction, and is responsible for the hardware addresses.

The MAC sublayer defines how multiple devices share access to the same media. The two main methods of access are:

- *With contention*, where devices can communicate when they need to. Ethernet is an example of a contention access method.

- *Token passing*, where communications can only occur when the device has the token, or communication frame. Token Ring, ARCnet, and FDDI are examples of token passing media access.

Layer 3: Network

The Network Layer establishes the route between the sending and receiving stations. This layer provides the switching and routing technologies to the layers above it. The Network Layer is a very complex layer because the networks where data must be routed to may be located on geographically diverse segments. These segments may be on the same LAN or countries apart and connected by many possible routes. Routing protocols that operate at the Network level (often times referred to as *Layer 3 routing*) typically select the optimal path between points. Routing and relaying systems currently operate only at Layer 2 or Layer 3; however, Layer 4 protocols are being developed. While routing at higher layers provides more options and control, it introduces extra overhead that slows the process down.

 exam preparation pointer

For the Network+ exam, you will need to know that routing occurs at the Network Layer

Layer 4: Transport

The Transport Layer is responsible for ensuring that data is sent and received successfully between two devices. Whereas the Data-Link Layer is only responsible for delivering frames from one device to another, it's the Transport Layer's job to detect transmission problems. In other words, if 5MB of data are sent, the Transport Layer assures that 5MB of data are received. If packets are lost during routing, the Transport Layer, Layer 4, initiates the retransmission request. Layer 4 determines how a *reliable* connection between the devices will be achieved. Establishing a reliable connection involves specific issues such as how the connections are established, maintained, and terminated. While transporting data, mechanisms to detect connection breaks and methods of recovering from these breaks are also defined. The Transport Layer also establishes the *flow control*, which prevents one system from overrunning another with data.

 exam preparation pointer

The first four layers deal with data *transportation* and the next three layers deal with data *application*.

Layer 5: Session

The primary function of the Session Layer is to provide the controls for communication between applications. Another very important service of the Session Layer is to map names to network addresses so that the applications can communicate with devices by name instead of through cryptic addresses. In practice, the services within this layer are usually incorporated into the Transport Layer.

Layer 6: Presentation

The Presentation Layer performs the data manipulation functions necessary to provide a common application interface and to provide services such as encryption, text compression, and reformatting. Layer 6 defines the manner in which software applications enter the network. The network *redirector* operates at this level, making files on a file server visible to the client computer.

 concept link

The network redirector is a software component that is installed on a client workstation. The job of the redirector is to determine if a resource (a file or printer, for example) is present on the local PC, or someplace else on the network. If the required resource is local, the redirector simply enables the request of the program to be passed on to the local operating system (Windows 95/98, for example) for processing. If, however, the resource is on the network, the redirector *intercepts* the request and passes it on to the network operating system.

Layer 7: Application

The Application Layer defines the *network applications* that support the end-user programs. Services such as FTP (File Transfer Protocol) and network management are handled in the application level. Common functions at this layer are opening, closing, reading and writing files, transferring files and e-mail messages, executing remote jobs, and obtaining directory information about network resources. However, this layer does not support *user applications* such as word-processors, spreadsheets, and so on. In fact, this level of functionality is not addressed within the OSI model.

The IEEE 802 Standards

In February 1980, the Institute for Electrical and Electronic Engineers (IEEE) formed a standardization group termed the 802 project (named after the year and month the group began). From their work, the 802 committee defined 12 specifications, identified by the following categories.

802.1 Internetworking and Management

802.2 Logical Link Control

802.3 Carrier Sense with Multiple Access and Collision Detection (CSMA/CD)

802.4 Token Bus LAN

802.5 Token Ring LAN

802.6 Metropolitan Area Network (MAN)

802.7 Broadband Technical Advisory Group

802.8 Fiber-Optic Technical Advisory Group

802.9 Integrated Voice/Data Networks

802.10 Network Security

802.11 Wireless Networks

802.12 Demand Priority Access LAN (For example, 100Base VG-AnyLAN)

exam
preparation
pointer **For the Network+ exam, you should know that the 802 specification contains twelve categories and that 802.3 (Ethernet) and 802.5 (Token Ring) are the two most common. You will not be expected to define the remaining ten.**

LOWER LAYER DEVICES AND FUNCTIONS

While the Network+ exam expects you to understand the functions of the entire OSI model, it focuses primarily on the first four layers. These layers deal specifically with the physical components of the network (the NIC and cable, for example) and with data routing. Therefore, the remaining discussion of the OSI layers examines the components and functions that operate at these four layers.

Physical Layer Devices

In addition to the NIC and the cable, there are many other devices that operate at the physical layer. The most common of these devices are:

o Hubs

o Transceivers

o Multistation Access Units (MAUs)

o Repeaters

While I touched upon many of the physical layer devices briefly in Chapter 1, it is important to discuss them in greater detail because they are critical for data to transverse a network.

Hubs

Hubs are normally located at the center of an Ethernet network within a star topology. Hubs generally do nothing more than pass the data packets around the LAN. Hubs create a single collision domain that may create problems if many hubs are stacked together to add additional network device connections. Hubs are generally inexpensive (ranging in price from $30 to $200), and require little if any configuration. Hubs are generally *passive*, meaning that they add nothing to the data signal, although more expensive hubs can also be *active*; they will regenerate the strength of the data signal before passing it on. To stay within proper Ethernet specifications, active hubs do not extend cable length capabilities, but rather boost the voltage of the data signal to compensate for outside distortions. An active hub may be useful in situations where noise exterior to the cable degrades the electronic pulses of the data. Note however, that this process will not correct any data errors, only regenerate them.

Transceivers

Transceivers are most commonly used to convert the physical connection from one Ethernet type to another. For example, if you have an older coax NIC and you need to connect to a Category 5 twisted-pair topology, you can use a transceiver. Most often the transceiver will attach to an AUI port on older NICs to enable conversion to a twisted-pair topology. However, transceivers will not convert topology or protocol types, such as connecting Ethernet to Token Ring.

MAUs

In Chapter 1, I discussed the basics of Token Ring, and introduced the concept of the Multistation Access Unit, or MAU. Although it is not completely analogous to a hub, it might be helpful to think of a Token Ring MAU as the equivalent of an Ethernet HUB. Logically thinking, the MAU is placed at the top of a Token-Ring ring and is the central point for packets traversing the LAN. Like a hub or a switch, MAUs have a specific number of devices that can be attached, including other MAUs that are *daisy-chained* to provide additional device ports. Just as Ethernet has collision domains that effect LAN performance, Token Ring has ring domains with similar effects. If there are too many devices connected into a stack of MAUs, the time it takes for any one device to get control of the token to communicate may become unacceptable. Therefore designing the physical layout of your topology, including the separation and bridging of ring segments, becomes increasingly important. Recently, Token Ring switching has become available. As with Ethernet switching, Token Ring switching provides a dedicated connection between two devices, in effect making a private *ring* for just those two computers. File servers attached to a switch with 16/32Mbps NICs can achieve 32Mbps receiving speeds while transmitting data at 16Mbps simultaneously on a second segment.

Repeaters

I covered the active hub so you already know what a repeater is. Independent of a hub, a repeater can be placed on a network cabling system to regenerate, or strengthen, the signal. In an Ethernet environment, repeaters are most commonly used in areas that contain large amounts of electrical interference where the electric impulses may be weakened. For other uses, especially in serial communications where end users use *dumb* terminals instead of PCs, repeaters can greatly increase the distance these terminals can be located from the main server. An important thing to remember about repeaters is that they *repeat everything*. The devices do not perform data conditioning or error checking. If bad packets come into a repeater, bad packets, albeit with a stronger signal, will leave the repeater.

Especially in an Ethernet environment, you should ask yourself if there is a better method to achieve the desired results before you deploy repeaters. Fiber optic cable is usually a better alternative, and as the cost of fiber components decreases, repeaters may end up more expensive than fiber components, and, with repeaters, you introduce an additional point of failure on the LAN.

A Physical Layer scenario

Many of the Network+ exam questions provide a typical networking situation and ask you to select an appropriate course of action. The goal is to see if you understand how to deploy a systematic approach to troubleshooting.

The Network+ exam deals specifically with connection problems relating to the physical layer of the OSI model, as discussed below. In this scenario, assume you have just installed a NIC into a computer but you are unable to connect to the network. The first step of the troubleshooting process is to look at the physical layer components.

First, check all possible points of failure with the cabling. Depending on your topology, you'll need to check a number of things:

- On a bus type network, make sure the T connector on the NIC is secure, and that both ends of the cable are attached. If this is the last device on the bus, make sure the terminator is attached to the outside of the T. Check to make sure other computers on this segment are operational. If not, the problem might be caused by a connection break someplace else on the cable system.

- On a star topology, make sure that the cable is plugged into the NIC and the wall jack, if appropriate. If you have access to the hub, make sure that connection is securely in place. Most NICs and hubs have link lights that illuminate when both ends are properly connected. If you don't have a link light, try attaching the cable into another port on the hub, and if necessary, replace the patch cable between the NIC and wall plate with a known good cable.

The next step in the troubleshooting process is to check the NIC and the NIC configuration. There are a number of possible card conflicts depending on the type of card used:

- If the NIC is not a Plug and Play card, it will most likely have jumpers, or software, to configure it. If there are physical jumpers on the card, check the documentation to be sure the IRQ, DMA, and I/O base addresses are set to the configurations you expect. Software-based configurations provide the same functionality as jumpers but they are accessed through a program provided by the manufacturer. In order to avoid conflicts with other cards in the PC, you will need to make sure these three settings have not already been assigned. Most current PCs enable you to reserve IRQs, DMA, and I/O addresses in the CMOS setup. Check your system's documentation for specific instructions.

o On Plug and Play devices, or after you have configured the board as discussed above, boot into the computer's setup routine. Make sure that the card is properly identified (if your firmware provides this feature) and that the IRQ, DMA, and I/O base address you configured on the NIC are available. Make adjustments as necessary. A common situation with older, ISA based cards, occurs when the system's resources default to Plug and Play devices instead of legacy ISA devices. Often times you will need to change the settings to redefine the IRQ to the settings on your NIC.

o If the computer has a number of other add-in boards, it is quite possible that you will not have a free IRQ for the NIC. This is especially common with systems that have two printers and a sound card. The printers use IRQ 5 and IRQ 7, and the sound card will typically reserve IRQ 10. These are the most common IRQs for NICs, especially non-Plug and Play ISA cards. (See Table 2-2 for a list of typically assigned IRQs.) In some cases, you may need to permanently remove an existing option board in order to connect to the LAN.

TABLE 2-2 TYPICALLY ASSIGNED IRQs

IRQ	SYSTEM DEVICE
0	System timer
1	Keyboard
2	Available: Connects to IRQ 9
3	Serial COM2 and COM4
4	Serial COM1 and COM3
5	Secondary printer port LPT2 (Also commonly used for sound cards)
6	Floppy disk
7	Primary printer port LPT1
8	Realtime clock
9	VGA, 3270 emulation
10	Available
11	Available
12	Available

IRQ	SYSTEM DEVICE
13	Math coprocessor
14	Primary IDE controller
15	Available but commonly used for secondary IDE controller

- In 32-bit Windows operating systems (Windows 9*x* and NT), you can also check the resource status from the Systems Settings option in the Control Panel. If your NIC conflicts with another device, you will see a yellow warning sign next to the NIC icon on this screen. If you review the details of the device, Windows usually tells you which device is using the conflicting resource. It is then a matter of manually changing the settings on one or the other devices. (Again, you may need to permanently remove the conflicting device to free the resources up for the NIC.)

- After you check the settings previously mentioned you want to check the hardware itself. You normally do this with diagnostic software supplied (by the vendor) with the card. A common diagnostic test is known as a loop back test. This requires a special loopback adapter that connects to the NIC just like the patch cable. (I discussed how to make loopback testers in the section "Wiring considerations," in Chapter 1.) The diagnostic software then verifies that the firmware on the NIC is functioning as expected on the local computer.

- If you do not succeed in connecting to the network, you should verify that you have not exceeded the maximum number of permitted connections to your server(s). Some systems, like Novell Netware for example, do not provide an error message when all licensed connections are used. Instead, the server simply refuses to acknowledge requests for new connections until someone else logs off. If possible, have another user log off the LAN, wait a few minutes to make certain the connection has been freed up, and try your PC again.

If all of the above tests do not provide a solution, the next step in the troubleshooting process involves other computers, and possibly the network server itself.

Other Physical Layer concepts

It is often desirable, or necessary, to have a single NIC capable of using more than one protocol. A *driver interface* enables this to happen. Two primary driver interfaces exist: NDIS and ODI.

- **Network Driver-Interface Standard (NDIS)** is the standard for Windows NT, 95/98, OS/2, and Windows for Workgroups.

- **Open Data-Link Interface (ODI)** was jointly developed by Apple computers and Novell, and is the standard for all Netware and Appletalk systems.

Network cards and drivers can communication in *full- duplex* or *half- duplex* mode. Full duplex provides the capability to send data out on the transmit wires of twisted-pair cable, and receive data on the receive wires at the same time. This greatly increases overall throughput and should be enabled on file servers whenever possible. Half duplex, on the other hand, is capable only of transmission or reception at a single time.

exam preparation pointer

The terms *full duplex* and *half duplex* will most likely be on the Network+ exam. You should be aware that implementing full duplex is a property of both the hardware and the software driver.

The term *bandwidth* is commonly used in the network world. The technical definition of bandwidth is the difference between the highest and lowest frequencies of a given range. Media that has a larger distance between the high and low ends can achieve faster data transmissions. Therefore, 100BaseT has a bandwidth of 100 Mbps where 10Base2 (coax) has a bandwidth of only 10 Mbps.

Two common transmission forms that apply to communications are *broadband* and *baseband*:

- **Broadband** enables multiple communication channels to simultaneously share the same media bandwidth, such as voice, video, and data. ISDN and xDSL WAN communication services are examples of broadband transmissions.

- **Baseband** transmission uses a single frequency; therefore, the entire channel is dedicated to a single data signal. Most LANs use a baseband technology, as do dial-up modem connections.

Data-Link Layer Devices

Remember that the Data-Link Layer, handles the point-to-point transfer *and* validity of data across the physical media. Many devices can be deployed to accomplish this transfer process although the end result is basically the same. The basic goal is to send data from one device to another, preferably as quickly as possible. In this section I look at the most common Layer 2 devices, and how they are used.

Bridges

When a collision domain becomes too large, it is necessary to *segment* the cabling system in some way to reduce the amount of traffic contending for the shared media. One device that works well for this is a *bridge*. The bridge, a device that connects two or more LAN segments of the same type, is responsible for directing traffic between the segments. For example, a bridge can connect two Ethernet segments but it cannot connect a Token Ring Segment with an Ethernet segment. Bridges create and maintain tables of addresses for the devices on the network. A bridge learns which addresses were successfully received through which particular output ports by monitoring which station acknowledged receipt of the address. While bridges create multiple *collision domains,* all bridged segments are still in one *broadcast domain.* Bridges work at the data-link layer and are *protocol independent.* Because of this, they are faster than routers. (Discussed in the next section.)

A bridging example

Figure 2-1 shows an example of bridging. The LAN consisting of three segments, or collision domains: S1, S2, and S3. Station A has data to transmit to station D so station A builds a frame that identifies station D as the destination address. Station A also includes its own address in the frame's source address field.

When station A transmits the frame, the bridge copies the frame from segment S1, then reads the source address — station A, in this case. Because the bridge copies the frame from the port attached to segment S1, it enters station A in its filtering database as existing on segment S1. Because the bridge has not yet determined where the station is located, it forwards the frame to all active ports except the one connected to S1 (the segment from which the frame came in). Station D sees that the frame is addressed to it, and sends back an acknowledgement. The bridge copies this frame and now knows that station D is on segment S2. From this point on, the bridge will forward all traffic between these devices directly through the proper ports. If station A sends data to station B, the bridge forwards nothing; thus, keeping the other segments free of unnecessary traffic. Using this method, the bridge eventually learns the location of all connected devices. This is known as *transparent bridging* because the directing of traffic is transparent (it is not visible) to the end user.

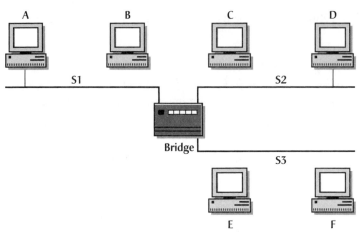

FIGURE 2-1 Example of a transparent bridge LAN

Source Route Bridging

Token Ring networks use a different bridging protocol known as *Source Route Bridging*. This protocol differs from transparent bridging in that the bridge itself does not contain the routing table, but the devices do. For example, in Figure 2-2, station A wants to talk to station D. Assuming station A has not communicated with D previously, A will send a *Hello* packet out on the wire. Bridges using Source Routing only copy frames that contain source-routing information in the packet header. Because this Hello Packet contains source-routing information, bridge B copies the frame and transmits it on to Ring 2. When station D sees the frame is addressed to it, it places its MAC address into the header and sends it back through the bridge to station A. Station A will now update its internal routing table so all further communication between these stations can occur directly. When more than one bridge must be crossed, each bridge will add its address to the header so that the full route to the destination is known.

 The routing table is held in RAM, so once the PC is reset, the table is erased and route discovery must occur again.

In order to minimize traffic, stations usually try to find the required device on the local ring by first sending the frame out without any source-route information. If the frame comes back without the destination device acknowledging it, the station knows that the device is not on the local ring.

FIGURE 2-2   **Example of Source Route Bridging**

Because the primary goal of designing a network is to provide redundancy in case of a device failure, many networks use multiple bridges to improve the chances of an available route between segments. When two or more paths exist, these bridging protocols can run into trouble, as I address in the next section.

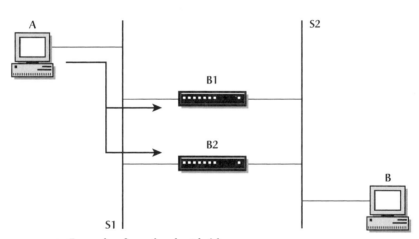

FIGURE 2-3   **Example of a redundant bridge**

Examine the situation in Figure 2-3. Two bridges (B1 and B2) are deployed between segments S1 and S2. In case one bridge fails, the other bridge provides a route between the two segments. Suppose station A sends data to station B: both bridges will copy the frame from segment S1. Because station A has not been discovered by either bridge yet, both bridges create an entry in their address table defining station A as existing on segment S1.

Now suppose that bridge B1 is a little faster than B2. B1 forwards the packet to segment S2 just slightly before B2 does. B2 now sees the frame forwarded by B1 and sees that the source device is station A. Because B2 has recorded station A as being on segment S1, it now assumes that station A has been physically moved to segment S2 and updates its address table. B2 will now forward the frame back out to segment S1 identifying it as existing on segment S2. Now bridge B1 picks up the frame forwarded by B2 and thinks that station A now exists on segment S2. When each bridge forwards the packet back to segment S1, each will in turn pick up the packet, assume the station has moved again, and update the address table. This is known as *bridge looping*. In order to avoid a complete collapse of the network (the wire would be consumed by the same frame being sent around and around), the protocol states that after any packet has crossed 16 bridges or routers, it is to be considered *lost*, and therefore, it is discarded.

Because Source Route Bridging already has path routing information within the packet, it is easier and less troublesome to create redundant paths with Token Ring networks. If there are multiple parallel bridges on a Token Ring network, multiple Hello packets reach the destination node (one from each redundant bridge). This node sends a response back to the original source node for each Hello packet it receives. The source node then picks the best path for all future communications.

The spanning tree protocol

In order to overcome the bridge-looping problem on an Ethernet network, the *spanning tree protocol* can be implemented. This protocol enables redundant pairs of bridges to dynamically adjust themselves to either be actively forwarding packets, or to be in stand-by mode. The bridges exchange information between themselves to determine which route is the most efficient, and then the remaining bridges stop forwarding packets. While in nonforward mode, the bridges constantly check for activity from the active bridge. If the activity ceases for a predetermined amount of time, the bridges force a *topology change* request. At this point, all bridges clear their routing tables and are dynamically reconfigured based on the new available routes. This route table exchange is known as *convergence*.

Routes can be manually predetermined by configuring the bridge with a *cost*. When the route discovery procedure occurs, the cost of the route takes precedence over the route distance. For example, if the network administrator adds a cost of four to a bridge, even though that route may be shorter, the other bridge will be the active bridge because its cost will be lower.

When a packet crosses a bridge (or router), the distance is measured as a *hop*. For example, if a packet is forwarded by two bridges and a router to reach its destination, the distance between the sending station and the destination is said to be three hops.

Data-Link Layer addressing

An essential component of the network is its capability to locate devices. Most of these locating devices use a NIC, whether as an add-on or built-in card. Each NIC has a hardware address burned into its *programmable read-only memory* (PROM). This address is typically called the MAC address since it is the responsibility of the Media Access Control sublayer of the Data-Link Layer to maintain hardware addresses. The MAC address is 6 bytes long; the first 3 bytes conform to the standards of the IEEE specification, and the last 3 bytes are assigned by the manufacturer. Therefore, each device has a unique hardware address. Because most computer systems have one physical network connection, they have only a single link-layer address. On the other hand, routers, bridges, and other devices connected to multiple physical networks can have multiple link-layer addresses. When all is said and done, transporting data between two devices is accomplished by locating the MAC addresses of the sending and receiving stations on the network.

 Most typical protocols, including TCP/IP and IPX, use higher level addresses for connected devices (although they are eventually resolved to the MAC address). TCP/IP uses an IP addressing scheme that I discuss in Chapter 3, and IPX uses an internal address made up in part by the MAC address and the network number.

Fragmentation and connection services

Depending on the routing service used, packets may be *fragmented* in the routing process. Fragmentation usually occurs when the maximum size of each packet cannot be defined or agreed upon before transmission. When a packet becomes fragmented, each fragment is assigned a *sequence* number so that the original packet can be reassembled at the receiving end.

When two devices communicate according to the OSI model, they communicate *peer-to-peer*, meaning that a given layer from a protocol stack on one computer communicates to the corresponding layers on another computer. This communication can be *connection orientated* or *connectionless*.

A *connectionless* service uses a dynamic method of routing data along the best path and is faster than connection services. The data path is determined as the packet is being sent. Packets are automatically re-routed around failures. A connectionless protocol is typically considered *nonreliable* because there is no guarantee that packets will arrive at the intended destination. And because packet sizes are not prenegotiated, packets often become fragmented in a connectionless service, and sequencing of the fragments occurs. A common analogy to describe connectionless services is the act of mailing a letter. When you drop your letter into the mailbox, you are fairly certain that it will reach its designation, but there is no *guarantee* that it won't be lost someplace in transit.

Connection orientated implies that some form of message negotiation takes place *before* data is sent and received. This pre-exchange sets up a virtual connection between the two peer OSI layers. Until the session is terminated, all further data sent between these nodes follows this virtual connection. Typically, connection-orientated routing is considered *reliable*; it is virtually a guarantee that packets are delivered. Packets sent via a connection-oriented service do not get out of order during transport because they are not fragmented. Fragmentation is not necessary since the maximum packet size can be negotiated prior to transmission. Using the postal analogy above, a connection-orientated service is like sending your letter via certified mail. There are extra steps taken to assure delivery including tracking it from post office to post office, and having the recipient sign a document stating that the letter arrived intact.

Network Layer Devices

The Transport and Network Layers of the OSI model handle the transmission of data across the network. These layers, together, take the data packets, often called *datagrams*, that are sent and received from the upper layers and route them around the network. Typical devices that operate at this level are switches, brouters, and routers. Let's examine each of these devices in more detail.

Switching hubs

Switching hubs, or switches, have become very popular in the past few years because of the additional functionality they provide over a normal hub. Due to their increased popularity, the price of switches is dropping quickly, costing as little as $200 for a small four-port switch. Recall that Ethernet uses a collision scheme where only one device at a time can access the cable to send or receive data. When two devices attempt to send data at the same time, a collision occurs, and both devices have to wait momentarily until one of them can successfully control the wire. A switch has *router-like* intelligence built into it in the sense that it can automatically build a table of locations for every device connected to it. Using this table, the switch can then create a virtual path between any two devices, in effect enabling those two devices to access a *cable segment* for their use only. This technology greatly reduces the possible number of collisions that devices must deal with. As I discuss later, this functionality is very much like the services a router provides, but a switch is more useful in a LAN situation where routers typically deal with wide area networks (WANs). There are two basic methodologies used in switching known as *cut-through* and *store-and-forward*. When you analyze the specifications of a switch, it is important to know which, or both, of these features are supported. It is also important to know which method the manufacturer uses when they publish the speed specifications of their switch.

Cut-through is the fastest, and is the preferable method on a well-tuned network. In cut-through mode, the switch waits for an incoming data packet only long enough to have the source and destination portion of the frame in memory. It basically *cuts into* the data packet to read where the data came from, and where it is supposed to be heading. With this information, the switch can then create the direct path (if it is not already established) and simply send the remaining data packets on through. While this seems pretty logical, there is a potential problem: Data frames add error-checking information *to the end* of the frame, thereby eliminating any error detection capabilities of a switch in cut-through mode. By the time the switch realizes a frame has been corrupted in transit, the switch has already passed 95 percent of the frame on to the destination device! In this case, the receiving device must handle the error detection itself, and send a request back to the sending device to retransmit the data. In an environment where many errors occur, the cut-through method may, in fact, increase traffic and reduce network performance due to retransmits.

The store-and-forward method, on the other hand, accepts the entire data frame *before* sending it on to the destination device, thus enabling the switch to verify the validity of the data frame. If there is an error in the packet, the switch can request the retransmission; this reduces the distance the frame must travel, and eliminates much of the error correction duties of a destination device. This additional error checking hinders speed, however, because the switch must wait for the entire frame of data before it can check for errors and pass the good frames on.

Most quality switches employ both technologies, and, in fact, implement an automatic determination method. The switch will begin in cut-through mode, but automatically converts to store-and-forward mode if a predefined threshold of errors is met. Suppose, for example, that a switch is programmed to change modes when 5 percent of the packets entering in from a specific device generate errors. In this case, a quality switch watches for the number of erroneous data packets any particular device is generating, and switches from cut-through to store-and-forward when five percent of the traffic contains errors. Most of the time, you will need a network management program running on the LAN in order to detect this mode change. However, end users will generally tell you the network is slower when a switch goes into store-and-forward mode after being in cut-through mode for sometime.

note **Some switches route packets based on the OSI Layer 2 MAC addresses instead of the OSI Layer 3 network address, and are therefore called *layer two switches*. Layer two switches are faster than layer three switches, but layer three switches offer better forwarding decisions, such as type of traffic, quality of service, and so on. Obtaining this routing information requires digging into the packet's header which increases processing time and slows down the routing function. Layer two switches cannot route between networks, but layer three switches can.**

Brouters

In environments where both routable and nonroutable protocols exist, the *brouter* is an excellent solution. If a packet contains routable information, the brouter will route it; otherwise, if there is not brouter, the packet will be bridged. Brouters usually cost more than a bridge or a router, so this cost is not justified if you do not need both functions. Some examples of nonroutable protocols are NetBEUI and SNA.

Routers

Routers are used to connect two or more (potentially extended) segments. The segments may or may not be of the same topology or protocol. (In other words, the router may be on a LAN or WAN, or placed between an Ethernet LAN and a Token-Ring LAN). Routing information must be contained within the data packet (as you'll see, not all protocols are *routable*). Broadcasts and multicasts are never propagated across a router because the exact destination information is not contained within the packets. Using the postal analogy again, the router is like a mail carrier. The mail carrier needs to know the exact street address on his or her route in order to deliver the mail. Routers are only interested in local hardware addresses, and they keep track of the network segments and share this address information with other routers.

Like bridges, routers can be used to segment LANs in order to balance traffic, but unlike a bridge, routers can be used to filter traffic for security purposes. The router's capability to filter out specific packet types, or packets from unknown locations, gives it very basic firewall capabilities. (I discuss firewalls in more detail in Chapter 5) Most routers are specialized devices optimized for communications; however, router functions can also be implemented by the network operating system (NOS) within the file server. For example, the NT and NetWare NOSs can route from one subnetwork to another if each segment is connected to a separate NIC in the file server.

Routers often serve as an internetwork backbone, interconnecting all networks in the enterprise. This architecture connects several routers together via a high-speed LAN topology such as Fast or Gigabit Ethernet. As networks become more and more complex, the need to extend network services across larger and larger geographic areas increases, and routing of data becomes a critical factor in network technology. Where bridges connect to network segments, routers typically connect two or more LANs. These LANs can be physically located in the same building, or across countries, continents, or hemispheres. When a router connects to geographically dispersed areas, the network is usually termed a *wide area network*, or WAN. There are any number of ways routers on each end can be connected, but the most common way is through dedicated lease lines, packet switching technology such as frame relay, or the Internet.

 exam preparation pointer **The Network+ exam requires you are familiar with the basic components of a WAN and the fundamental routing concepts**.

Regardless of which physical lines connect the WAN, the device used to connect the in-house line to the external digital circuit is known as a *Digital (or Data) Service Unit/Channel Service Unit* or DSU/CSU. The DSU/CSU is similar to a modem, but it connects a digital circuit rather than an analog circuit. The CSU/DSU takes the digital signal and optionally strips off optional channels for voice lines. The data flow is then fed out to another port, commonly with a V.35 serial cable (see The V.35 Serial Interface sidebar), which is then attached to the router. The router has a single LAN connection, either BNC for coax, or RJ-45 for twisted-pair. This combination of devices accounts for the physical connection between WAN components. Refer to Figure 2-4 to see how these components might look in a typical WAN configuration.

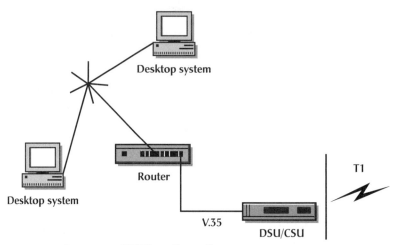

FIGURE 2-4 A common WAN configuration

Gateways

When it is necessary to connect two networks of different protocols, for example TCP/IP and IPX, you need a *gateway*. The gateway device can be a specialized box or it may be implemented by the NOS. While gateways are normally discussed along with transport layers, gateways actually operate at all levels of the OSI model.

Basic Routing Concepts

Routers use flat lookup tables stored in RAM to make forwarding decisions. These tables are either *static* or *dynamic*. Static routing requires a network administrator to physically calculate the routes between segments and enter these addresses into the router's databases. Static routing is only recommended for small networks with only one or two routers.

THE V.35 SERIAL INTERFACE

V.35 is a standard for *data transmission at 48Kbps using 60 to108KHz group-band circuits*. This basically means that V.35 is a very fast, high-speed serial interface designed to support both higher data rates and connectivity between *Data Terminal Equipment* (DTE) or *Data Communication Equipment* (DCE) via digital lines. The V.35 connector is made up of 24 pins that combine several telephone circuits to provide the high-speed interface between these devices and the DSU/CSU. Although V.35 is specified to support speeds from 48 to 64Kbps, much higher rates can be achieved. Theoretically, a V.35 cable can achieve speeds up to 100Kbps at a length of 120m (4000 feet). These speeds are obtained by the V.35's design to combine both balanced and unbalanced voltage signals on the same interface.

V.35 Serial Cable

Dynamic routing uses special routing protocols that enable routers to exchange data with each other. The two most common routing protocols are *Routing Information Protocol* (RIP) and *Open Shortest Path First* (OSPF). RIP performs route discovery based on *hops,* or the number of routers that must be crossed to reach various segments. OSPF bases its routing calculations on the available *bandwidth* rather than hops. These routing protocols exchange their tables with adjacent routers so that each router on the network knows how to get a data packet from any one point to another. Based on routing tables, any router on the network should be able to direct a packet either to the desired segment (if that segment is attached to the router) or on to another router that forwards the packet based on its routing tables.

Even with this table exchange, there are many possibilities that can occur to keep a router from knowing which router to send data to. Therefore, a concept called the *default route* is used. Every router should be configured with a default route. When a packet is received with a destination address that the local router does not have in its routing tables, it simply passes the packet on to its default route and the receiving router deals with the problem. When designing a routed network, it is important that special attention be paid to the default routes of each router. A data packet typically is passed on by a maximum of 16 routers or *hops*, before the packet is considered undeliverable and is discarded.

When a client workstation is configured for IP, a *default gateway* address is usually defined within the TCP/IP properties. When the workstation needs to send data beyond its local network, the data flows to this default gateway (the router) ; the workstation lets the router handle the process of finding the data's destination location. This is typical on a LAN where Internet access is required. Because Internet addresses will always go beyond a private LAN, a router is used to pass the data to the Internet systems. In the default gateway scenario, the router has a local IP address (a private address for the LAN) and a public address connected to the Internet.

concept link

Default gateways used in TCP/IP networks will be covered in more detail in Chapter 3.

Not all protocols are *routable* however. IP and IPX can be routed because their packets contain segment address information, but other protocols, such as NetBEUI (used frequently in Microsoft networking) and SNA (Systems Network Architecture, used on IBM networks) are not. A nonroutable protocol cannot transverse across a network and its data packets destined outside the local LAN are discarded.

exam preparation pointer

The Network+ exam requires you understand that IP is a routable protocol, and NetBEUI is not.

Comparing Bridges, Switches, and Routers

These three devices are not necessarily competing technologies, but rather complementary ones. The primary difference between the devices is the layer at which they operate. Bridges and switches are Data-Link Layer devices, and routers operate at the Network Layer. Therefore, segments connected by bridges all have the same network address whereas routers create separate network addresses for connected segments on the same network layer. Where Data-Link Layer devices are used, packets do not contain addressing information to tell them when the destination device is located, whereas when Network Layer devices are used, destination addresses are provided in the packet header.

Bridges and switches are designed to connect LAN segments and to break up collision domains in order to provide more useable bandwidth. Because routing information is not available at the bridge level, routers are used to connect multiple networks. Routers segment broadcast domains and offer security because they can filter out packets based on protocol type or address. One school of thought is to "Bridge/switch when you can, route when you must."

EXAM PREPARATION SUMMARY

In Chapter 2 the main focus was standards within the PC networking field, especially the OSI model. I explained how data is passed between computers, whether the computers are connected locally or are continents away. I discussed the many devices used in networks to connect PCs together, and explored the processes of moving data across various physical components. I recommend you review the key concepts in this chapter to make sure you understand the material that you just read. You should be able to:

- Define the OSI model and identify the protocols, services, and functions that pertain to each OSI layer

- Understand how network cards are usually configured, including jumpers and Plug and Play

- Understand the basic steps in troubleshooting physical layer problems when a workstation will not connect to the network

- Identify and understand the use and differences of the following components:

  - Hubs
  - MAUs
  - Transceivers
  - Switching Hubs (switches)
  - Repeaters

- Identify the concepts of bridges and bridging, and the functions and characteristics of the MAC addresses

- Understand the following routing and network layer concepts:
  - The fact that routing occurs at the network layer
  - The difference between a router and a brouter
  - The difference between routable and nonroutable protocols

o The concept of default gateways

o The difference between dynamic and static routing

APPLYING WHAT YOU'VE LEARNED

The following review questions give you an opportunity to test your knowledge of the information presented in this chapter. The answers to the assessment questions are in Appendix A. If you miss questions, review the sections in this chapter that cover those topics before going further.

1. What is the OSI model, and why is it important?

2. Name the seven layers of the OSI model:

    1. _____

    2. _____

    3. _____

    4. _____

    5. _____

    6. _____

    7. _____

3. At which layer are hardware addresses maintained?

4. Which layer of the OSI model is responsible for packaging and transmitting data on the physical media?

5. Which layer of the OSI model is responsible for creating, maintaining, and tearing down of the data transportation connections?

6. Which layer of the OSI model is concerned with network applications such as Telnet and FTP?

7. Which layer of the OSI model is concerned with user applications such as word processing and spreadsheets?

8. At which layer of the OSI model are functions of TCP and IP defined?

9. How many categories are defined by the IEEE 802 committee?

10. What networking system is described by the 802.2 standard?

11. What networking system is described by the 802.5 standard?

12. Name four physical layer devices:

    1. _____

    2. _____

    3. _____

    4. _____

13. What are two types of Ethernet hubs?

    1. _____

    2. _____

14. What is a transceiver typically used for?

15. How many Ethernet collision domains are created when you connect two active hubs together?

16. When is a repeater useful to extend cable length signals?

17. Why is there a limit to the number of MAUs that can be connected together in a standard Token Ring network?

18. How many devices can communicate simultaneously within a Token Ring LAN?

19. What are three common items that must be configured correctly when installing a Network Interface Card (NIC)?

20. When you troubleshoot connection problems, you can confirm that physical layer devices are communicating by visually inspecting _____ on the NIC and hub.

21. What is the name of a common test performed on a NIC with vendor supplied diagnostic software?

22. Name two driver interfaces that enable a NIC to communicate on more than one protocol.

23. Bridges operate at the _____ OSI level.

24. Which bridging method is commonly used in Ethernet with only one bridge?

25. Where are bridging address tables maintained when using source-route bridging?

26. What bridging protocol can be used to prevent bridge looping when more than one physical path exists between two or more network segments?

27. Which two methods do switching hubs use to transport data between devices?

   1. _____

   2. _____

28. Which method of transporting data with a switch is fastest?

29. Can switching hubs propagate broadcast packets on the network?

30. How many physical addresses can be assigned to a NIC?

31. What are the two types of routing connections?

32. Which type of routing connection would typically fragment data packets?

33. Which types of connections are usually established across the layers of a WAN?

34. When would a brouter be useful?

35. Which type of device is used to connect an external digital signal to an in-house line?

36. Name two routing protocols and the characteristics they use to determine routes:

   1. _____

   _____

   2. _____

   _____

37. Which device is required to connect networks using different protocols, such as IPX and TCP/IP?

38. What can be defined within a router to assure that packets addressed to networks the router is unaware of can be forwarded on?

39. At which layer of the OSI model does routing occur?

40. What type of routing table is used when routers are not configured to share address tables?

The Fundamentals of TCP/IP

About Chapter 3

As the world of networking evolves, so too do communication standards. The Internet has been one of the largest and most profound influences in transforming the PC of the 90s; we turn to the World Wide Web for everything—from banking, to shopping, to staying in touch around the world via e-mail. With the use of the Internet comes a renewed interest in the protocol TCP/IP, the *language* of the Internet. Chapter 3 discusses this language in great detail, and explores the fundamental protocols used in PC networking.

Actually, TCP/IP is not a single network protocol (remember that a protocol is the set of rules that two or more computers agree on to facilitate communications), but a suite of protocols and applications, all of which I will discuss in this chapter. TCP/IP is extremely well suited for LANs and WANs; it is quite versatile and a good choice for many configurations. At least for the foreseeable future, TCP/IP will be the dominant network communications suite, and you can be sure it will appear in a large percentage of questions on the Network+ exam.

The original goal behind the TCP/IP communications standard was to create an easy method to establish connections between many dispersed computers. Back in the mid-1960s, computer networks only existed in the minds of a few scientists. It was the scientists' dream to create a computer communication system that would facilitate collaborative research across universities worldwide. In the late 1960s, the United States Defense Department's Advanced Research Project Agency funded a project to do just this. Because the Department of Defense provided the funds, many people incorrectly assume the Internet was originally designed to protect national security in the face of nuclear war. The truth is, although the military realized the potential security features of a national or worldwide computer network, the original goal was, and always has been, unrelated to national defense. Research scientists, not military personnel, worked on the early development of the Internet.

When the concept of this *connected network* was first proposed, standards for computer to computer communications did not exist. Therefore, it was necessary to develop a new protocol to handle the diversity of the various computer *languages*. Because it was impossible to re-engineer existing systems to a new standard, some compromises had to be made, especially in relation to security. Also, because the primary long distance links would be voice grade telephone systems, the protocol had to be as efficient as possible in order to keep retransmission requirements to a minimum. Due to the many demands for a fast, efficient low-overhead suite of protocols, *Transmission Control Protocol / Internet Protocol*, or simply TCP/IP, was developed. Since its conception, TCP/IP has been improved and enhanced, and is now considered by many the protocol of choice for today's networks.

In Chapter 3, I take an in-depth look at the TCP/IP suite. I discuss IP addressing and routing concepts, the various protocols that make up the full TCP/IP suite, how e-mail is delivered from place to place, and the large number of TCP/IP utilities available to assist in implementing and maintaining a TCP/IP network. This chapter is a cornerstone of the Network+ exam. Many of the other topics covered in the exam, and existing in real-life networking, revolve around the TCP/IP suite. As you read through Chapter 3, be sure that you fully understand the material.

DEFINING THE TCP/IP STANDARDS

The standards for TCP/IP are published in a series of documents called *Request for Comments*, or RFCs. These documents define network services and implementations, and often summarize policies. TCP/IP standards are not developed by a committee, but rather through consensus. No single company or entity *owns* the TCP/IP protocol. Anyone can submit a document for publication as an RFC. Each RFC is reviewed by a technical expert, a task force, or the RFC editor and is then assigned a classification, or state. Table 3-1 lists the five states of RFCs.

TABLE 3-1 RFC CLASSIFICATION STATES	
CLASSIFICATION STATE	**DESCRIPTION**
1. Required	These are agreed standards; items that *must* be implemented on all TCP/IP based hosts.
2. Recommended	These specifications are highly recommended; it is highly suggested these items be implemented.
3. Elective	These policies are optional; most items in this class are applications that are agreed upon, but never widely used.

Continued

TABLE 3-1 *(continued)*	
CLASSIFICATION STATE	DESCRIPTION
4. Limited use	These items are not intended for general use; they may be proprietary in nature.
5. Not recommended	These concepts are not recommended for implementation in any form.

Common TCP/IP Vocabulary

Several acronyms are commonly used when speaking TCP/IP *lingo*. I'll discuss each of them in more detail as I get farther into the protocol suite; but first, I briefly define the terms so you may become familiar with them:

- **Hosts**: Any device, or node, connected to a network running the TCP/IP protocol. A computer is a host, as are routers and print servers.
- **TCP**: *Transmission Control Protocol*. Provides a connection-orientated packet delivery.
- **UDP**: *User Datagram Protocol.* Provides a connectionless packet delivery service.
- **IP**: *Internet Protocol.* Provides address and routing functions.
- **ICMP**: *Internet Control Message Protocol.* Reports messages and errors regarding packet delivery.
- **FTP**: *File Transfer Protocol.* Copies files between computers using a standard method.
- **Telnet**: *Terminal Emulation protocol.* Enables a connection to a PC using a text-based screen. Many Unix boxes use Telnet as their access method to the server.
- **SMTP**: *Simple Mail Transport Protocol.* Defines methods of sending and receiving e-mail.
- **SNMP**: *Simple Network Management Protocol.* Permits SNMP enabled devices to send and receive status information.
- **ARP**: *Address Resolution Protocol.* Finds a computer's numerical *address* given a computer *name*.

- **RARP**: *Reverse Address Resolution Protocol*. Returns the computer's *name*, given a computer *address*. (The opposite of ARP.)

The TCP/IP Suite

Recall that TCP/IP is a suite, or collection of protocols, and not a single protocol itself. Of the suite, Transmission Control Protocol (TCP) and Internet Protocol (IP) are two of the best-known protocols. They operate at the lower levels of the OSI model, but the suite also includes higher level specifications such as e-mail, file transfer, and terminal emulation. Table 3-2 shows the relationship between some of the more important Internet protocols and their corresponding OSI layers.

TABLE 3-2 INTERNET PROTOCOL SUITE AND THE OSI MODEL

OSI Layer	*Protocol*
Application	FTP, Telnet, SMTP, SNMP
Presentation	FTP, Telnet, SMTP, SNMP
Session	FTP, Telnet, SMTP, SNMP
Transport	TCP, UDP
Network	IP (IP routing protocols)
Data Link	ARP, RARP (address resolution protocols)
Physical	Not specified

Internet Protocol (IP)

IP is the *mailroom* of the TCP/IP suite—the place packet sorting and delivery takes place. At this layer, each incoming or outgoing packet is referred to as a *datagram*. Each IP datagram contains the source IP address of the sender and the destination IP address of the intended recipient. Unlike the MAC addresses, the IP addresses in a datagram remain the same throughout a packet's journey across an internetwork.

Network addressing

To fully understand TCP/IP and how information is passed around the network, you need to understand how each network device is defined. No matter which network protocol is used, IPX, IP, AppleTalk (for Apple Computers), and so on, each device on the network needs a unique address. Some protocols, such as IPX, automatically assign addresses when the device is connected to the network. IP, however, requires that you, the network administrator or engineer, assign a *unique* address to everything you add to your LAN or WAN. No two devices can have the same address. There are utility programs available to assist in the process of assigning addresses, but for now assume that you will assign them manually. This process is known as *static* IP address assignment. Static means that the addresses are preassigned and can only be changed manually. An IP address is a logical address as opposed to a physical address. For example, if you replace a defective NIC with a different one, the *physical* MAC address changes, but you keep the same *logical* IP address.

IP address classes   IP addresses are first defined as *classes*. Under the current version of IP, there are four classes of address ranges: A, B, C, and D. D is never used in a production environment so I do not discuss it here. The class of a given IP address tells you how many *network segments* are available, and the maximum number of *hosts*, or IP devices, that can be on each network segment. It's important to understand that a single LAN may be composed of many *network segments*. This is to say that you can have a single LAN in your office, but it may contain many network segments, created by routers (see Figure 3-1). Also, each segment is identified uniquely within an IP address.

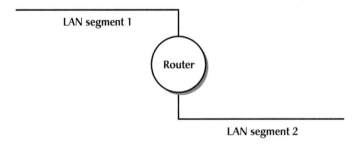

FIGURE 3-1 Example of a network with two segments separated by a router

An IP address is a 32-bit number divided into a network portion, and a host portion. You will commonly see IP addresses given in *dotted decimal notation* with four sets of three decimal numbers from 0 to 255, or four sets of eight bit binary numbers called octets. For example 192.168.100.121 is a valid IP address. When address resolution or routing occurs, the computer always uses the address in its binary form. IP is typically discussed in dotted decimal notation because it is easier for humans to deal with. The *first octet* identifies what the address class is. The decimal ranges for standard IP classes are shown in Figure 3-2.

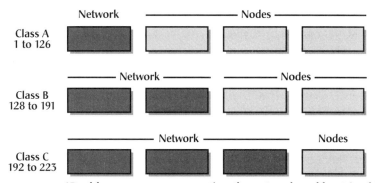

FIGURE 3-2 **IP address ranges representing the network and host (node) portion for each class**

There are a few rules you need to know about addresses before going further:

1. You may have noticed that the class ranges above seem to have skipped 127. In IP, the address 127.0.0.1 is reserved for testing purposes. You cannot use an IP address starting with 127 because it refers to the local device only (or loopback, if you will).

2. Neither the network portion nor the host portion can be 0 or 255.

3. Any IP address can be used on a private network but you must obtain a registered address if you wish to connect your computers to the Internet.

An organization known as the InterNIC is responsible for assigning IP addresses for public use. In recent years, so many people and organizations now use the Internet that IP addresses are in short supply. In fact, all the class A and B addresses have been assigned. Only Internet Service Providers (ISPs) are able to obtain new class C licenses anymore. If you need an IP address, or a block of addresses to connect your network to the Internet, your only option is to lease one from a service provider. You can contact the InterNIC by e-mail for more information at: `info@internic.net`

Referring to the fourth column in Table 3-3, you find that the two addresses, 5.100.10.2 and 5.100.10.12 are Class A, and both of the devices assigned to these addresses reside on network segment number 5. You know that both are Class A addresses because the value of the first octet (the network portion) is between 1 and 126. Because both numbers begin with 5, you know that both IP addresses are on the same network segment (5), and that the last three octets refer to the host number.

Given the addresses 192.168.10.101 and 192.168.11.101, you can tell that the addresses are Class C addresses (the value of the first octet falls between 192 and 255), and that they are *not* on the same network. Because Class C addresses use the first *three* octets to identify the network portion of the address, these two addresses define network segments 10 and 11. Both addresses have the same *node* number (101), but they exist on two different network segments.

Class C licenses do not offer nearly as many devices on any one segment as a Class B or Class A license does. In fact, the maximum number of devices, or nodes, is limited to 254. Remember that neither a network nor a node address can be 0 or 255 so there are only 254 legal addresses available in the host portion of a Class C address. If you design a *private* IP network, you must pay particular attention to your current and future needs. If your network is going to contain a large number of segments, then a Class B or C addressing scheme is likely best; however, if you need more nodes and not as many segments, a Class A or B address range is more appropriate. Refer to Table 3-3 for a list of the possible number of hosts and networks available for each address class:

TABLE 3-3 THE NUMBER OF HOSTS AND NETWORKS FOR IP ADDRESS CLASSES			
ADDRESS CLASS	*NUMBER OF NETWORKS*	*NUMBER OF HOSTS PER NETWORK*	*RANGE OF NETWORK IDS*
Class A	126	16,777,214	1 – 126
Class B	16,384	65,534	128 – 191
Class C	2,097,152	254	192 – 223

All *hosts* located on the same physical network segment must be assigned the same network ID in order to communicate. If you have more than one network connected by routers, you need to assign a network ID for *each* wide area connection. Pay close attention here to be sure you understand the following illustration.

As you can see in Figure 3-3, LAN (A) and LAN (B) are connected via routers. The segment between A and B must also be given a unique network address. In the figure, the network address of 192.1.10 is assigned to LAN (A), 192.1.20 to routed LAN (C), and 192.1.30 is assigned to LAN (B). Because the router has two physical connections, the network on each connection must have a unique IP network address. You'll see more on why this is important when I discuss IP routing later in the chapter.

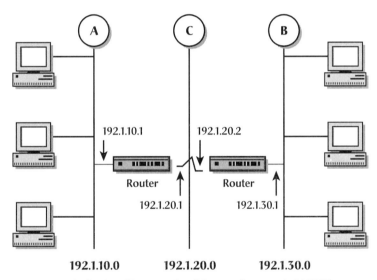

FIGURE 3-3 Assigning IP network addresses in a routed WAN

 in the real world

There are no set rules for assigning IP addresses, but many people try to group the numbers in a meaningful way. For example, if you use a Class B address scheme, you may reserve the 3rd octet to identify the operating system. You may have all Windows 95 PCs use IP addresses between 10 and 99; all NT PCs, between 100 and 199; and so on. Likewise, it is often wise to reserve either the low or high-end numbers for various devices. For example, you may want to reserve host IDs from 1 to 10 for routers, and from 11 to 20 for file servers. It can be very difficult to reassign IP addresses down the line, so spending a little time up front to logically plan your numbering pattern will probably save many hours in the long run.

IP addressing and communication problems   Two common problems often occur with IP addressing. The first happens when two devices on the same network segment have different network IDs. This is most likely to happen with Class C addresses, and when the IP address scheme is *subnetted* (see next section in this chapter for more on subnetting). Devices need to be on the same network segment in order to communicate, so keep an eye on your addresses.

The second most common problem happens when two devices on the same network segment are assigned the same host ID address. When a workstation boots up, it broadcasts it's IP address on the local network. If another device already has that address, all sorts of problems can occur. Typically, the station just entering the LAN receives an error stating that the IP address is already in use and further networking on IP will be suspended. However, you cannot always count on this outcome, and it is likely that both devices will be negatively impacted until the situation is resolved.

Subnets and subnetting   There are times when a single IP address does not provide enough segments or hosts by itself. You can add a second IP address in these situations, but if you have a registered IP block, you may find it is quite expensive. IP provides a method known as *subnetting* to divide a single IP address block into multiple segments. Using a *subnet mask*, a single IP address block can be partitioned in such a way that it modifies the normal placement of the host portion to create additional or fewer networks. In order to accomplish the subnetting of an IP number, the IP devices compare the actual data bits of the entire 32-bit address to a 32-bit mask number.

Whenever you use an IP address, you must also supply a *subnet mask*. As with the IP number, this mask is also a 32-bit number referenced in dotted decimal notation. The mask is used to compare the bits of two IP addresses to determine if they are on the same network. Table 3-4 outlines the *default subnet mask* for the three IP classes. Simply stated, the subnet mask *masks out,* or *covers-up*, the network portion of the IP address to determine if the host is local or remote. When examining the default subnets, the number 255 (eight binary ones) is used to identify the network portion of the IP address, and a 0 is used for the hosts portion. For example, the Class C address of 192.168.10.1 has a *default subnet mask* of 255.255.255.0. This identifies that the network portion of this address is contained completely within the first three octets of the IP address. The 0 in the subnet mask indicates that the host portion of the address begins with the fourth octet.

TABLE 3-4 DEFAULT SUBNET MASKS BY IP ADDRESS CLASS	
IP ADDRESS CLASS	*DEFAULT SUBNET*
Class A	255.0.0.0
Class B	255.255.0.0
Class C	255.255.255.0

exam preparation pointer

Each host on a TCP/IP network *requires* a subnet mask — either the default mask for the address class, or a custom mask.

exam preparation pointer

The Network+ exam expects you to know the default subnet masks for the three classes of IP addresses. The exam does not include the advanced concepts of subnetting although other certification exams do. The following section, "Advanced subnetting concepts," is not necessary information for the Network+ exam.

Advanced subnetting concepts   In order to understand advanced subnet masking, you need to use base 2 arithmetic. If you look at the binary representation of the default subnet masks, you get the values outlined in Table 3-5.

TABLE 3-5 DEFAULT SUBNET MASKS IN BINARY AND DECIMAL REPRESENTATION		
ADDRESS CLASS	*BINARY SUBNET MASK BITS*	*DOTTED DECIMAL NOTATION*
Class A	11111111 00000000 00000000 00000000	255.0.0.0
Class B	11111111 11111111 00000000 00000000	255.255.0.0
Class C	11111111 11111111 11111111 00000000	255.255.255.0

In order to subnet a standard IP address, you must borrow some of the bits from the host portion of the address. For example, if you change the subnet mask of a Class B address to 255.255.240.0, the binary equivalent is:

```
11111111 11111111 11110000 00000000
```

As you look at the subnet masks in their binary format, it is easier to see how the mask can be used to identify changes in the default value of the network portion. For example, look at Class B addresses 130.110.20.50 and 130.110.30.60 to see how the subnet is used to determine if the hosts (20.50 and 30.60) are on the same network or not:

IP Addresses	Subnet Mask	Same Network?
130.110.20.50	255.255.0.0	Yes
130.110.30.60	255.255.0.0	Yes

In this example, both addresses are on the same network (130.110). It seems quite obvious that the network portion is the same assuming the default subnet mask is used. However, if the subnet mask is changed to 255.255.255.0, these two addresses will reside on *different* networks because the subnet mask dictates that the first *three* octets are being used to identify the network portion.

IP Addresses	Subnet Mask	Same Network?
130.110.20.50	255.255.255.0	No
130.110.30.60	255.255.255.0	No

To compare these numbers in binary format, the protocol uses an ANDing process. The IP address is ANDed with the subnet mask to compare each bit and to determine if the addresses identify the same network or not. This ANDing process results in either a 0 or a 1 when two bits are compared, as follows:

1 AND 1 = 1

1 AND 0 = 0

0 AND 0 = 0

0 AND 1 = 0

Taking your two Class B addresses and converting them to binary, you get the following address tables:

130.110.20.50	10000010 11011110 00010100 00110010
255.255.255.0	11111111 11111111 11111111 00000000
ANDed results	**10000010 11011110 00010100 00000000**

130.110.30.60	10000010 11011110 00011110 00111100
255.255.255.0	11111111 11111111 11111111 00000000
ANDed results	**10000010 11011110 00011110 00000000**

When doing a bit by bit comparison of the ANDed results, the protocol identifies the network portion of the address up to the point that the bits differ. By comparing your ANDed results above, you see that the bits differ starting with the third octet. In this example, a host device with the address 130.110.30.60 is routed to another network based on the subnet mask even though both addresses are Class B.

Tables 3-6 and 3-7 help you quickly determine which subnet mask to use to obtain the desired number of hosts and networks when the default mask is insufficient. The left column, "# of Bits," indicates how many of the left most bits are taken away from the default host number to identify the segment. This of course means there are less numbers available to identify hosts on that segment. You do not get something for nothing here; you get more segments, but less hosts per segment. Notice how the custom mask numbers tend to repeat themselves from octet to octet. (While there are other numerical possibilities, they are not shown on the table because they are invalid due to reserved numbers.)

TABLE 3-6 QUICK REFERENCE CHART FOR CLASS B SUBNETS

# OF BITS	MASK IN DECIMAL	# OF SEGMENTS	# OF HOSTS
0	255.255.0.0	0	65534
2	255.255.192.0	2	16382
3	255.255.224.0	6	8190
4	255.255.240.0	14	4094
5	255.255.248.0	30	2046
6	255.255.252.0	62	1022
7	255.255.254.0	126	510
8	255.255.255.0	254	254
9	255.255.255.128	510	126
10	255.255.255.192	1022	62
11	255.255.255.224	2046	30
12	255.255.255.240	4094	14
13	255.255.255.248	8190	6
14	255.255.255.252	16382	2

TABLE 3-7 QUICK REFERENCE CHART FOR CLASS C SUBNETS

# OF BITS	MASK IN DECIMAL	# OF SEGMENTS	# OF HOSTS
2	255.255.255.192	2	62
3	255.255.255.224	6	30
4	255.255.255.240	14	14
5	255.255.255.248	30	6
6	255.255.255.252	62	2

Dynamic addressing and management   On small networks, manually assigning IP addresses (static addressing) is not a big issue, but in large organizations, it can become a full-time job! Whatever the case may be, you should always
maintain detailed documentation of your IP addressing. As the network changes
you will frequently need to refer to your documentation in order to avoid address
conflicts and other issues.

IP addresses do not have to be statically assigned. The TCP/IP suite provides
another protocol to assist in the assignment and management of IP addresses for
network devices. *Dynamic Host Core Protocol*, or DHCP, enables you to assign IP
addresses *as needed*. Basically, a network server runs a DHCP service, which is a
database of IP addresses. When an IP-based device attaches to the network, the
DHCP service assigns the device an unused address from the available pool, called
a *scope*. Figure 3-4 provides a simple look at what happens in the DHCP process.

PC 3 boots up and begins the process of attaching to the network. The NIC
driver sends out a broadcast message looking for a DHCP server. The server
responds back, telling PC 3 that it has an IP address to lease out. PC 3 then
acknowledges the DHCP offer and obtains an IP address from the pool of addresses
the DHCP server is responsible for. In addition to the IP address, the DHCP server
also supplies a subnet mask. and possibly a *default gateway,* and *DNS address.* (I
look at the properties of the gateway and DNS address shortly.) Note that the IP information provided here is *leased* to the PC, and not permanently assigned. The
assigned address has a *lease life* that is, by default, 72 hours. At the halfway point,
36 hours, the device contacts the DHCP server and request a renewal of the IP
address. If the server responds, the lease is refreshed, and, again, in effect for 72

hours. If the renewal is ignored or refused, the device waits for one-half of the remaining lease life (18 hours) and requests another renewal. This process happens at each half-life point until the address is either renewed or the lease expires. If the lease expires, all TCP/IP based services for that device cease. The expiring lease concept makes it possible to accommodate more hosts than there are valid IP addresses. Further, mobile users can also login to different networks and receive valid IP addresses.

If more than one DHCP server exists on the network segment, all servers respond to the broadcast request. Because multiple DHCP servers can exist, it is up to the PC to send a second request to the server of its choice (usually the first one to respond), and to acknowledge it has received the servers IP information. The other DHCP servers do not receive an acknowledgment and therefore do not assign any addressing parameters.

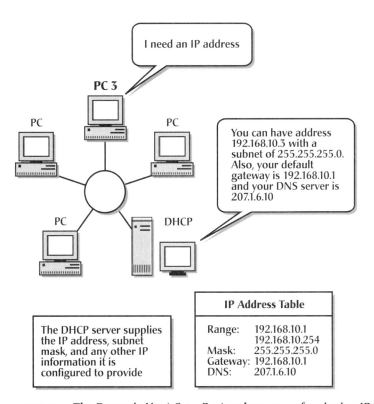

FIGURE 3-4 The Dynamic Host Core Protocol process of assigning IP information

It is important to understand the flow of the DHCP assignment process. A minimum of four conversations take place when a device requests a dynamic address:

1. The PC sends out a broadcast message looking for a DHCP server.
2. The DHCP server responds to the broadcast *if* it has available addresses to lease.
3. The requesting device acknowledges and accepts the DHPC's offer to supply the address information.
4. The address data is assigned to the requesting device.

DHCP services *cannot* span across network segments. Therefore, if your LAN contains more than one segment, you need to either place a DHCP server on each segment or configure a separate service to assist the DHCP server. Some NOSs and some routers provide a service called *DHCP Forwarding*, which acts as a middleman or relay, between segments. DHCP Forwarding can assist in the dynamic IP addressing process across multiple segments. For example, a router that supports DHCP forwarding will listen for the address request from a device connected to one of the router's segments. The router will then make the address request on behalf of that device on a segment where a DHCP server resides. When the DHCP server offers the address information, the router will accept the data, and forward it on to the requesting device. Neither the device nor the DHCP server ever *talks* directly to each other, nor are they aware that the router acted as the middleman. When you design a network under these conditions however, it is important to make sure that no single device failure prevents the DHPC service from transversing the network segments. If a single device, such as a NIC in a file server connecting to two segments, fails, an entire portion of your users will be unable to access the network!

DHCP addressing should be reserved for client devices only. If you use DHCP for file servers, routers, switches, or other connectivity devices, you will create a number of potential problems. If the leases expire on any of these components you will likely loose large portions of your network. Likewise, it is important to always know the addresses assigned these devices. Always use static IP addressing on servers and network components and make sure these addresses are excluded from your IP pool on the DHCP server(s).

Name resolution

Few people in society are willing to work in a binary dialog; the decimal system even confuses some people. In order to keep up the *user-friendly* tradition, it is necessary to provide a method for people based on computer names rather than numbers. You can image how difficult it would be for someone to find a particular file located on a PC identified only as 192.168.10.2! It is much easier to find the file if you can identify the location as *John's PC*. The process of associating names and address is known as *name resolution*, and names on the Internet are often called a *Universal Resource Location,* or URL. The TCP/IP specification includes a number of tools to help you use names instead of numbers on your networks.

Resolving names using ARP   The *Address Resolution Protocol*, or ARP, is the easiest way to resolve a host name to its IP *and* hardware address. ARP is a broadcast protocol and maintains its own *cache*, a small table kept in RAM. ARP is the fundamental method of resolving an IP address to the device's MAC (hardware) address required in order for host-to-host communications to occur. Once the IP and MAC addresses are obtained, both are stored in the ARP cache to improve performance. The ARP resolution is a four-part process consisting of an ARP request and an ARP reply, as outlined below:

1. When a device tries to communicate with another device on the network, the ARP process is initiated. ARP first looks in its ARP cache to see if an entry for the requested host exists. If one is found, the process is complete.

2. If no entry is found in the cache, the ARP protocol builds a broadcast packet that basically asks, *"Who has this IP address, and what is your hardware address?"* The packet consists of the source host's IP address and the IP address of the desired host to locate.

3. Because the packet is sent as a broadcast, all devices *on the local segment* receive and process the request. After checking the address, every device whose IP address does not match simply ignores the packet.

4. When the target device receives the packet, it sends an ARP request back directly to the sending device (because the IP address of the sending device is already known, this response does not need to be broadcast to all devices). The returned packet includes the target's hardware address. Both the hardware and IP address are inserted into the ARP cache for possible future use, and communication between the two devices can now commence.

In the event that the destination address is not on the local segment, the ARP packet addresses the destination to the default router and the router initiates the same form of ARP request across the remaining segments.

Most devices enable you to view and modify the ARP cache. On a Windows NT server, the command `arp -a` displays the current cache contents. To delete an entry, you can use the command `arp -d <ip_address>` where `<ip_address>` is a valid IP address contained within the cache. To add a permanent address, you use the `-s` parameter with the IP and MAC address of the host. For example, `arp -s 130.110.20.50 02-60-6b-8a-28-91`. Other devices and operating systems work similarly.

in the real world

ARP cache requests are typically retained only for a maximum of ten minutes. As entries are added to the cache, they are *time stamped*. If an entry is not reused after two minutes, it is purged from the cache; otherwise the entries will be deleted after ten minutes.

Host files   For small networks, each device can have a small file known as a *host file*. The host file is a simple text file that contains IP addresses and the computer names the addresses correspond to. A simple host file may look like this:

```
# This is a sample HOSTS file used by Microsoft TCP/IP
#
# This file contains the mappings of IP addresses to host
# names. Each entry should be kept on an individual line. The
# IP address should be placed in the first column followed by
# the corresponding host name.
# The IP address and the host name should be separated by at
# least one space.
#

102.54.94.97     rhino.acme.com           # source server
38.25.63.10      x.acme.com               # x client host
206.175.162.15   sales.idgbooks.com       # great books
192.41.63.54     info.net-engineer.com    # great resource site!
127.0.0.1        localhost
```

When a TCP/IP request is made to locate the computer named `sales.idgbooks.com`, the protocol opens the hosts file and reads sequentially through the list of names until it (hopefully) finds `sales.idgbooks.com`. Internally, IP routing is now accomplished using the IP address.

A major draw back to the host file method of name resolution is the effort required to keep each file up-to-date. Any change on the network requires a change to all host files. For example, if you use host tables for your company network, each PC's host table needs to be modified every time a new computer is added to the network. Not only is this time consuming, the method is also very prone to typographical errors.

Domain Name Service   In large environments, such as the Internet, the need to resolve hundreds or even millions of computer names cannot possibly be done with simple host files. Therefore, the TCP/IP suite provides a service known as *Domain Name Service,* or DNS. This is similar in nature to host files in that entries are stored as a database that cross references IP addresses to their computer names. However, it is impractical to search such a huge list of entries sequentially; to overcome these problems, DNS servers are based on a hierarchical formula. Every computer on the Internet has a unique name that ends in a *top-level domain name*. For example, `idgbooks.com` has the top-level domain name, COM. The most common top-level domain names are:

- `com`: Commercial
- `org`: Organizations, primarily non-profit
- `edu`: Educational institutions
- `gov`: Government institutions
- `mil`: Military sites
- `net`: Network — usually an Internet Service Provider, or ISP

Beginning with the high level domains, DNS servers can break down any given address into smaller and smaller pieces until a specific server is located, as depicted in Figure 3-5.

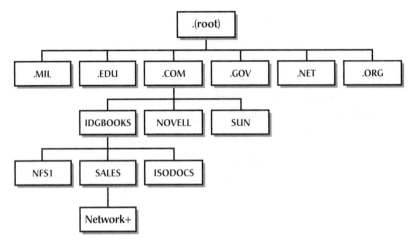

FIGURE 3-5 **Graphic example of the domain tree**

When a request is made to a primary DNS server, the root is queried first. The result is returned as a list of other servers containing servers within their domain name (such as COMs, GOVs, EDUs, and so on). These servers are then queried further to locate the next lower portion of the target name, and so on until the full name is resolved. The process is demonstrated with the following example:

Suppose you want to view a file located on a server named `networkplus. sales.idgbooks.com`. This is a fictitious server in IDG Books Worldwide's (a commercial company) sales department. In order to find its Internet address, four different servers may potentially have to be queried, as follows:

1. A query is made to a central server (the root) to find out where the `com` server is. `com` is a server that keeps track of commercial organizations. The root server then provides the names and Internet addresses of several servers for `com`. (There are several servers at each level, to allow for the probability that one might be down.)

2. One of the `com` servers is asked for the address of the `idgbooks` server. Again, names and Internet addresses of several servers for `idgbooks` are provided. Most likely, not all of those servers are physically located at IDG Books, to allow for the possibility that the company's computer(s) may be unavailable.

3. `idgbooks` is asked for the addresses of the `sales` servers.

4. One of the `sales` servers is asked for the address of the `networkplus` computer. The end result is the Internet address for `networkplus.sales.` `idgbooks.com`. Each level is referred to as a *domain*, and the entire name is called the *domain name*.

While this discussion has primarily focused on Internet name resolution, DNS servers are equally important in private IP networks.

 DNS services are not included with versions of NT prior to 4.0 nor in Netware prior to 5.0 although third party DNS services can be used in these environments.

NetBIOS name resolution   NetBIOS, *Network Basic Input/Output System*, is a native networking protocol in Microsoft DOS and Windows networks. Although the protocol itself is not part of the TCP/IP suite, it is a fundamental part of Windows-based networking and it can *ride on top of TCP/IP* within a Windows environment. Therefore I feel it is appropriate to include a short discussion of NetBIOS and its functionality.

As an application runs it may make calls for certain resources (files, printers, and so on). It is the redirectors job to determine if the resources are local (on the node) or remote (on the network). If the resource is on the network, the redirector makes a call through the transport driver interface to the network transport protocol to talk to the network device (resource). NetBIOS is a transport driver interface. (So is Windows Sockets, which I discuss shortly.) Name management is the only NetBIOS function that is not duplicated by the TCP/IP suite, hence the interest in using NetBIOS over TCP/IP.

NetBIOS, when combined with it's native transport layer protocol NetBEUI, is nonroutable. Recently however, NetBIOS is being combined with the routable transport protocols of IPX or TCP/IP to create an interface for applications at the session layer (Layer 5). Name management not only helps a system find the computer it wants to communicate with but also the proper service operating on that computer. NetBIOS names are 15 characters in length and assigned when the Windows operating system is installed, or when a NetBIOS service starts. (There is actually a 16th character [one byte] that is entered by each service running on the computer.) For example, when Windows NT is first installed, you are asked to give the server a name. This is a NetBIOS name that makes connecting to the server easier than accessing it strictly by its IP or IPX address. Similarly, all Windows client operating systems (Windows 3.*x*, Windows for Workgroups, and Windows 95/98) ask for a computer name when any networking components are installed. On an all Windows network, NetBIOS is fairly efficient and easy to maintain; you only need to make certain that each computer is assigned a unique name. NetBIOS name resolution is the process of successfully mapping a computer's NetBIOS name to an IP address. Typically, this resolution is accomplished in one of two ways, either by broadcasts on the local segment, or by a table lookup. When a computer needs to locate another NetBIOS device to obtain its IP address, the NetBIOS protocol performs the following queries in this order:

1. The Net BIOS protocol looks in the NetBIOS *name cache*. Each time a NetBIOS name resolution is successful, the protocol keeps the name and IP address in a local cache (RAM). If the current request exists in this cache already, name resolution is accomplished here.

2. If a NetBIOS name server such as a Windows Internet Name Server (WINS — discussed below) exists, NetBIOS queries that server for the computer name.

3. NetBIOS performs a *local broadcast* next. This process simply involves the protocol sending out a message to all local devices asking the specified computer to return it's IP address if the specified computer name exists on the segment. Remember that a local broadcast is not propagated across routers.

4. If there is no response from the local broadcast, NetBIOS attempts to look up the computer name from a local HOSTS file. Windows-based computers use two such files: LMHOSTS, which is proprietary to Microsoft, and the UNIX standard HOSTS file. Both perform the same function; both cross-reference IP addresses to computer names.

5. If all else fails, NetBIOS attempts to resolve the computer name using a DNS server.

in the
real world

If your network uses NetBIOS as the primary network protocol, and you are trying to fine-tune the LAN for performance, keep in mind the resolution process above. You can greatly increase NetBIOS communications by implementing a WINS server instead of a DNS server simply because of the order in which NetBIOS looks up names. Without a WINS server, each new connection between NetBIOS devices will generate a segment wide broadcast that can greatly increase unnecessary traffic on the network segment.

Windows Internet Name Server   *Windows Internet Name Server,* or WINS, is a Microsoft specific enhanced NetBIOS name service. WINS is used to register NetBIOS computer names and resolve their IP address, both local and remote, and to reduce broadcast traffic associated with NetBIOS using TCP/IP. When a PC configured as a WINS client enters the network, it registers itself to the WINS server. This registration is dynamic and includes the device's NetBIOS name and IP address. When a WINS-enabled client initiates a request to communicate with another device, the query request is sent to the WINS server instead of using a broadcast. The protocol attempts to locate the primary WINS server three times (using ARP), and if unsuccessful, makes three more attempts for a secondary WINS server (if one has been configured). If there is still no response from a WINS server, normal name resolution begins using the standard ARP process.

IP routing

IP routing is the process of sending data across disperse networks through routers. As datagrams are passed to the IP protocol from UDP and TCP above, and from the network card(s) below, the datagrams are labeled with a source and destination IP address. The IP protocol examines the destination address on each datagram, compares it to a locally maintained *route table*, and decides what action to take. There are three possibilities for each datagram:

- It can be passed up to a protocol layer above IP on the local host.
- It can be forwarded via one of the locally attached NICs.
- It can be discarded.

The route table maintains four different types of routes. They are listed below in the order that they are searched for a match:

1. Host (a route to a single, specific destination IP address)
2. Subnet (a route to a subnet)
3. Network (a route to an entire network)
4. Default (used when there is no other match)

The route table may be viewed from the command prompt as shown in Figure 3-6.

```
Microsoft(R) Windows 98
   (C)Copyright Microsoft Corp 1981-1998.

C:\WINDOWS>route print

Active Routes:

  Network Address          Netmask  Gateway Address        Interface  Metric
          0.0.0.0          0.0.0.0    209.181.196.6    209.181.196.4       1
        127.0.0.0        255.0.0.0        127.0.0.1        127.0.0.1       1
    209.181.196.0  255.255.255.248    209.181.196.4    209.181.196.4       1
    209.181.196.4  255.255.255.255        127.0.0.1        127.0.0.1       1
  209.181.196.255  255.255.255.255    209.181.196.4    209.181.196.4       1
        224.0.0.0        224.0.0.0    209.181.196.4    209.181.196.4       1
  255.255.255.255  255.255.255.255    209.181.196.4          0.0.0.0       1

C:\WINDOWS>
```

FIGURE 3-6 The route table

The route table shown here is for a computer with the class C IP address of 199.199.40.123. It contains the following seven entries:

1. The first entry, to address 0.0.0.0, is the default route. A default route is always selected when a destination is unknown. If a packet is sent out on the default route, it is up to the next router to determine how the datagram is to be handled.
2. The second entry is for the loopback (or *self*) address, 127.0.0.0.
3. The third entry is a network route, for the network 199.199.40. (The last octet of 0 indicates the whole network as opposed to a host on a network indicated by a valid host ID as the fourth octet). The local NIC is specified as the path to this network.
4. The fourth entry is a host route for the local host. Note that it specifies the loopback address, which makes sense because a datagram bound for the local host should be handled internally.
5. The fifth entry is for the subnet broadcast address (again specifying the local interface because broadcasts are always local).
6. The sixth entry is for IP multicasting. Remember that multicasts are similar to broadcasts except that a specific group of hosts are contacted instead of all hosts.
7. The final entry is for the broadcast address.

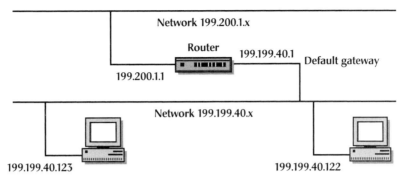

FIGURE 3-7 An IP routing example

For example, referring to the network diagram in Figure 3-7, the PC at address 199.199.140.123 sends a packet to host 199.199.40.122. The table is first scanned for a host route (not found), then for a subnet route (not found), then for a network route (that is found). The packet is sent via the local interface 199.199.40.123. If a packet is sent to 199.200.1.1, the same search is used, and no host, subnet, or network route is found. In this case, the packet is directed to the default gateway by inserting the MAC address of the default gateway into the destination MAC address field.

The route table is maintained automatically in most cases. When a host initializes, entries for the local network(s), loopback, multicast, and configured default gateway are added. More routes may appear in the table as the IP layer learns of them. For instance, the default gateway for a system may advise it of a better route to a specific network, subnet, or host. Routes also may be added manually.

Transmission Control Protocol (TCP)

TCP provides transport functions that ensure the total amount of bytes sent is received correctly at the other end. TCP provides for reliable host-to-host communication and has mechanisms built-in to inform you if a transmission fails (for example, if a router is down and no other routes to the destination exist). Reliable transportation is a good thing. With TCP, you don't need to worry about the data getting through; it is like sending a registered letter in that you are sure that it reaches its intended recipient. However, there is a cost for reliable transportation; TCP has a lot of overhead that increases network traffic, and decreases performance of the network as a whole. It is necessary for many forms of communications and not as necessary for others. The next section covers the protocol used when reliability is not a primary issue.

TCP is used by a number of other programs and utilities contained within the TCP/IP suite. Specifically, file transfers using FTP, terminal emulation using Telnet, and e-mail delivery using SMTP all use TCP as their transportation methods. (I discuss these utility programs a little bit later).

concept link   **Recall from the previous discussion of NetBIOS that its native transport protocol is NetBEUI, which is nonroutable. However, NetBIOS can be combined with TCP/IP, which is routable. For NetBIOS to function over TCP/IP, NetBIOS must use ports. For example, the NetBIOS name service that I discussed uses port 137 with the UDP protocol (covered later).**

TCP communication between two hosts is much like human communication via the telephone in that the complexities between callers is not as important as a clear, uninterrupted connection. One of TCP's responsibilities is to create an interface between the host-to-host layers and upper layer processes. The IP address takes you to the host, but how do you get to the proper process running on that host?

To identify specifically where data is to be transmitted, a *port number* identifies each protocol. The port number is appended to the IP address of the computer. For example, if you download a file from the Internet using the FTP protocol, TCP establishes a connection between your computer and the Internet computer using Port 21 [xxx.xxx.xxx.xxx/port 21]. A large number of port numbers, often referred to as *well-known ports*, are reserved for specific protocols. The most commonly used port numbers are:

- FTP   Port 21
- Telnet   Port 23
- SMTP   Port 25
- HTTP   Port 80

exam preparation pointer   **The Network+ exam will likely expect you to know the four *well-known port* numbers.**

Port numbers are assigned by a group know as the *Internet Assigned Number Authority*, or IANA, and are specified in an RFC document titled, *Assigned Port Numbers, RFC 1700*.

When the unique IP address and the port number are used to identify a specific connection between two hosts, a *socket* is created. Sockets provide an application program interface (API) between processes and the TCP/IP suite. Programmers can use these API to enable their programs to interface to the network. You may be familiar with a Windows socket standard called *WINSOCK*, which is Microsoft's API standard that enables programmers to write applications directly to the services TCP provides.

Application Protocols of the TCP/IP Suite

As mentioned earlier, TCP/IP is a suite of protocols. The following items discuss the various protocols that round out the suite. You may find many of these to be familiar, such as FTP, which is commonly used to send files across the Internet, and Telnet, which is commonly used to connect terminals to a UNIX-based PC.

User Datagram Protocol (UDP)

Like TCP, UDP is a transportation mechanism, but unlike TCP, UDP is *unreliable*. This is not to say that UDP is a *lower-class* mechanism, but simply that the data it transports is not of the nature that you *need* confirmation it has been delivered. UDP uses a *best effort* delivery method, and does not inform the other protocols if a packet is undeliverable. The primary use for UDP transmission is speed. Because error checking is omitted, there is very little overhead associated with the UDP protocol. Among the services that use UDP are *Trivial File Transport Protocol* (TFTP), *Simple Network Management Protocol* (SNMP), *Domain Name Services* (DNS), *and Network File Systems* (NFS). A good example of UDP is live video and audio services on the Internet. If a datagram is lost during video or audio transmission, there simply isn't enough real time to retransmit the dropped data and remain *live*.

File Transfer Protocol (FTP)

FTP is the standard method of sending files between computers over a TCP/IP-based network. Most commonly found on the Internet, FTP is reliable and offers some basic security features. The FTP protocol provides a command set that permits such things as connecting to a network using a user name and password, and navigating the directory structure. FTP can be invoked from a command line environment, a graphical interface, or even from a Web browser by preceding the server address with ftp:// (For example, you can enter `ftp://microsoft.com` to access publicly available programs from Microsoft). Many FTP sites permit anyone to use the login name *anonymous* to access and download files. The anonymous FTP directory is isolated from the rest of the system and generally does not accept uploads from users. Many of these anonymous sites use your e-mail name as the password so they have some indication of who is accessing the files.

Unlike e-mail programs that require graphic and program files be *attached*, FTP is designed to handle files directly and does not add the overhead of encoding and decoding the data. FTP services can be installed on most Unix, Windows 95/98/NT, and NetWare systems.

As mentioned above, *Trivial File Transfer Protocol*, or TFTP, uses UDP as its transportation mechanism and does not have directory or password capabilities.

Hypertext Transport Protocol (HTTP)

HTTP is the communication protocol that connects servers on the World Wide Web and transmits Hypertext Markup Language (HTML) pages to a client browser (such as Netscape Navigator or Internet Explorer). Most browsers assume the address you enter has HTTP connections; if you type `www.idgbooks.com`, the browser automatically inserts the http:// portion for you. The HTTP protocol is undergoing many changes to make it more efficient and useful so there is no need to discuss the protocol in much detail here.

Post Office Protocol Version 3 (POP3)

Most client e-mail packages in use today use *Post Office Protocol 3*, or POP3, especially with the proliferation of dial-up access. POP3 provides a message store that holds all incoming mail on a central server until the recipient connects to the server and downloads it. POP3 is very simplistic, and offers little security beyond basic user name and password. When a connection is established and verified, all pending messages and file attachments are downloaded at the same time. This way, you can read your e-mail and view any file attachments without having to remain connected to the Internet.

Simple Mail Transport Protocol (SMTP)

Before e-mail reaches your central holding point and waits to be retrieved from a POP3 client, the servers that transport the e-mail data around the Internet need a protocol. *Simple Mail Transport Protocol*, or SMTP, is just such a standard. SMTP is a TCP/IP protocol that defines the message format, and the methods to store and forward the mail. Servers use SMTP to route messages throughout the Internet to mail servers which then provide message storage for incoming mail.

Simple Network Management Protocol (SNMP)

With the ever-increasing size and complexity of Network systems, a standardized method of managing the multitude of components has become a necessity. In 1988, the Internet Engineering Task Forced developed the *Simple Network Management Protocol*, or SNMP, to enable simple, but extensible network management. Devices enabled with the management client components monitor various network devices and gather information about the components. These client components are known as *management agents*. A PC running special management console software is also required to complete the SNMP process. The management agents are programmed with certain *thresholds*, which are minimum or maximum acceptable values. When one of these values falls outside the range of a threshold, the agent issues a *trap*, thus notifying the management console of the problem. SNMP is based on a GET/SET paradigm. The Management Console can request information from an agent (GET) or, if sufficient security is given, alter the value of a threshold (SET).

The variables that an agent has responsibility for are maintained as a simple database called a *Management Information Base,* or MIB. Manufacturers of manageable devices create these MIBs within the confines of the SNMP guidelines. Some of the most common management software packages are HP OpenView, Novell's ManageWise, Microsoft's Systems Management Server (SMS), and Compaq's Insight Manager.

CONNECTING TO THE NETWORK

I briefly discussed the various components required to connect to the network and now I take a look at specific configuration issues. Although the Network+ exam is *non-vendor* specific, in reality, Windows 9*x* and Windows NT based PCs make up the bulk of most PCs connecting to the network. Therefore, I look closely at what is necessary to configure these operating systems for network connectivity, as well as discuss other options generic to any type of client. The basic configurations discussed in this section are the same whether you're connection to a private network, the public Internet, or both.

Proxy Services

Connecting your network to the Internet presents many challenges. As you've seen, obtaining enough public IP address can be difficult and costly. Security issues also arise because it is important to keep your data safe from prying eyes and malicious individuals. One useful method to both provide Internet services to a group of network users, and to employ a fairly strong security measure is to use a *proxy*. A proxy, sometimes also called an *application level gateway*, is an application that separates the connection between sender and receiver. Proxy servers help prevent hackers from obtaining internal addresses and details of a private network. Often times, proxy servers employ a service called *network address translation*, or NAT. NAT simply takes a private IP address from a network client and converts it to a single, public IP address before sending it out to the Internet. This method permits a virtually unlimited number of users to access the Internet simultaneously with only a single registered IP address. As Internet requests are converted and sent out to the Internet, the Proxy server tracks their internal origins to maintain the connections to the appropriate users.

Proxy servers are available for many services. Some of the more common proxies are HTTP for Web access, FTP file transfers, and SMTP proxy for e-mail. Some Web proxies also incorporate Web page caching to improve Internet browsing on the World Wide Web. When a user requests a Web page for the first time, the data is stored in the proxy's cache so that the next request can be obtained locally, and therefore, much faster. For companies that maintain their own Web servers, reverse proxy can be deployed. This technology pushes the contents of the Web server out to cache so Internet users don't actually access the primary hosting server. Figure 3-8 presents a visual overview of how a proxy server might look in a network environment.

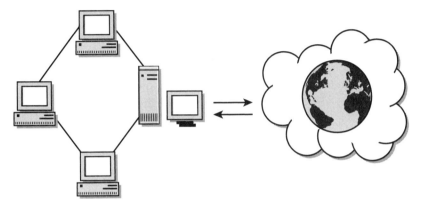

FIGURE 3-8 Simple overview of a proxy server in a network environment

A proxy server offers another big advantage. The requirement to install TCP/IP on each client is not longer necessary because the proxy server performs all of the Internet access for you. If you don't need TCP/IP for other services, you can simply configure your Web browsers, FTP clients, e-mail clients, and so on to access the proxy server. The proxy is then configured for both your normal LAN protocol (IPX perhaps) and TCP/IP to handle all of the Internet access.

Configuring TCP/IP on a Windows Client

32-bit Windows operating systems offer built in support for TCP/IP. The protocol must be installed and configured, however, before you can use it on your network. For both Windows 9*x* and NT, you install, configure, and maintain TCP/IP settings from the Network applet. Figure 3-8 shows what this dialog box looks like.

 note **This section often refers to 32-bit Windows operating systems. These include Windows 95, 98, and Windows NT.**

▼ ▼ ▼

TO OPEN THE NETWORK DIALOG SCREEN FROM THE CONTROL PANEL, COMPLETE THE FOLLOWING STEPS:

1. Click on Start.

2. Click on Settings.

3. Click on Control Panel.

4. Click on Network.

5. The Network dialog box appears, as shown in Figure 3-9.

■ ■ ■

 tip You can also open this dialog box by first right-clicking on the Network Neighborhood icon on the desktop, and then selecting Properties.

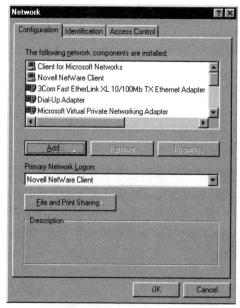

FIGURE 3-9 The Windows 9x Network dialog box

▼ ▼ ▼

TO CONFIGURE TCP/IP ON A WINDOWS 9X CLIENT, COMPLETE THE FOLLOWING STEPS:

1. Click Add.

2. Click Protocol, as shown in Figure 3-10, and then click Add.

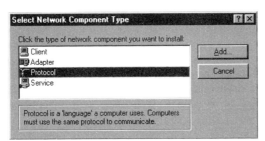

FIGURE 3-10   To add a protocol, first select the Protocol option in the Select Network Component Type dialog box

3. Click Microsoft in the Manufacturers list, and TCP/IP in the Network Protocol list, as shown in Figure 3-11.

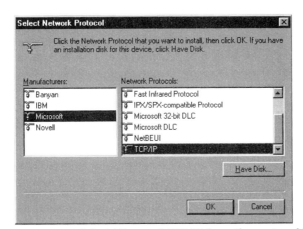

FIGURE 3-11   Select Microsoft TCP/IP from the protocol list

■ ■ ■

note   **When adding a protocol, you will need the original Windows 9x in-stallation CD, diskettes, or file location of the CAB files on a con-nected hard drive.**

Once the protocol is installed, the main Networking dialog box is redisplayed. If a DHCP server is accessible, you do not need to further configure the TCP/IP settings. However, if you use static IP addressing, you will need to perform additional tasks (as follows).

▼ ▼ ▼

TO ASSIGN THE STATIC IP ADDRESS, COMPLETE THE FOLLOWING STEPS:

1. Click the TCP/IP line that corresponds to your network adapter, and then click on Properties.

2. Click the radio-button labeled Specify an IP Address.

3. Enter a unique IP Address, and corresponding Subnet Mask in the boxes provided, as shown in Figure 3-12.

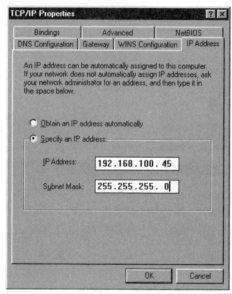

FIGURE 3-12   Defining a specific IP address

4. If your network uses WINS for name resolution, click on the WINS Configuration tab, shown in Figure 3-13, to enable WINS and provide the IP address of your WINS server.

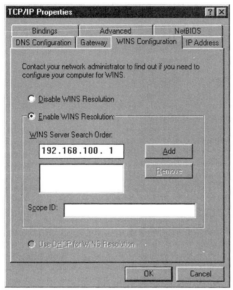

FIGURE 3-13 Enabling WINS services and setting the IP address of the local WINS server(s)

5. The Gateway option enables you to define the default router for internetwork routing. This may point to a router that is connected to the Internet or to another part of your WAN. In either case, you should define a default gateway on your PC, as shown in Figure 3-14, if you have a router and need access to other LAN segments.

in the real world

When troubleshooting connectivity problems across a WAN, one of the first steps should be verifying that the PC has a properly defined default gateway.

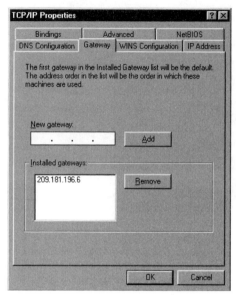

FIGURE 3-14   Setting the TCP/IP default gateways in Windows 9*x*

6. If your network has a DNS server for name resolution, or you are statically configuring TCP/IP for Internet access, you must provide a proper DNS server IP address. Click on the DNS Configuration tab to display the dialog box. You can then choose to Enable DNS or Disable DNS. Click the radio button to enable DNS services, as shown in Figure 3-15. Next you must provide a Host name, which is usually the PC name defined in the Identification page or the user's login name. The Domain name is the name of the network domain you are accessing. Normally, if you are configuring IP on a dial-up adapter (modem), the Domain name is your Internet Service Provider, and if you're configuring the local NIC, the Domain name is the Network Domain that you log into. The last part of this dialog box enables you to define the IP addresses of your DNS servers. You can define more than one, which is recommended in case your primary DNS server is unavailable. Most ISPs provide at least two DNS servers.

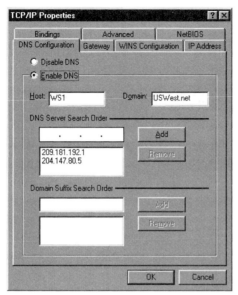

FIGURE 3-15 Setting DNS properties in Windows 9*x*

7. The last item that you may need to configure is the NetBIOS page. If you are in an NT-based network, and you run any application that uses NetBIOS, you will need to check the box on this page to enable TCP/IP to *encapsulate* NetBIOS packets. As you may recall, NetBIOS is a nonroutable protocol so NetBIOS packets by themselves are not sent across the WAN link. Using a method known as *encapsulation*, nonroutable packets can be wrapped, or encapsulated, into a routable frame type, such as TCP/IP. The router looks at the packet as a TCP/IP frame and sends it across the WAN link. Another service on the other end sees the encapsulated packet and strips off the TCP/IP headers leaving the NetBIOS packet in tack.

8. Close the TCP/IP Properties screen and allow Windows to reboot. When Windows restarts, you should have TCP/IP connectivity.

---------------------------------- ▼ ▼ ▼ ----------------------------------

TO CONFIGURE TCP/IP ON A WINDOWS NT CLIENT OR SERVER, COMPLETE THE FOLLOWING STEPS:

1. From the Network Dialog box, click the Protocols tab.

2. Click Add.

3. From the list of Network Protocols, Click TCP/IP, and then click OK.

---------------------------------- ■ ■ ■ ----------------------------------

 You may need the original Windows NT installation CD.

Once the protocol is installed, the main Networking Dialog screen is re-displayed. If a DHCP server is accessible, you do not need to further configure the TCP/IP settings.

---------------------------------- ▼ ▼ ▼ ----------------------------------

IF YOU USE STATIC IP ADDRESSING YOU WILL NEED TO PERFORM THE FOLLOWING TASKS:

1. Enter a unique IP Address, and a corresponding Subnet Mask and Default Gateway in the boxes provided, as shown in Figure 3-16. The Gateway option enables you to define the default router for internetwork routing. This may point to a router that is connected to the Internet or to another part of our WAN. In either case, you should define a default gateway on your PC if you have a router and need access to other LAN segments

2. If your network has a DNS server for name resolution, or you are statically configuring TCP/IP for Internet access, you must provide a proper DNS server IP address. Click on the DNS Configuration tab to display the dialog box, as shown in Figure 3-17. You need to provide a Host Name, which is usually the PC name defined in the Identification page, or the user's login name. The Domain name is the name of the network domain you are accessing. Normally, if you are configuring IP on a dial-up adapter (modem), the Domain name is your Internet Service Provider, and if you're configuring the local NIC, the Domain name is the Network Domain that you log into. The last part of this dialog box enables you to define the IP addresses of your DNS servers. You can define more than one, which is recommended in case your primary DNS server is unavailable. Most ISPs provide you with at least two DNS servers.

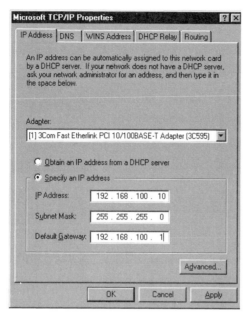

FIGURE 3-16   Setting static IP information in Windows NT

Microsoft TCP/IP Properties

IP Address | DNS | WINS Address | DHCP Relay | Routing

Domain Name System (DNS)

Host Name: Domain:

ntserver   uswest.net

DNS Service Search Order

204.110.184.5

Up↑
Down↓

Add...   Edit...   Remove

Domain Suffix Search Order

Up↑
Down↓

Add...   Edit...   Remove

OK   Cancel   Apply

FIGURE 3-17   Enabling DNS and setting DNS properties

3. If your network uses WINS for name resolution, click on the WINS Address configuration tab, shown in Figure 3-18, to enable WINS and provide the IP address of your WINS servers. You may supply IP addresses for both a primary and secondary WINS server. Additionally, you can check the DNS enable box to enable DNS to perform all of your name resolutions.

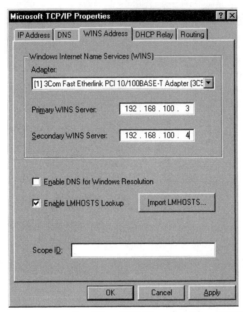

FIGURE 3-18   Enabling WINS and setting WINS properties

■ ■ ■

If you need to makes changes to your TCP/IP settings, you can follow these steps for the operating system you're using and simply change the items you need. Remember that any changes, especially IP addresses, should be manually documented thoroughly.

TCP/IP TESTING AND TROUBLESHOOTING UTILITIES

The TCP/IP suite specification provides many tools to assist in testing and troubleshooting connectivity problems. You will need to use these tools often when dealing with an IP network.

The Ping Utility

Ping is probably the most used of the tools mentioned. Ping was named after the sound a sonar detection device makes on military submarines. The purpose of the sonar is to send a signal at a potential target and listen for the *ping* sound it makes upon its return after successfully bouncing off the target. You can use ping to see if another IP device on the network is active. For example, go to a DOS prompt and type

```
PING xxx.xxx.xxx.xxx
```

where the xxxs represent the IP address that you wish to test. If the device is active, and reachable from your PC, the utility returns a message. The specific message varies depending on the version of the ping program you use. In addition to the confirmation message, the ping utility also returns the number of milliseconds it took to send and receive the *ping* from the target device. If the ping is unsuccessful, you will see a message saying that the request timed out, or that the destination host was unreachable.

The following is an example of the output from the ping.exe program in Windows 98:

```
C:\ping 209.181.192.1


Pinging 209.181.192.1 with 32 bytes of data:
Reply from 209.181.192.1: bytes=32 time=24ms TTL=253
Reply from 209.181.192.1: bytes=32 time=26ms TTL=253
Reply from 209.181.192.1: bytes=32 time=25ms TTL=253
Reply from 209.181.192.1: bytes=32 time=25ms TTL=253
Ping statistics for 209.181.192.1:
    Packets: Sent = 4, Received = 4, Lost = 0 (0% loss),
    Approximate round trip times in milliseconds:
    Minimum = 24ms, Maximum =  26ms, Average = 25ms
```

exam
preparation
pointer

You can use the ping utility to see if IP is correctly configured on your local device. From a DOS prompt, type `ping 127.0.0.1` **(this is the reserved** *local device* **IP address). If your results are successful, then IP is properly functioning on this device.**

When using ping to determine if you can reach a specific host, you should start with the farthest device in the chain. For example, if your IP address is 192.168.10.100 and you want to ping the address 208.162.105.10, which is on a network connected by two routers, your first attempt should be to ping the device itself. If you are successful, you know that IP is correctly configured between your two devices. If the test fails, you should start pinging the middle devices from the outside in. Refer to Figure 3-19.

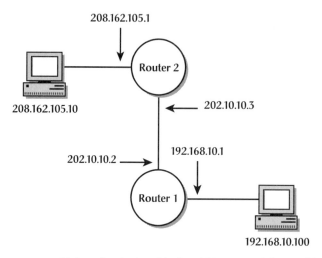

FIGURE 3-19 Using ping to troubleshoot IP connectivity problems

Figure 3-19 demonstrates the pinging method I describe above:

o If you fail to ping the target host, continue the process by pinging IP address 208.162.105.1: If this succeeds, then the problem is at the target PC (208.162.105.10).

o Next ping 202.10.10.3: If this succeeds, then Router 2 is the problem and it does not know how to get to the 208.162.105 network segment.

o Next ping 202.10.10.2: If this succeeds, then the problem lies in the local router, Router 2. If this fails, you should perform the next ping test to see which side of your router is having the problem.

o Next ping 192.186.10.1: If this fails then the problem is a local IP configuration issue.

Ping is also an excellent tool to verify that you're receiving proper name resolution. If you ping a host by name, (for example, PING IDGBooks.com) you should get a successful result indicating that name to IP resolution is functioning properly. If the ping utility returns the error message *unknown host,* or *destination host unreachable*, then name resolution is not being performed. You can now use ping, or other tools to troubleshoot your name resolution problems.

The Tracert Utility

Tracert goes a bit farther than ping in that it also tells you how many *hops* away the target device is. Remember that a *hop* is a router that forwards the request on to another segment, so four hops means that the tracert packet had to be forwarded by four routers in order to reach its destination.

Tracert is especially useful in troubleshooting router problems. Because the results of a tracert show each router hop, you can quickly determine which router in a path has failed to forward the packet. Tracert also provides the response time; this helps you see how efficient a specific route is. If you notice that a particular router is slow, you can further diagnose why there is a hang up at this point.

For example, the following command shows how to use tracert from a command prompt, and a sample of what the results might be:

```
tracert 209.181.192.1

Tracing route to stcd.uswest.net [209.181.192.1] over a
maximum of 30 hops:

1     28 ms     29 ms     27 ms   209.181.195.254
2     29 ms     29 ms     28 ms   209.181.203.6
3     28 ms     29 ms     29 ms   stcd.uswest.net [209.181.192.1]

Trace complete.
```

This shows that the route to device 209.181.192.1 crossed 2 routers (209.181.195.254 and 209.181.203.6). Likewise, you can see that the time it took to reach each of these routers is all under 30 milliseconds. Not too bad!

The Ipconfig and Winipcfg Utilities

The ipconfig utility quickly displays the current TCP/IP settings defined on your local PC. *Ipconfig.exe* is a DOS-based program. Under Windows 95/98, Microsoft also offers a graphical version called *winipcfg.exe*. These are especially useful utilities when you use DHCP to tell you what IP address and other ancillary information your network card obtained. These utilities not only return your IP address but also the subnet mask, default gateway address, and DNS server addresses for all network cards in your computer. The following is a sample output of the ipconfig utility run from the DOS prompt on a Windows 98 PC:

```
Windows 98 IP Configuration
0 Ethernet adapter :
  IP Address. . . . . . . . . : 209.186.192.3
  Subnet Mask . . . . . . . . : 255.255.255.248
  Default Gateway . . . . . . : 209.186.192.6
```

The winipcfg program is shown in Figure 3-20.

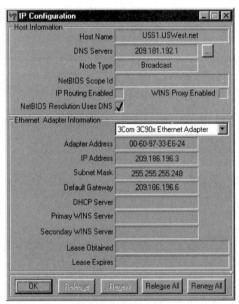

FIGURE 3-20 Example display from the WINIPCFG
utility in Windows 9*x*

The Netstat Utility

Netstat displays protocol statistics and current TCP/IP network connections. Options to the netstat command enable you to see all connections and listening ports, Ethernet statistics, TCP or UDP connections only, and the contents of the routing table in memory. As with most of the other TCP/IP utilities, the netstat program is run from a DOS prompt. The following command line parameters are currently supported by the Windows 95/98 version of the program:

```
netstat  [?] [-a] [-e] [-n] [-s] [-p proto] [-r] [interval]
```

- `-?`: Displays all available command line options.
- `-a`: all connections and ports.
- `-e`: Displays Ethernet statistics.
- `-n`: Displays addresses and port numbers in numerical format.
- `-p proto`: Displays connections for the protocol specified by *proto*. *Proto* may be TCP, UDP or IP. If used with the –s option, the display shows protocol statistics.
- `-r`: Displays the routing table.
- `-s`: Displays per-protocol statistics. By default, statistics are shown for TCP, UDP, and IP.
- `interval`: Redisplays the selected statistics, pausing between each display the number of seconds defined by *interval*. If omitted, netstat displays the current configuration only once.

Telnet

Telnet is a remote terminal emulation protocol that provides text-based access to a host running a telnet service. Most UNIX networks use or permit Telnet, as do many active hubs, switches, dedicated print servers, and routers. Telnet is also a very useful tool to test full TCP/IP connectivity. While ping is a good tool to test basic TCP/IP functionality, Telnet is a more reliable test as a connection-oriented session is actually created. (Note that the device you wish to test must be running a Telnet service.) To use Telnet, click the Telnet icon in the Accessories program group or at the command prompt in Run, type **telnet**.

▼ ▼ ▼

TO CONNECT TO A REMOTE COMPUTER USING THE 32-BIT WINDOWS TELNET CLIENT SOFTWARE, FOLLOW THESE STEPS:

1. Click Remote System from the Connect menu.

2. In the Host Name field, type or select the name of the remote system you want to connect to.

3. In the TermType field, type or select a string to be used if your host uses TermType negotiation.

- If you're not sure which emulation to use, click VT-100 (ANSI). Many telnet servers follow the VT-100 format.

- After you change the emulation, Telnet adjusts your system so that your computer, keyboard, and terminal perform the same as the specified terminal.

4. Click Connect.

■ ■ ■

in the real world

While the free Telnet client supplied with Windows 95/98 and NT is very useable, it is limited to the very basic features. There are literally hundreds of more robust Telnet clients available for download from the Internet. Most of these packages are free. To locate them, choose your favorite Internet search engine and search on the keywords: +Telnet +Free.

ARP

You may recall that ARP, or Address Resolution Protocol, is the first method used when attempting to resolve a host name to an address. Once these resolutions are made, the data is stored in cache memory to improve performance. The ARP command utility enables you to display and modify the IP-to-physical address translation tables. In fact, the ARP utility enables you to make permanent entries to frequently accessed hosts, preventing them from being flushed out of the cache even if they have not been referenced with the allotted time (two minutes by default). The format for using the ARP utility is as follows:

```
ARP      -s inet_addr eth_addr [if_addr]
```

```
ARP      -d inet_addr [if_addr]
ARP      -a [inet_addr] [-N if_addr]
```

- **-a**: Displays current ARP entries by interrogating the current protocol data. If `inet addr` is specified, the IP and physical addresses for only the specified computer are displayed. If more than one network interface uses ARP, entries for each ARP table are displayed.

- **-g**: Same as `-a`. (Windows 3.*x* and some other operating systems do not support the `-a` parameter).

- `Inet_addr`: Specifies an internet address.

- **-N if_addr**: Displays the ARP entries for the network interface specified by `if_addr`.

- **-d**: Deletes the host specified by `Inet_addr`.

- **-s**: Adds the host and associates the Internet address `inet_addr` with the physical address, `eth addr`. The physical address is given as 6 hexadecimal bytes separated by hyphens. The entry is permanent.

- `Eth_addr If_addr`: Specifies a physical address. If present, this specifies the Internet address of the interface whose address translation table should be modified. If not present, the first applicable interface is used.

For example:

```
> arp -s 157.55.85.212 00-aa-00-62-c6-09
```

adds a static entry.

```
> arp -a Displays the arp table.
```

NBTSTAT

NBTSTAT displays a list of NetBIOS computer names that have been resolved to IP addresses, protocol statistics, and current TCP/IP connections using NetBIOS over TCP/IP. The command line format for the NBTSTAT utility is:

```
NBTSTAT [-a RemoteName] [-A IP address] [-c] [-n] [-r] [-R]
[-s] [-S] [interval] ]
```

- ○ -a **(adapter status)**: Lists the remote machine's name table given its name.

- ○ -c **(cache)**: Lists the remote name cache including the IP addresses.

- ○ -n **(names)**: Lists local NetBIOS names.

- ○ -r **(resolved)**: Lists names resolved by broadcast and via WINS.

- ○ -R **(Reload)**: Purges and reloads the remote cache name table.

- ○ -S **(Sessions)**: Lists sessions table with the destination IP addresses.

- ○ -s **(sessions)**: Lists sessions table converting destination IP addresses to host names via the hosts file.

- ○ RemoteName: Remote host machine name.

- ○ IP address: Dotted decimal representation of the IP address.

- ○ Interval: Redisplays selected statistics, pausing interval seconds between each display. Press Ctrl+C to stop redisplaying statistics.

ROUTE displays or modifies the local routing table. The format for this command line utility is:

```
ROUTE [-f] [-p] [command [destination] [MASK subnet_mask]
[[gateway]]
```

- ○ -f: Clears the routing tables of all gateway entries. If this is used in conjunction with one of the commands, the tables are cleared prior to running the command.

- ○ -p: When used with the ADD command, makes a route persistent across reboots of the system. By default, routes are not preserved when the system is restarted. When used with the PRINT command, displays the list of registered persistent routes. Ignored for all other commands, which always affect the appropriate persistent routes.

- ○ Command: Specifies one of four commands:

  - ○ PRINT: Prints a route.

  - ○ ADD: Adds a route.

  - ○ DELETE: Deletes a route.

  - ○ CHANGE: Modifies an existing route.

- ○ Destination: Specifies the host to send command.

- MASK: If the MASK keyword is present, the next parameter is interpreted as the subnet_mask parameter.
- Subnet_mask: If provided, specifies a sub-net mask value to be associated with this route entry. If not specified, it defaults to 255.255.255.255.
- Gateway: Specifies gateway IP address.

EXAM PREPARATION SUMMARY

This chapter presented the fundamentals of the TCP/IP protocol suite. A solid understanding of this material provides you with the foundation necessary to master the Network+ exam. Because TCP/IP plays a major role in all modern networking, you can be sure that the Network+ exam will cover this topic in depth. Likewise, many vendor specific certification programs expect you to understand the fundamentals of TCP/IP.

This chapter began with a list of TCP/IP specific terms. The definitions and proper uses of each should become second nature to you. Next I discussed IP addressing, name resolution, routing, and how to configure a Windows 32-bit client to use TCP/IP. The last section of this chapter introduced you to the other utilities and protocols that round out the TCP/IP suite as well as what troubleshooting information the various utilities can provide. I recommend you review the key concepts in this chapter to make sure you understand the material that you just read.

- Know that TCP/IP is a suite of protocols supported by nearly every operating system and is used by millions of hosts worldwide
- Understand the classes of IP addresses
- Understand what a subnet mask is used for, and the common masks for each of the three IP address classes
- Understand the main protocols that make up the TCP/IP suite, including TCP, UDP, POP3, SMNP, SMTP, FTP, HTTP, and IP
- Understand the purpose and use of DHCP, HOST files, DNS, and WINS
- Understand the hierarchies of the NDS protocol, including the concept of domains and domain names
- Understand the concept of a default gateway in IP routing

- Understand configuration concepts of TCP/IP, including configuration of the workstation and when to use a proxy service

- Explain how and when to use the following TCP/IP utilities to test, validate, and troubleshoot IP connectivity:

ARP	Telnet
NBTSTAT	Tracert
NETSTAT	ipconfg / winipcfg
FTP	ping
ROUTE	

- Understand the concepts of the Transport Layer, specifically the distinction between connection and connectionless transport, and the purpose of name resolution

APPLYING WHAT YOU'VE LEARNED

The following review questions give you an opportunity to test your knowledge of the information presented in this chapter. The answers to these assessment questions can be found in Appendix A. If you miss questions, review the sections in this chapter that cover those topics before going further.

1. What are devices connected on a TCP/IP network commonly referred to as?

2. Name two protocols in the TCP/IP suite that function at the Transport Layer of the OSI model:

3. IP is responsible for sorting and _____ packets.

4. What is the first octet range for a Class A IP address?

5. What is the first octet range for a Class B IP address?

6. What is the first octet range for a Class C IP address?

7. What is the reserved *loopback* IP address that can be used to test the configuration of the local IP device?

8. Is the IP address 132.10.0.15 valid?

9. Is the IP address 192.168.10.0 valid?

10. What is the *maximum* number of host IDs available on a Class C address?

11. How many network addresses are needed when routers connect two LANs?

12. If two devices on a LAN are unable to communicate, what two common IP addressing problems should be investigated first?

13. What is the default subnet mask for a Class A address?

14. What is the default subnet mask for a Class B address?

15. What is the default subnet mask for a Class C address?

16. When is a subnet required?

17. How many bits are subnets comprised of?

18. The process of subnetting can be useful to create additional _____.

19. What are the two methods used to assign IP addresses?

20. What is DHCP used for?

21. In addition to IP addresses, what information can a DHCP server assign?

22. What does a host do first to request a dynamic IP address?

23. What is the default lease life of a dynamically assigned IP address?

    A. Permanent

    B. For as long as the host is connected to the network

    C. 72 hours

    D. 36 hours

24. How many network segments can a single DHCP server provide services to?

25. Describe the basic concept of name resolution.

26. What is the primary protocol used for name resolution?

27. Which type of address does ARP resolve?

28. What is the first thing ARP does when attempting to resolve a host name?

29. By default, ARP entries are retained in memory for:

    A. Two minutes, unless they have been reused, then they'll be retained up to ten minutes

    B. Thirty-six hours, unless they are renewed half way before being purged

    C. For as long as the PC remains connected to the network

    D. Five minutes unless a manual request is made to keep the tables longer

30. What is the file name that resides locally on a host, and contains host names and their IP addresses?

31. What name resolution protocol is most commonly used in large environments, including the Internet?

32. Name four popular top-level domain names:

33. What is the primary DNS server known as?

34. What is the order in which a server named `rocky.bullwinkle @cartoon.com` is located in a typical DNS request?

    A. Root ⇛ Cartoon servers ⇛ Characters

    B. Root ⇛ COM servers ⇛ Characters ⇛ Rocky server

    C. Root ⇛ COM servers ⇛ Cartoon servers ⇛ Bullwinkle servers ⇛ Rocky server

    D. Rocky server ⇛ Bullwinkle server ⇛ Cartoon server ⇛ COM servers

35. In which operating systems would you typically find NetBIOS?

36. NetBIOS is routable:

    A. Never

    B. Only on an IP network

    C. Only on an IPX network

    D. When combined with NetBEUI or TCP/IP

37. What are the five methods NetBIOS uses to resolve names to addresses?

38. What is the order that a router uses to search for a path in the routing table?

    A. Default, network, subnet, host

    B. Host, subnet, network, default

    C. Host, network, subnet, default

    D. DNS, WINS, Host files, default

39. What is the difference between a multicast and a broadcast?

40. TCP is:

    A. Connectionless and reliable

    B. Connectionless and unreliable

    C. Connection-orientated and reliable

    D. Connection-orientated and unreliable

41. What are the commonly used port numbers known as:

42. When a unique IP address *and* port number are used to identify a specific connection between two hosts, a _____ is created.

43. UDP is:

    A. Connectionless and reliable

    B. Connectionless and unreliable

    C. Connection-orientated and reliable

    D. Connection-orientated and unreliable

44. Name two services that use UDP as their transport protocol:

45. What is the function of the FTP protocol?

46. What is the difference between FTP and TFTP?

47. Where are you most likely to see the Hypertext Transport Protocol (HTTP) used?

48. What is the basic message handling method of the POP3 protocol?

49. What protocol is used between e-mail servers?

50. What is the standard protocol for network management features?

51. When a managed threshold is exceeded, a management agent issues a:

    A. Warning

    B. Trap

    C. Alert

    D. Credit

52. What are two main benefits of a proxy server?

53. What is the first recommended check when troubleshooting connectivity problems across a WAN link?

54. What simple utility can you use to see if a TCP/IP device is active?

55. What is an easy method to use to see if name resolution is functioning on a TCP/IP network?

56. What information does TRACERT provide that ping does not?

57. What utility can you use to see the local IP address, subnet mask, and default gateway of every NIC in your host?

58. What utility provides you with current TCP/IP network connection statistics?

59. What utility could you use to access a router or a UNIX server using a text-based connection?

60. What utility provides a list of NetBIOS names and IP address that have been resolved on the network?

Remote Access Technologies

About Chapter 4

I n this chapter I take a look at the various options available to provide network access to users away from the office. Whether the user calls in from her or his home PC, or from the road on a laptop, there are a number of technologies to give her or him access to the corporate network. I begin with the most common access methods, and their advantages and disadvantages. Next I look at how the actual connects can be made, such as using the public telephone system or a high-speed digital connection, and the various protocols that provide the data connection. Because many of the techniques require dial-up access using a modem, I examine the steps necessary to install and configure a modem in the Windows 32-bit environment.

REMOTE ACCESS TECHNOLOGIES

Thanks in large part to the Internet, people are now more accustomed to using computers to communicate beyond their immediate area. In fact, it is nearly impossible to purchase a new computer nowadays that doesn't include a built-in modem. The business place is no exception. Sales people, managers, and just about any other employee who uses the network in the office, want and often need access to the corporate LAN outside the office. Remote access is so dominant, in fact, that most hotels and motels now have in-room telephones with modem attachments. Another sign of this *connected world* is evident in mainstream operating systems that offer built-in remote access services. Windows 9*x* offers built-in dial-up networking, NT contains remote access server (RAS), NetWare has NetWare Connect, and UNIX (and its free lookalike Linux) provides a number of similar services.

Remote access has become an expected extension to the corporate LAN, but as necessary as it is, providing the proper service is often still difficult. End users have become accustomed to faster and faster connection speeds and naturally expect similar results when calling in from home or on the road. Software licensing issues must be reviewed carefully, as well, as many accepted standards have changed with the explosion of dial-up connectivity. And of course, once you open up the LAN to permit authorized persons access, you have new security issues to deal with as well.

REMOTE ACCESS CONCEPTS

There are many options available to provide remote connectivity to users outside of the corporate LAN:

- **Remote Node**: Enables the remote location to attach to the LAN as if the telephone line was merely an extension of the network cable. When users connect using remote node, they are prompted to log into the network, and they gain access to network drives just as if they were stationed at their office PC.

- **Remote Control**: This method uses both a *remote* (home) PC and a locally connected, or *host* PC (usually the user's office computer or a dedicated PC in the office that is always on for remote control purposes). All of the actual processing occurs on the host PC back at the office. Screen displays, keystrokes, and mouse actions are the only things sent between the two computers.

- **WinFrame or Terminal Server**: Citrix Systems, Inc. developed a hybrid version of Microsoft Windows NT *v*3.51 that uses the multithreading capabilities of NT to enable a remote access service similar to remote control. Although Microsoft licensed the NT code to Citrix, they did not sign over the rights for competing products, so Microsoft recently started delivering a similar product for NT *v*4.0 known as Terminal Server. Both products provide the best benefits of remote control without the need to dedicate a PC for each user that wishes to dial-in. A single WinFrame or Terminal Server can support one or more users simultaneously.

- **Virtual Private Networks (VPN)**: While VPN technology is not really an *access method*, the technology is often used in conjunction with remote access. As powerful and inexpensive as the Internet has become, companies have looked for ways of using the Internet for remote connections. Virtual private networks, or VPNs, promise to deliver simplified remote access without the expenses associated with traditional methods. Using the Internet as a transport medium, VPN hardware and software products establish a secured *pipe* between two computers using data encryption. Because there are no official standards defined for VPN technology at this time, the data encryption function is proprietary to the solutions being implemented. Most solutions are based on the public key encryption methods (discussed in Chapter 5); the encryption is done by software at the PC level while other solutions use special hardware at each end to provide the data encryption. Once authentication is established, the remote PC can be used to transfer data to and from the LAN safely and securely. Standards for VPNs are still being established, but many vendors offer very useable proprietary products today.

In this chapter I take a closer look at these remote access technologies, discuss their software and hardware requirements, and explain some of the most common troubleshooting tips.

Remote Node

Remote node is the method of connecting an outside PC to the corporate LAN to provide network services to the outside PC just as if it were locally connected. Figure 4-1 shows how a remote user on a laptop computer enters the network as if the computer is directly connected to the LAN. Remote node technology is often referred to as RAS, or *Remote Access Services*. Some NOSs (network operating systems) incorporate RAS within the operating system; other hardware vendors have specialized devices that attach to the LAN and provide RAS services independently of the operating systems (the LanRover hardware option from Sheva is a good example). When NT is compared with NetWare, RAS has been a distinct feature of NT, although Novell offers a similar feature in their NetConnect product.

Remote node advantages are that is fast for data transfers, easy to implement, and does not generally require additional software on the client PC. Typically the remote user uses the Windows 95, 98, or NT dial-up networking feature to initiate a session to the RAS server, although numerous free or low-cost dial-up applications exist for just about any other desktop operating system. And recently, software packages are being offered to increase the speed of data transfers across RAS connection even further. By synchronizing data files between the host and remote PCs, these software additions can selectively transfer only data that has been modified. For example, if a salesperson on the road dials into the corporate LAN and downloads an 800KB inventory file, the process may take one to three minutes, depending on the connection speed. Next, when the salesperson places an order that modifies only a few records in the database and sends the file back to the LAN, the synchronizing program only transmits the newly modified records instead of the entire 800KB file, and thus saves a considerable amount of time throughout the day!

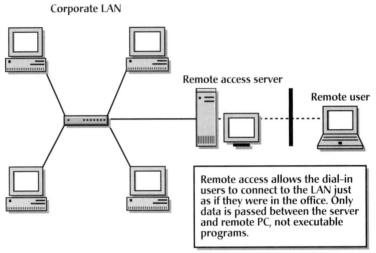

Corporate LAN

Remote access server

Remote user

Remote access allows the dial-in users to connect to the LAN just as if they were in the office. Only data is passed between the server and remote PC, not executable programs.

FIGURE 4-1   Example of remote node access to a corporate network

Advantages to remote node

Advantages to remote nodes are as follows:

o They are generally simple to install and configure. Either the NOS provides the service, or third party hardware offerings make installation go quickly.

o The client side is easy to install. 32-bit Windows operating systems have dial-up networking built in, and many simple and inexpensive third party applications exist for other systems.

o They have good transfer speeds when only data and printing are required.

o Synchronizing software can cut the transfer times of modified data back to the LAN from 1 to 99 percent.

Disadvantages to remote node

Disadvantages to remote nodes are as follows:

o Executing *programs* across the data link is unacceptably slow. All programs must reside on the remote PC for performance to be useable.

- Separate software licenses will probably be required for every dial-in user because the programs need to be located on the remote PC.

- Remote users cannot easily access data stored on their office desktop PCs.

Remote Control

Remote control requires the network act as a host for the remote PC . (See Figure 4-2.) For illustration purposes, I assume a person is using remote control technology to connect to their office LAN from their home. The office PC (usually the person's desktop computer in the office) is called the *host* and the home PC is the *remote*. Whereas the remote *node* requires programs to be stored and executed locally (at home), remote control uses very little of the local resources. Programs are executed on the host (office) PC, but all network resources available on the host PC are also available on the remote PC, including disk storage and printers. Recent improvements to data compression, modem technology, and physical telephone components (such as fiber optic cables) have made remote control response times similar to what a user may be accustomed to in the office. Two of the most popular remote control software packages are Symantec's pcANYWHERE and Stac's Reachout products.

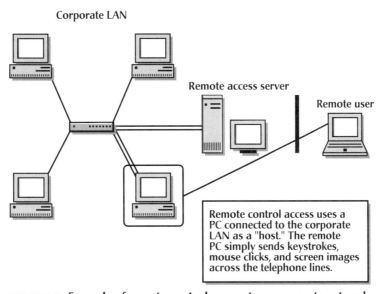

FIGURE 4-2 Example of remote control access to a corporate network

Because remote control actually *takes over* another PC, helpdesk and other support personnel find this technology invaluable. If an end user experiences problems, the helpdesk person can take control of the user's PC and perform troubleshooting without having to leave his or her desk! In large buildings, or across counties, the capability to perform remote support can save an organization several thousands of dollars and greatly improves the response time to problems.

Another inherent feature of remote control software is its capability to display the remote user's actions simultaneously on the host PC. Using this feature, the helpdesk person actually shows the end user how to accomplish a particular function within their application. Likewise, an instructor can take control of students' computers to demonstrate a process without leaving the front of the room or using expensive overhead projectors.

Most remote control software has full-duplex capabilities that enable users on both ends to communicate, or *chat* in real time. This feature is useful during training or troubleshooting because communication between the two sides is necessary.

Advantages to remote control

Advantages to remote control are as follows:

- Performance is greatly improved overall, especially when executing programs.

- Dial-in users have easy access to files on their office desktops when their desktop acts as the host.

- Software requires only one license because the programs are all located and executed on the host computer.

- Support personnel can fix problems more easily from their location by taking control of the problem PC.

- Instructors can control student PCs for training purposes, regardless of where the PCs are physically located. This can save organizations thousands of dollars in travel expenses and enable a single instructor to reach more students at the same time.

- Remote control software is easy to configure and well supported by vendors. It has been in the marketplace for years and is very reliable.

Disadvantages to remote control

Disadvantages to remote control are as follows:

- The software is proprietary and not normally part of the operating system. This can add overhead costs and take up valuable memory resources in older computers.

- Communications requires two computers. A host PC must be configured to answer the remote dial-in request, and the host PC is not available for other purposes when it is controlled by remote access.

- Host PCs must be configured separately for each user. Each person that wants remote control for his or her office PC must have a modem and a telephone line installed at their computer. (Recent improvements regarding this scenario are covered in the next section.)

- Bypassing LAN access methods by directly dialing into a host PC may compromise corporate security policies.

The best features of remote node and remote control

Remote control software typically configures each PC that acts as a host with dedicated telephone lines and individual modems. Often times, companies dedicate a single PC running the host software to enable remote access through a single telephone line and modem. This helps keep costs down, but it also prevents users from accessing data stored locally on their office PCs and prevents multiple users from accessing the host at the same time. In order to make remote control software a bit more useable, a number of vendors have added features to take advantage of remote node technology. Recent changes make it possible to install the *host* portion of the software on many different machines while using a common remote node (RAS) connection for remote users to dial into. The NOS, third party software, or a third party hardware/software product can supply the actual RAS connection. Once the connection is established, the user can select a host PC from a list to take control of it using LANs native protocol (TCP/IP or IPX, for example). Figure 4-3 shows how this technology is implemented. By using a common RAS connection to provide the initial connection to the LAN, multiple remote users can simultaneously implement remote control technologies that provide better performance in many cases. This combination also provides an easy method of enabling multiple users to access the LAN without having to dedicate PCs specifically to remote control services.

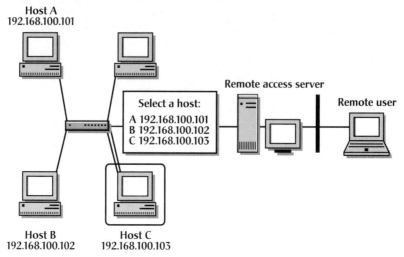

FIGURE 4-3 Example of using remote node and remote control to access a corporate network

Advantages to using combined remote node and remote control

The advantages to implementing a combination of these remote technologies are as follows:

- Concentrates modem telephone line locations into a single area.
- Permits dial-in access from various connection methods, such as analog phones, ISDN, xDSL, and more. (See the next section for more information.)
- Can be configured to provide generic host machines as well as specific desktop hosts.
- Can be configured to use a company's PBX (private internal telephone network), thus, eliminating the need to remember and use specific telephone numbers to dial-in.

Disadvantages to using combined remote node and remote control

The disadvantages to implementing a combination of these remote technologies are as follows:

- Does not eliminate the need for multiple modems or telephone wires, although the number of multiple lines can be reduced if they are used in conjunction with an internal PBX system.

- May require additional security measures to ensure users don't use hosts they should not have access too.

Multiuser NT Access

As I mentioned earlier in this chapter, WinFrame and Microsoft's Terminal Server (TS) software provides a proprietary solution based on the Windows NT server operating system. This technology requires a true server PC to act as a dedicated *communications server*. By exploiting NT's capability to run multiple, simultaneous sessions, users can dial into a WinFrame or a TS server and run application programs directly on the server. In order to achieve near-LAN speed performance, these hybrid versions of NT add custom changes to the core NT operating system. Citrix developed a proprietary technology called *Independent Computing Architecture*, or ICA, which conceptually works the same way as remote control does. As with remote control, only screen images, keystrokes, and mouse commands are passed through the connection, although the ICA protocol is much more efficient. In fact, the remote WinFrame client can run just about any 32-bit Windows program acceptably well on as little as a 286 class PC. Even across a 14.4 Internet connection, programs execute reasonably well on a WinFrame server.

Advantages to ICA

Advantages to ICA are as follows:

- Performance is ICA's number one feature. Applications can be run across even slow Internet links at reasonable levels.

- Multiple connections to a single server eliminate the need for numerous host components on each user's desktop.

- Legacy devices such as 286-, 368-, and 486-based PCs can act as the remote computer without a loss of performance. This feature alone may save a company money because it can extend the useful life of older computers.

- ICA permits direct dial-in, as well as Internet connections, with good security features.

Disadvantages to ICA

Disadvantages to ICA are as follows:

- WinFrame is a hybrid of Windows NT *v*3.51. It will not support applications specifically written to *v*4.0 specifications. Terminal Server will run on either NT v3.*x* or 4.*x*, and only supports remote client devices that meet the minimum specifications for Windows for Workgroups, or the 32-bit Windows family. (This limits clients primarily to 486 and Pentium computers.)

- Both WinFrame and Terminal servers require hefty server hardware. A Pentium 166MHz PC with 96MB RAM will support about five users. Dual- or four-processor machines with as much as 256MB of RAM are necessary to support 15 or more users.

- Older software, especially DOS-based software and programs that need direct access to the hardware, will not operate correctly, if at all.

- There are no industry-accepted standards for WinFrame or Terminal Server, so all of the support and products are proprietary.

- *Chat* sessions between the host and the remote are not possible, nor is file synchronization available.

Remote Access Connectivity Methods

Regardless of which remote access method you use, some form of medium must be used to connect the remote PC and the LAN. This connection can be done through satellite systems, microwave signals, or other wireless protocol, but by far the most common method is to use existing telephone cables. Within this realm of the physical media, various transport protocols and other routing methods can be used to increase the bandwidth, transfer speeds, and reliability of these links. The next section looks at the most common transport methods in use today and their advantages and disadvantages.

Plain old telephone system (POTS)

As I mention above, the plain old telephone system is by far the common method of connecting remote users. This is because there is practically nothing else to buy, nearly every software and hardware device supports it, and until people become accustomed to faster speeds, telephone system performance is generally acceptable. POTS exists throughout the world, so access between any two points is usually possible. Further, most of the world's public telephone networks have been upgraded from their original analog systems to digital. The result is access that is more reliable and more compatible to data compression technologies used in to-day's higher analog modems. Unfortunately, though, not all POTS lines have been converted to digital. The infamous *last mile*, the amount of cable from your home or office to the telephone company's central office (CO) generally is still analog. And it's this *last mile* that prevents high-speed digital access at reasonable prices to many residential and small business users.

Advantages to POTS

Advantages to POTS are as follows:

- Wide availability. Nearly any location you want to access a host from has a standard telephone jack nearby.

- Price. Calls are often free for the end-user, either through a local number or a toll-free number paid for by the company.

- Supported by all modems and software applications.

- Acceptable speeds when applications and hardware use data compression and other bandwidth-saving technologies.

Disadvantages to POTS

Disadvantages to POTS are as follows:

- Speeds higher than 53Kbps are simply not possible. Although modern modems are capable of 56Kbps transmission speeds, the FCC limits analog communications to a maximum speed of 53Kbps. And even at 53Kbps, the *modulation/de-modulation* process incurs a performance penalty when a computer's digital signals are converted to analog and vice-versa for trans-mission over the telephone line.

- Long distance calls can quickly add up, making prolonged remote access expensive.

Integrated Services Digital Network (ISDN)

ISDN is an international telecommunications standard for transmitting voice, video, and data (hence the word *integrated*) over digital lines running at 64Kbps (kilobits per second). Telephone companies commonly use a 64Kbps channel for digitized, two-way voice conversations. ISDN is a reasonably inexpensive way to replace slow modem technology for speeds up to 128Kbps before compression. With compression, it is quite possible to achieve throughput speeds of from 256Kbps to more than 1Mbps. Digital lines are almost totally error free, which means that the slowdowns and errors typically encountered in today's modern transmissions are no longer a problem.

ISDN uses two 64Kbps circuit-switched channels identified as channel B, or *bearer,* and channel D, or *delta*. The B channel carries voice and data, while the D channel is used for control signals. These control signals trigger the telephone company's computers to make calls, put calls on hold, or activate special features such as call forwarding or video conferencing. The D channel also receives information about incoming calls, such as the identity of the caller.

ISDN's basic service is called *Basic Rate Interface*, or BRI. BRI is made up of two 64Kbps B channels and one 16Kbps D channel. BRI is sometimes known as 2B+D. As the word *basic* implies, 2B+D has minimal capacities and can run on the same copper twisted-pair wiring found in most homes. With BRI Service, the same pair of wires that provides two primary, high speed (64 Kbps) communications channels can be used simultaneously, as well as independently, to carry any combination of data, image, video, or voice calls. By combining these channels, data transfer at up to 128 Kbps may be achieved. BRI Service can also provide a third, auxiliary channel for low to moderate speed data communications that is ideal for point of sale, remote monitoring, or telemetry applications.

concept link

It may be of interest to note why B channels have a bandwidth of 64Kbps when normal speech frequencies go up toward 4,000Hz. To digitally encode the amplitude of analog signals, speech frequencies must be sampled at twice their maximum frequency. Thus normal human speech needs to be sampled 8,000 times per second. At the time this technology was developed, encoding schemes used only eight bits to store the value of each sample. Eight bits times 8,000 samples per second equals the 64Kbps bandwidth of a B channel. Today, however, speech-encoding methods enable us to use channels with much less bandwidth.

No special handling is required when voice calls are made between ISDN phones and conventional telephones—the network manages the necessary conversions. When conducting data calls, in order to use the B Channels for digital communications, ISDN-based equipment is required at both ends of the communications path; this is also the case with conventional modem connections or fax machine transmissions.

The first level of Primary Rate Interface, or PRI, consists of 23 B channels and a D channel, and has a total transmission rate of 1.544Mbits/second. PRI is also known as 23B+D. Each 64Kbits/second B channel carries user information such as voice calls, circuit-switched data, and video. The 64Kbits/second D channel carries the control, or signaling, information. PRI requires special wiring that is not normally found in residential settings.

Connecting ISDN to a personal computer or network requires a network terminator (NT1) and ISDN terminal adapter. The NT1 plugs into the two-wire line from the telephone company and provides four-wire output to the terminal adapter. The NT1 is typically built into the terminal adapter.

ISDN comes as either a dial-up or a dedicated connection. Dial-up ISDN requires that your terminal adapter call the ISDN receiver to establish a connection. Dedicated ISDN, on the other hand, uses routers on both ends for the connection. The advantage to the dedicated connection is that it can be shared by multiple users, whereas dial-up connects to a single PC. This is not to say that dedicated ISDN is *always on*. The time to initiate a dedicated connection is somewhat faster than dial-up, but it still requires an initiation process be performed when you need access. Because most telephone companies charge by the minute for ISDN, you do not want the connection to remain open when there is no data begin transmitted.

Advantages to ISDN

Advantages to ISDN are as follows:

- Offers much higher speeds than basic analog connections.
- Digital signals are nearly error free and eliminate the need for modulation/de-modulation of analog signals.
- Less expensive than dedicated leased digital phone lines.
- Can generally be run on the existing copper wires within a building.
- Data and voice can be transmitted simultaneously on the same ISDN line.

Disadvantages to ISDN

Disadvantages to ISDN are as follows:

- Not available in all areas and not widely accepted. As other technologies emerge, ISDN may not become the *de-facto* digital standard.
- More expensive than standard analog systems; this includes higher costing ISDN devices on both ends of the call line.
- Software compatibility issues. Currently, not all remote access applications support ISDN connections, although most will in the very near future.

Digital Subscriber Line (xDSL)

DSL is my personal favorite. Although it is not yet widely available, DSL services are gaining momentum. DSL is a modem technology that increases the digital speed of ordinary telephone lines anywhere from 56Kpbs to over 8Mbps! Ordinary analog modems do not support DSL signals, but a DSL modem costs under $200, and it is well worth the cost for the increased speeds. xDSL modems use digital coding techniques to squeeze up to 99 percent more capacity out of a standard telephone line without interfering with your regular telephone services. This means you can be simultaneously talking on the telephone while sending a fax or surfing the World Wide Web. DSL runs on normal copper wiring so there is no need to install new cabling into the home or office. The DSL modem separates the voice and data signals from the wire and passes the appropriate data over to the telephone, a NIC, or a hub/switch on the LAN. The generic term for the various flavors of DSL technology is xDSL. The other variations include:

- **ADSL**, or Asymmetric DSL, provides faster download speeds, preferable with the Internet usage and video.
- **HDSL**, or High data rate Digital Subscribe Line, has modems on either end of one or more twisted pair wires that deliver speeds up to 1.55Mbps.
- **RADSL**, or Rate Adaptive, provides a guaranteed minimum speed that may increase as demand for the technology decreases.
- **UDSL**, or Unidirectional HDSL, has been proposed by a European company, but there have been no signs of interest from anyone else.

- **VDSL**, or Very high data rate Digital Subscriber Line, is a modem for twisted-pair access that operates at data rates from 12.9Mbps to 52.8Mbps with a corresponding maximum reach ranging from 4500 feet to 1000 feet. VDSL service requires cabling of 24 gauge twisted pair wire.

- **VADSL**, or Very high speed ADSL, is either the same as VDSL or a subset of VDSL, if VDSL includes symmetric mode transmission.

Advantages to xDSL

Advantages to xDSL are as follows:

- Has very high speed. *All* digital transfer rates are from 56Kbps to over 8Mpbs.

- Runs over standard copper wires and does not require additional cabling.

- Costs are minimal. DSL service costs as little as $40 per month for a 256Kbps connection. For services of 1Mpbs and higher, costs typically remain under $300 per month (as compared to T1 connections that can cost $1,000 or more monthly).

- Does not require a dedicated data line because voice and data are carried over the same copper wire.

- Provides an *always-on* connection to the Internet. DSL does not require you *dial* a service provider. Your Internet connection is always available.

Disadvantages to xDSL

Disadvantages to xDSL are as follows:

- Not yet available in all areas. The end user's telephone connection must be within 15,000 feet (3 miles) of the telephone company's central office.

- The number of ISPs to offer xDSL service is still quite limited.

Remote Access Protocols (Line Protocols)

Network protocols can be transported over communications media they were not originally intended for. These remote access protocols, or line protocols, actually encapsulate the network protocol packet. When the line protocol reaches the dial-up server, the line protocol packet is stripped away and the network protocol packet is sent onto the network.

Point-to-Point Protocol

A data link protocol (Layer 2 of the OSI Model) provides dial-up access over serial lines. A Point-to-Point Protocol (PPP) is designed for simple links that transport packets between two hosts. The links provide full-duplex, simultaneous, bi-directional operation, and deliver packets in order, and PPP provides a common solution to connect a variety of hosts, bridges, and routers. In fact, it has become the de facto standard for dial-up Internet connections. PPP can encapsulate multiple network-layer protocols, such as IPX and AppleTalk; this makes it very easy to use for connections into a private network as well. The PPP protocol was designed to be easy to configure, and generally, the standard defaults handle all common configurations. By this, I mean, the protocol's self-configuration is implemented through a negotiation mechanism where each end of the link describes to the other its capabilities and requirements. In order to establish communications over a point-to-point link, each end must first send *Link Control Protocol* (LCP) packets to configure and test the data link. After the link is established, the peer may be authenticated. Next, PPP must send *Network Control Protocol* (NCP) packets to choose and configure one or more network-layer protocols (such as TCP/IP or IPX). Once each of the chosen network-layer protocols has been configured, *datagrams* (a packet of information with associated delivery information) from each network-layer protocol can be exchanged. The link remains configured for communications until explicit commands close the link down, or some external event, such as an inactivity timer expiring occurs. The PPP protocol also is capable of automatically reestablishing, or *camping*, a failed connection.

Serial Line IP

Serial Line IP (SLIP) is an older data link protocol for dial-up access to TCP/IP networks. SLIP is commonly used to gain access to the Internet, and it can also be used to provide dial-up access between two LANs. SLIP transmits IP packets over any serial link (dial-up or private lines) and simply defines a sequence of characters that frame IP packets. SLIP does not provide addressing, packet type identification, error detection/correction, or compression mechanisms. Because the protocol does so little, it is usually very easy to implement. SLIP is commonly used on dedicated serial links and sometimes for dial-up purposes and is usually used with line speeds between 1200bps and 19.2Kbps. It is useful for enabling mixes of hosts and routers to communicate with one another (host-host, host-router, and router-router are all common SLIP network configurations).

Three major drawbacks to SLIP (that PPP provides) are its lack of addressing, packet type identification, and error detection/correction. With SLIP, both computers in the link need to know each other's IP addresses for routing purposes. This causes problems because there is a growing lack of public IP addresses, and most ISPs dole out dynamic addresses upon connection.

Without a packet type identifier field, SLIP is only capable of transmitting a single network-layer protocol. So for example, in a configuration with two DEC computers that both run TCP/IP and DECnet, there is no hope that TCP/IP and DECnet can share one serial line while they use SLIP.

The majority of remote connections used today rely on the public telephone system, and the bulk of these connections are through analog phone lines. These lines are susceptible to noise and other interference that can corrupt data packets in transit. Since the SLIP protocol does not provide error detection/correction, other higher-level protocols on the end devices are responsible to request retransmission of bad data. This can add quite a bit of unnecessary overhead to the remote connection.

Virtual Private Networks

Many people have concerns about transporting sensitive information across a shared IP network, such as the Internet, because that traffic can be intercepted or modified by hackers. At the same time, the Internet is a natural transport medium to reduce long distance data transportation costs. To address these issues, *Virtual Private Networks*, or VPNs, can be implemented. VPNs are pathways, or tunnels, established by hardware and software technologies, that create virtual point-to-point connections through a shared IP-based network. VPNs behave as if they were direct dial-up or leased line connections, even though they function in switched, or routed, networks. The data passing through these virtual tunnels are encrypted while delivering the security, management, and control of dedicated links.

At the core of VPNs is a technique referred to as *tunneling*. Tunneling enables VPN traffic to be routed through an IP network irrespective of the type of network or device the traffic originates on. In this sense, VPNs operate independently of other network protocols, and tunneled traffic may consist of IP, IPX, AppleTalk, or any other type of packet.

Essential to the tunneling technique is the tunneling protocol. The *Point-to-Point Tunneling Protocol* (PPTP) was codeveloped by 3Com and Microsoft. It has become the first widely available protocol for establishing VPNs. All 32-bit Windows operating systems support PPTP, enabling most desktops to initiate a VPN. PPTP supports both client-to-LAN (such as mobile user to campus LAN) and LAN-to-LAN (such as sales office to campus LAN) tunneling by taking a packet of any other protocol and encapsulating it in a PPTP packet.

 tip **The Microsoft Dial-Up Networking 1.2 upgrade supports PPTP. All the improvements to Microsoft's Dial-Up Networking are included in the OSR2 release of Windows 95.**

Basic Modem Configurations

Because the bulk of remote communications that are currently used are based on analog modems, it is critical to understand the basic configuration and troubleshooting techniques for these devices. Great strides have been made in the Plug and Play technology of modems, but many real world problems still require manually configuring the hardware and their associated devices. For the remainder of this chapter, I go over the basic components of serial-based modems and how they are properly configured.

Serial ports

As mentioned above, the bulk of remote communications take place over serial connections with analog modems. External modems are typically connected to the serial ports on the back of the computer. These ports are usually 9- or 25-pin connectors. DOS and Windows natively recognize the serial ports as COM (communication ports) 1 through 4. In order to avoid conflict with other serial devices, modems should be configured to use either COM1 or COM2. Internal modems create a new COM port when they are installed into the computer. If the system board already has COM1 and COM2 enabled as external connections, the modem must be set to COM3 or COM4. Unless both external COM ports are in use, it is wise to disable one of these ports to enable the internal modem to be configured as one of the first two COM ports. With Plug and Play devices in a Plug and Play operating system (such as Windows 95/98) internal modems automatically are configured for the next available COM port. On non-Plug and Play systems, the COM port of an internal modem is typically configured with jumpers on the card, or by a software utility provided by the manufacturer.

Regardless of how you configure your modem's COM port, it is necessary to identify which serial ports are already in use before installing the new modem. Assuming that your COM ports are integrated in your motherboard, the safest method is to check the serial port configuration in the computer BIOS or CMOS setup screen. The method used to view and configure the serial devices varies from PC to PC, so you may need to refer to the motherboard's documentation. Remember that in order to avoid conflict with other serial devices, it is important to make certain that COM1 or COM2 is available for use by the modem.

If you install an internal modem, and you want both external ports available, I recommend you configure COM1 on the 9-pin connector for the mouse, and configure the second serial device as COM3 or COM4. Most newer BIOSs will permit this; if yours does not, you may need to disable the second serial device altogether. Another option is to install a PS/2 or bus mouse instead of a serial mouse. Your motherboard may already provide a PS/2 connection, or you can purchase a bus mouse with an add-in ISA card.

If you are installing an external modem, you only need to make sure the physical port is unused and is defined as COM1 or 2 in the BIOS setup. You should also set the speed of the port to the maximum permissible in your BIOS configuration.

In Windows 95/98, you should also check the configuration of the serial devices from the System applet in the Control Panel, as depicted in Figure 4-4.

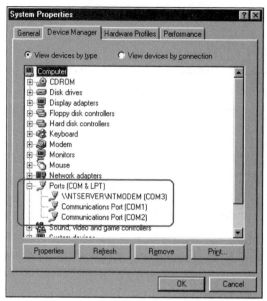

FIGURE 4-4   Ports settings found in Windows 9*x* Device Manager

▼ ▼ ▼

**TO ACCESS THE PORT SETTINGS IN WINDOWS 9X DEVICE MANAGER, FOLLOW
THESE STEPS:**

1. Click the Start button.

2. Click Settings.

3. Click Control Panel.

4. Click System.

5. From the System Properties window, click on the Device Manager tab,
expand Ports and highlight the port configuration you want to see, and click
the Properties button.

■ ■ ■

For an external modem, you want to see the COM port listed here. If it is not
here, run the *Add New Hardware* utility from the Control Panel before proceeding.

For internal modems, you do not want to see the COM port listed here. When
the modem is installed, and Windows performs its auto-detection (or you manually configure it) the modem creates a new COM port in the process. If the modem

COM port exists in this screen, you need to remove it (highlight the desired port and then click Remove), and readjust the settings in the computers BIOS.

IRQs

Most devices in the computer require an *interrupt* line. There is a fixed amount of interrupts available, and conflicts between devices using the same interrupt can cause many headaches. Before installing a serial modem, you must make sure the modem is configured to use a free interrupt. There are predefined default interrupts for each COM port. Unless your system has been manually configured otherwise, your modem should be configured according to the table below.

TABLE 4-1 DEFAULT SERIAL PORT INTERRUPTS

COM PORT	IRQ
1	4
2	3
3	4
4	3

You can see from this table that COM1 and COM3, and COM2 and COM4 each share an interrupt. This is why it is advisable to keep the modem on COM1 or 2. If your modem is configured for COM3, and your mouse for COM1, it is very likely that either your mouse will quit working when you initiate a modem call, or your modem will drop the connection when you move your mouse. Interrupts can be shared, but it is best to share them with devices that are not likely to be used at the same time.

I/O Address

Just as the modem needs an available interrupt, it also needs a dedicated memory range known as the input/output address. Again, there are default settings for I/O addresses, as outlined in Table 4-2. Unless it is absolutely necessary, default address ranges should always be used.

TABLE 4-2 DEFAULT SYSTEM I/O ADDRESS

I/O ADDRESS RANGE	DEVICE TYPICALLY FOUND IN THIS RANGE
000–01F	DMA controller 1
020–03F	Interrupt controller 8259A
040–05F	Timer
060–06F	Keyboard controller
070–07F	Real-Time clock
080–09F	DMA Page registers
0A0–0BF	Interrupt controller 2
0C0–0DF	DMA controller 2
0F0	Clear math coprocessor busy
0F1	Reset math coprocessor
0F8–0FF	Math coprocessor
1F0–1F8	Fixed disk
200–207	Game I/O
278–27F	Parallel printer port 2
2E8–2EF	4th Serial I/O Port
2F8–2FF	Serial port 2
300–31F	Available/prototype card
360–36F	Available/network card
378–37F	Parallel printer port 1
380–38F	SDLC bisynchronous 2
3A0–3AF	SDLC bisynchronous 1
3B0–3BF	Mono display/printer card
3C0–3CF	Available
3D0–3DF	Color display card
3E8–3EF	3rd Serial I/O Port
3F0–3F7	Primary disk drive controller
3F8–3FF	Serial port 1

Windows 95/98 has another screen in the System Devices applet that shows all of the resources in use by every defined device.

▼ ▼ ▼

TO VIEW THIS LIST FROM THE CONTROL PANEL, FOLLOW THESE STEPS:

1. Click the System icon.

2. Click the Device Manager tab.

3. In the Device Manager window, highlight the Computer icon by clicking on it once, and then click the Properties button at the bottom of the window.

A Computer Properties list will be displayed similar to Figure 4-5 (below). From this screen, you can view the settings of the current IRQs, I/O addresses, DMA addresses, and memory allocations simply by clicking the associated radio button.

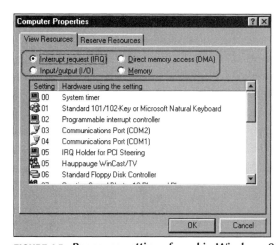

FIGURE 4-5 **Resource settings found in Windows 9*x* Device Manager**

■ ■ ■

So far we've only discussed Windows 95/98 configurations, but you're likely to run into other systems as well. Unfortunately, there is no set method to install and configure new hardware for every machine, so you may have to do a little digging into the manufacturer's documentation. However, all modems need the same types of resources that I've discussed in the previous pages. You'll need to make sure the COM port is properly defined, the IRQ and I/O addresses are set, and that none of these items conflict with other components in the system.

Modem Installation in Windows 9x

Windows 95/98 has greatly improved the process of installing modems. If a modem is physically installed when the operating system is installed, the modem should be automatically detected. Likewise, most PCI-based modems are automatically detected once Windows reloads, after the modem has been physically installed. However, for older modems, or if the modem isn't automatically detected, Windows 95/98 has an installation and diagnostic applet.

▼ ▼ ▼

TO DISPLAY THE MODEM DIALOG BOX IN WINDOWS 9X, FOLLOW THESE STEPS:

1. Click on Start.

2. Click Settings.

3. Click Control Panel.

4. Click Modems.

■ ■ ■

The screen shown in Figure 4-6 appears. From this screen you can see what modems are already defined in your computer, update the modem drivers, manually install new modems, and run some basic diagnostics.

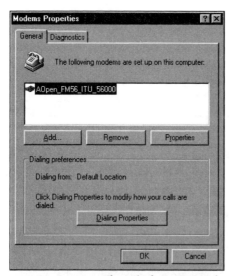

INSERT FIGURE 4-6   The Windows 9x Modem
Properties dialog box

To add a new modem, simply click on the Add button. The next screen asks you if you want Windows to attempt to automatically locate the modem for you. Normally you select this, but if the system does not detect your modem, or the manufacturer provides special Windows 95/98 drivers, you will elect that Windows does not search for new modems. Figure 4-7 shows the screen that appears when you choose to manually install a modem.

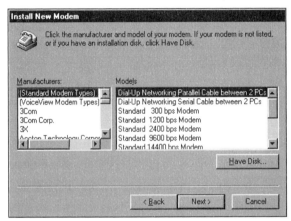

FIGURE 4-7   The Windows 9x modem installation dialog box

If the manufacturer and the model appear in the list, you can select them from here, otherwise click the Have Disk button and select where the files are located (normally from a floppy disk or CD). Windows then attempts to install the drivers. If the installation fails, you should review the settings for your modem as discussed in the last section.

The next step is to make sure that the modem responds to basic commands. You can run some basic diagnostics on the modem by clicking on the Diagnostics tab in the Control Panel. It shows what serial devices Windows has defined on each COM port. Select the modem you wish to test, and then click the More Info button. If the modem responds properly, you will see test results similar to the output shown in Figure 4-8.

Adjusting Modem Properties

There are a number of properties that you may want to set to achieve the best performance from your modem. Likewise, depending on other options you may have on your telephone service, you may need to make some minor adjustments to prevent the modem from disconnecting when you don't want it to.

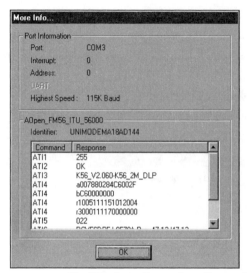

FIGURE 4-8 The Windows 9*x* modem diagnostics
dialog box

On the main Modem Properties window, highlight the modem in question,
and click the Properties button to display the screen shown in Figure 4-9.

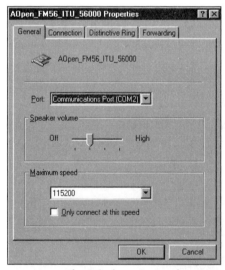

FIGURE 4-9 The Windows 9*x* Modem Properties
dialog box

From this screen, you can adjust the volume of the modem's built-in speaker
and the maximum speed a modem can establish a connection. The maximum

speed value should be set no lower than the actual maximum speed rating of the modem. If the speed is set to low, the modem will not function efficiently. The Only connect at this speed check box should *not* normally be checked. If you are only calling into one other modem, such as an office PC for remote control, you can select this option to instruct the modem to disconnect and retry the connection until the maximum speed is negotiated. The problem with checking this box for normal use is you are not assured that every modem you wish to dial into can handle the same speed as your modem. If you select a maximum speed of 115,200 bits per second (bps) with this option selected, and you attempt to call a service that only has 14.4 baud modems, the connection will never be established since the target modem can never connect at 115,200bps.

tip **When diagnosing connection problems, make sure you check the settings for the connection speed. It is better to set the speed *higher* than your modem supports since the connection will be established only as fast as the *slowest* of the two modems.**

The modem Connection tab screen shown in Figure 4-10 enables you to make other important modifications. Most current modem connections require 8 data bits, no parity (none), and 1 stop bit. These are signal timing and error detection settings for the serial transfers. Unless you have specific needs that require you to change these settings, use should use these defaults.

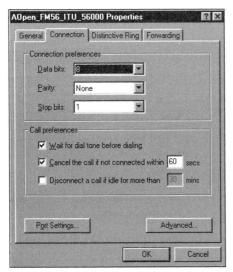

FIGURE 4-10   The Windows 9*x* modem Connection tab

The Call preferences section provides three useful options:

1. Wait for dial tone before dialing. This option should normally be selected if you're in North America, but may need to be unchecked if you are in other countries. Some telephone systems have unique dial tones that appear to be busy signals to some modems.

2. Cancel the call if not connected within so many seconds. This setting is up to the individual. The higher the value, the more rings the modem will wait for before giving up.

3. Disconnect a call if idle for more than so many seconds. Selecting this option may save you some money on your phone bills and minimize the frustration level of other people trying to call you! This option monitors the amount of traffic to and from the modem. For example, if you have this value set to 30 minutes and leave the modem connected for a two-hour long download (see DSL!), you do not loose the connection if you decide to go to bed instead of waiting for the download to complete.

Windows 98 has added a few more options to dial-up networking properties. If your telephone service provides special rings to identify different incoming calls, fax calls, personal calls, and so on, then you can define these ring types as shown in Figure 4-11. This option is used primarily when you permit incoming data calls to come in; for example, when you run the host portion of remote control software on a PC.

If your telephone has call waiting, another crucial setting is on the Forwarding tab screen, as shown in Figure 4-12. Call waiting, or call forwarding, is a feature the telephone companies offer to alert you that someone else is calling while you're on the telephone. Typically, you hear a faint clicking noise when the second call comes in. Unfortunately, this signal can confuse a modem, and it may assume that the telephone connection has been terminated. The PPP protocol then forces the modem to disconnect and try to reestablish the link again. On the Forwarding tab screen, you can insert the code that your local telephone company gives you to temporarily disable call waiting while you use the modem. This code differs between services and may require a second code to reestablish call waiting. You can usually find the code in your telephone book, or by calling your local telephone company. When a modem session begins, the call-waiting feature is disabled, and it is enabled when the modem breaks the link. Please note that in

Windows 95, call waiting can be disabled in the Dialing Properties screen rather than Modem Properties screen.

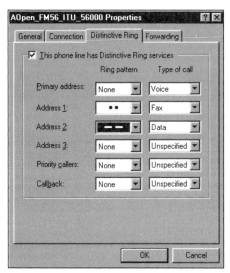

FIGURE 4-11 Setting Distinctive Ring Properties in Windows 9*x*

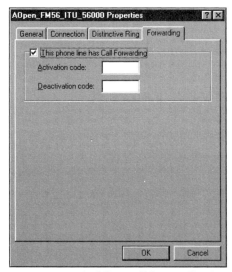

FIGURE 4-12 Disabling call forwarding in Windows 9*x*

EXAM PREPARATION SUMMARY

This chapter presented the fundamental concepts of remote connectivity. I discussed the various types of remote access, including remote node, remote control, and multi-user NT remote control, and listed the primary advantages and disadvantages for each method. Next I covered the various access methods, from POTS to ISDN, xDSL, and VPNs, and the pros and cons to each method. And last, I provided a step-by-step look at how to install, configure, and troubleshoot serial connections using analog modems with Windows 95/98.

It is important to review key concepts for this chapter in order to make sure you understand the material you just read. Key concepts include:

- The various types of remote access, including remote node, remote control, WinFrame, and Terminal Server
- Remote connections requirements
- ISDN, xDSL, and POTS attributes, advantages, and disadvantages
- The serial connection distinctions between PPP and SLIP
- The purpose and function of PPTP, and the conditions that make is useful
- Modem configurations, including serial ports, IRQ, I/O addresses, and maximum port speeds

APPLYING WHAT YOU'VE LEARNED

The following review questions give you an opportunity to test your knowledge of the information presented in this chapter. The answers to the assessment questions are in Appendix A. If you miss questions, review the sections in this chapter that cover those topics before going further.

1. Your customer has a number of salespeople that need access to the company inventory files. The data is accessed through a spreadsheet program that is loaded on each of their laptops. Which is the best remote access method to deploy?

   A. Remote control

   B. Remote node

   C. VPN

2. The key payroll person at a company will be on maternity leave for three months. During this time, she needs to process payroll from home. For security reasons, the payroll applications are only installed on her office PC. Which method of remote access is best?

   A. Remote control

   B. Remote node

   C. VPN

3. A company plans to upgrade a major piece of software that requires training 100 people. Rather than sending the instructor to six different cities over five months, the company would like to use technology to make training more efficient. What remote technology can you suggest to help train large numbers of dispersed employees?

   A. Remote control

   B. Remote node

   C. WinFrame or Terminal Server

4. A company opens a small branch office within the local dialing zone. The office needs three people to have access to the main computer to run the 32-bit Windows Version of Microsoft Office suite. It is not important that users are connected at all times, but they may need simultaneous access. The company's network hardware is centrally located with easy access to the company's PBX telephone system. Which remote solution would best suit these needs?

   A. Remote control

   B. Remote node

   C. WinFrame or Terminal Server

   D. VPN

5. When designing a remote access solution, the main requirement is easy access for remote users who may need access from many different locations. What connectivity method would be best to implement?

   A. ISDN

   B. POTS

   C. xDSL

   D. Carrier pigeon

6. How many channels are required for an ISDN line to operate?

   A. One B channel for BRI service

   B. 23 B channels for PRI service

   C. At least three; two B channels for data, and one D channel for signaling

   D. One digital pair for data, and One analog pair for voice

7. What is the major road-block to providing full digital service over POTS?

   A. The *last mile* of telephone cable is still copper

   B. The competition isn't strong enough to warrant full digital service

   C. Fiber optic lines do not reach rural areas

   D. It is too expensive for the telephone companies to implement

8. Name two advantages of xDSL technology:

   A. It runs on fiber optic cables and has increased bandwidth

   B. It is inexpensive and uses commonly available modems

   C. It provides high-speed digital access and is inexpensive

   D. It provides fast analog service and *always on* Internet access

9. What dial-up protocol is capable of passing multiple LAN protocols across the link?

   A. SLIP

   B. PPP

   C. TCP/IP

   D. POTS

10. Which dial-up protocol is considered self-configuring?

   A. SLIP

   B. PPP

   C. TCP/IP

   D. POTS

11. Which dial-up protocol requires that devices on each end know the other's address?

   A. SLIP

   B. PPP

   C. TCP/IP

   D. POTS

12. What protocol provides an encrypted connection between devices using Virtual Private Networking?

   A. PPTP

   B. PPP

   C. TCP/IP

   D. SLIP

13. What three configurations must be checked in order to avoid conflicts that could cause a modem to fail?

   A. Electrical flow, Analog signaling, and Plug and Play compatibility

   B. Serial COM ports, I/O addresses, and IRQ settings

   C. Serial COM ports, RAM, and Windows95 compatibility

   D. IRQ settings, COM ports greater than 4, and sufficient disk space

14. Where do you disable a COM port in order to install an internal modem on COM2?

   A. Windows95 Control Panel

   B. DOS prompt

   C. The system BIOS/CMOS

   D. Jumpers on the modem

15. What is the standard IRQ for COM1 and COM4?

   A. 1 and 2

   B. 4

   C. 3

   D. 4 and 3

16. What would happen if you installed an external modem on COM2 with an I/O address of 0F8-0FF?

   A. The modem would probably fail since this is a common I/O range for the math co-processor

   B. The modem might initialize but an Interrupt conflict with the Timer would cause it to fail when dialing

   C. The modem would work as long as the mouse was disabled

   D. The modem would work just fine at these settings

17. A customer calls to say that the new modem he or she just installed is not connecting to his or her Internet Service Provider. A dial-tone and the other modem answering can be heard, but the connection is dropped within a few seconds. What might be a logical reason for this?

A. The modems are incompatible

B. The modem is configured on the wrong COM port

C. The customer has call waiting and another call is disrupting the connection

D. The customer checked the *only connect at this speed* option and the ISP's modems are not as fast as the customer's

18. Where would you look to find what IRQs are already assigned on a Windows 95/98 PC?

A. The system BIOS/CMOS

B. Computer Properties in the Device Manager under Control Panel

C. Ports properties in the Device Manager under Control Panel

D. In each hardware device's documentation

19. Your customer calls to complain that their modem randomly disconnects from the Internet even though they have disabled all auto-disconnect features. The telephone company has tested the lines and is certain that there is no unusual noise. What option should you look at first when troubleshooting this problem?

A. Verify that the modem is plugged into a working wall jack

B. Enter the code to disable call waiting in the modem's property screen

C. If the modem is external, replace it with an Internal model

D. Test the line with an inexpensive tester to confirm that feed is analog and not digital

20. Remote node technology is a good solution when remote users need data from their personal PC in the office as long as they have applications loaded on their laptops?

A. True

B. False

Network Security

About Chapter 5

This chapter identifies good practices to ensure network security and provides a framework to follow in order to implement and maintain security policies. I look at basic NOS security features, standard password practices and procedures, data encryption use, and the basics of firewall technology to protect the Internet connected LAN from outside attacks.

The first part of this chapter discusses basic concepts and principles of network security. There is no perfect solution to keeping a network safe, but basic practices can go a long way. The second part of this chapter covers some of the user rights and policy settings that can be implemented in a Windows environment. I've focused in primarily on the Windows platform simply because it is probably the easiest platform for you to work with hands-on, but other operating systems such as NetWare and UNIX have similar security mechanisms.

THE IMPORTANCE OF NETWORK SECURITY

In a recent television advertisement, a woman and a man sit behind a maze of computer monitors. The woman points to one computer screen and exclaims, "This VP only makes half of what that VP makes . . . I wonder if he knows that?" In response, the man taps a key on the keyboard and announces, "He does now . . . I just e-mailed everyone in the company." Is this reality? It's arguable, but it does point out the fact that is it not only hackers on the Internet who jeopardize network security. In fact, most security breaches are caused by internal sources, yet many network administrators fail to realize this threat.

There is no magic wand for network security. Each network presents unique circumstances, and this eliminates the possibility of creating a generic security policy. However, network security **must** be a top priority before a system goes live. Unfortunately, in the real world, this is often not so. Security is frequently an after-thought, and many times, it is placed on the back burner. Security does not have to be an insurmountable task; in fact, it can be quite simple to implement when it is approached systematically and with a little forethought. The steps necessary to assure good security basically involve evaluating how vulnerable your system is, implementing the NOS features available to you, defining internal policies, and taking the time to review security measures on a regular basis.

UNDERSTANDING AND SELECTING THE SECURITY MODEL

A primary function of a network operating system (NOS) is to apply and enforce access restrictions to data and resources. Every NOS provides its own method of applying security, but most rely on the basic concept that each user has a unique *network* name and an associated password. Before access to any resource on the network is permitted, a user *logs in* by supplying his or her network name, and (hopefully) a password. If the user name exists, and the password matches the security record in the network database, the user is permitted access to the network.

There are a few fundamental principles that need to be followed. First, user's names must be unique, and second, a method of keeping passwords secret must be implemented. Note also that while the log in process provides access *to* the network, it does not necessarily provide rights to network resources. There are further security measures that may need to be implemented before a person can actually *do* anything on the network although the NOS has authenticated them.

User Naming Conventions

While there is no steadfast rule for creating user names, some forethought to naming conventions may save many headaches as the network grows. Names should normally be less than ten, but more than two, characters long. Many organizations use a combination of the users first and last names. For example, the naming system may be the users' first names and the first initial of the last names. With this convention, a person whose name is John Smith will have a network name of JohnS. This might be fine for a small company with only a few employees, but suppose John works in accounting, and there is an employee in sales named John Scholtz. The company ends up with two network names of JohnS!

To prevent this situation, some organizations simply use the first name, and as many characters of the last name as it takes to create a unique network name. Given the above situation, Mr. Smith would be JohnS, and Mr. Scholtz would become JohnSc. While this solves the problem, consider the VP who wants to send an e-mail message to John Smith. How is the VP going to know which John was created first, JohnS or JohnSc?

Another naming convention is to use employees' last names and the first initial of their first names. John Smith is then SmithJ, or if the order of the first initial of the first name and the last name is reversed, Jsmith. Again, both methods work, but it requires everyone in the office knows how to spell everyone else's last name. Smith is easy enough, but what about Wojciechowski? (It took me nearly two years to memorize how to spell my childhood friend's last name!)

A third convention is to use employment titles, such as CEO, HR, Sales, and so on. However, it's easy to see that this only works in very small organizations where employee are familiar with their coworker's titles, and still has the potential to create problems identifying the proper person. So what *is* the best method? There really isn't one. The important thing is to decide on one convention and stick with it. It won't take long for people to understand a specific convention, and they'll be capable of handling minor address issues, should they arise. Many network applications, such as e-mail systems, provide a user directory so that when you enter JohnS, a list of all users whose name begins with JohnS is displayed along with their full name. It is relatively easy then to select the correct recipient from the list.

Keeping Passwords Secure

While user names identify individuals, passwords assure the person logging in is who he or she claims to be. Obviously, this authentication is only as useful as our ability to keep passwords private. As with user names, it is important to set up a password, and it is important the password be neither too simple nor too complex. If passwords are easy to guess, they don't provide the intended security. Yet, if passwords are difficult for the authorized user to remember, the user will either write them down, or take other methods to record them, and this compromises the privacy of these passwords. For example, many years ago, I began a new job as a network administrator. I asked my new employer for the supervisor password (the account with full access to the LAN) but the previous administrator had failed to tell anyone what the password was. Nevertheless, it took me less than 30 seconds to properly log in to the network. I simply looked under the keyboard and sure enough, the password was there, taped to the bottom. This is the number one place people *hide* their password in case they forget it.

As with user names, there are no *rules* governing passwords, but there are some generally accepted standards. When you define a security policy, examine the benefits to the following guidelines and implement those guidelines capable with your installation.

- **Mix alpha and numeric characters**. It is much more difficult to guess a person's password if it contains both letters and numbers. A hacker often tries to guess passwords by using the names of children, pets, or other close relatives of valid network users. Similarly, birthdates, anniversaries, and telephone numbers are common guesses. By mixing numbers and letters, passwords become many times more secure. For example, the password Jimmy is much easier to guess than Jim99my.

- **Mix upper and lower case letters**. For the same reason you mix numbers and letters, mixing character case can increase security. For example, you might use JiMmy or jImmY. Before relying on this method alone, however, be sure your NOS is case sensitive so it makes a distinction between J and j.

- **Use a minimum length**. As a rule, passwords should be no less than four characters long. There are a number of *brute force* password cracking programs easily accessible from the Internet. These programs systematically try combinations of letters in order to find the right combination for the password. The more characters a password has, the longer it takes a password cracking program to find a valid combination. Passwords with three or less characters can normally be decoded in a relatively short amount of time.

- **Use a maximum length**. Passwords longer than eight characters offer minimal additional security, but they often make a password difficult to remember. When users can't remember their passwords, they begin to write them down where others may find them.

o **Force periodic changes**. Although users may feel it is inconvenient, passwords should be changed, at least, quarterly (every three months). This practice not only enforces the idea that passwords are important, but it may thwart a hacker who has already gained access. Suppose someone does learn a user's password and this knowledge goes undetected. At the very least, this hole will be plugged sometime in the near future!

o **Disallow the repetitive use of the same password**. If you require users to change their passwords every three months, but users simply switch back and forth between two passwords, security may be compromised. Most operating systems have the capability to enforce the frequency of password changes, and how often passwords can be reused. If you set a policy that requires password changes four times a year, then repetition should be permitted no more than every third change.

o **Limit the need for more than one password (when possible)**. If people need to remember multiple passwords, the likelihood that they will write them down, increases. For example, if you have both NetWare and NT on your LAN, set up identical user names and passwords for both systems. This way, whichever NOS is responsible to authenticate the user passes the user name and password on to the other operating system. If the user name and password are the same on both servers, the person only needs to login once for both systems.

o **Force accounts to automatically expire**. If the operating system provides for it, make sure user accounts expire within a few days of the required password change if users have not made password updates. For example, suppose an employee leaves the company and his or her computer account isn't purged. This person can potentially enter the system later, and even if they need to change their password (due to the force password change option), they are still able to access their old account. If the account automatically expires after the grace period of the last forced change date, only an administrator is able to access this account.

o **Always require passwords**! You might be surprised at how many people simply overlook this guideline!

One final item to consider when you deal with basic network security: Always create a *super-user* with administrator rights. In the event an administrator account is compromised, either by accident or by attack, the secondary, super-user account with complete network rights can save many hours of reconstruction or reinstallation of the NOS.

Security for Peer Resource Sharing

If you recall from Chapter 1, a peer-to-peer network is based on sharing resources locally rather than centrally. Even in a client/server network, it is often convenient to share files, printers, CD-ROM drives, and so forth on local workstations instead of dedicated file servers. This capability is the most requested feature of the Windows operating system, and it was added in Windows for Workgroups (*v*3.11) and refined in Windows 95/98. In order to protect shared resources at this local level, peer-to-peer security exists at two levels: *user-level* and *share-level*.

User-level security

User-level security uses a *security provider*, such as an NT or NetWare server. The local resources are registered with the primary NOS and access to these resources is granted or denied through normal NOS security mechanisms. This process is called *pass-through* security.

Share-level security

With share-level security, an owner of specific resources grants others access rights to the resources. The owner assigns various levels of access, such as *read-only* access (others can view but not modify files), *read-write* access (others can read and modify the data, but cannot create or delete files), or *full access* (others have complete rights to all file functions). In addition to permitting various levels of access, the owner can define which users have access, and decide whether or not those users need to provide a password before access is granted. NetWare does not provide this level of security between workstations. However, Windows-based clients on a NetWare network configured for peer-to-peer file and print sharing may implement the shared-level security model.

Configuring share-level access in Windows 95/98

Because Windows 95/98 is currently the most common operating system for peer sharing, I've included the steps necessary to share a directory or printer using share-level security. (Before you can share resources, however, you need to install the peer-level sharing components on the Network Properties page.)

---------------------------------- ▼ ▼ ▼ ----------------------------------

TO INSTALL WINDOWS 9.x FILE AND PRINT SHARING, FOLLOW THESE STEPS:

1. Click the Start button.

2. Click Settings.

3. Click Control Panel.

4. Click Network.

5. In the Network properties windows, click the File and Print Sharing button. The dialog box in Figure 5-1 will be displayed, enabling you to check which file and/or print resources you wish to share.

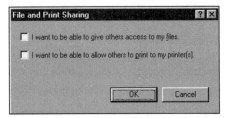

FIGURE 5-1   File and Print Sharing is configured in the Windows 9.x Network property page

---------------------------------- ■ ■ ■ ----------------------------------

 In order to share an entire drive, such as a CD-ROM drive, you need to enable *file sharing*.

Sharing disk resources in Windows 95/98

Once the File and Print Sharing option has been installed, you can share selected folders by using Windows Explorer or My Computer.

---------------------------------- ▼ ▼ ▼ ----------------------------------

**TO SHARE DISK RESOURCES IN WINDOWS EXPLORER
OR MY COMPUTER, FOLLOW THESE STEPS:**

1. Start Explorer by selecting it from the Program Menu, or double click My Computer on the Windows desktop.

2. Locate the directory to share and right-click on that folder's icon.

3. In the drop-down menu, click Sharing. The screen will look similar to that in Figure 5-2.

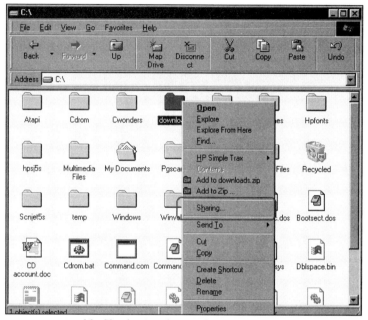

FIGURE 5-2 Enable file sharing for a selected folder using Explorer

■ ■ ■

Figure 5-3 shows the properties dialog box that is presented when folder sharing is selected. This is where all security is defined and maintained. The title bar of the dialog box indicates which folder is being used (downloads in the example).

▼ ▼ ▼

TO SET THE SHARE-LEVEL SECURITY PROPERTIES, FOLLOW THESE STEPS:

1. Click Shared As, and type the resource's Share Name. This is the name other users see on their computers when they look for available resources on the network. Filling in the Comment field is optional, but the field is displayed, along with the Share Name, when users browse the network.

2. Under Access Type specify whether you want users to have Read-Only, Full, or Depends on Password access.

3. If you wish to protect this resource further, you can optionally enter a Read-Only Password under Passwords for read-only access, full access, or both.

■ ■ ■

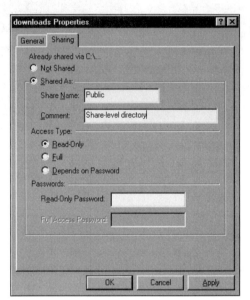

FIGURE 5-3 Setting the share-level security properties for a folder

  tip Directories can be shared, but hidden from the Network Neighborhood browsing list by adding a dollar-sign character ($) to the end of the share name, such as MyPrivateStuff$. In order for users to access this directory, they need to know the exact path name in *Universal Naming Convention* (UNC) format. For example, if this directory were located at the root of a PC named JohnS, the UNC path would be \\JohnS\MyPrivateStuff$. UNC paths begin with two backslashes, followed by the computer name and the directory path.

Configuring user-level access in Windows NT

User-level security requires a security provider such as an NT or NetWare server. All requests for access are filtered through the NOS's security database before access is granted or denied. As with Windows 95 and Windows 98, disks, directories (folders), files, and printers are all sharable in Windows NT; however, NT uses user-level security with NTFS (NT File System) only. A FAT-based NT Server can use share-level control but share-level is much more limited than user-level security. Whereas share-level only goes down to the directories, user-level sharing goes down to the files in the directory; it is much more granular, and offers more control.

Sharing disk resources in Windows NT

Once the File and Print Sharing option has been installed, you can share selected folders by using Windows Explorer or My Computer.

TO SET THE SHARE-LEVEL SECURITY PROPERTIES, FOLLOW THESE STEPS:

1. In Windows Explorer or My Computer, right-click the icons for the directory or printer you want to share and, in the context menu click Sharing. (The screen looks very much like Windows 95/98 as seen in Figure 5-2.)

2. Click Shared As, and then type the resource's Share Name. This is the name other users will see on their computers when looking for available resources on the network. Filling in the Comment field is optional, but the field is displayed, along with the Share Name, when users browse the network. (Again, this is the same with Windows 95/98.)

3. With user-level sharing, all licensed users can be granted access to shared resources (see Figure 5-4), or the number of concurrent users can be limited. In the User Limit section of the properties box, click either Maximum Allowed, or Allow, and enter the number of concurrent users you wish to have access.

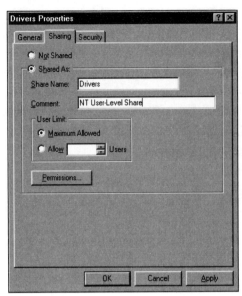

FIGURE 5-4   Setting the user-level security
properties for a folder under NT

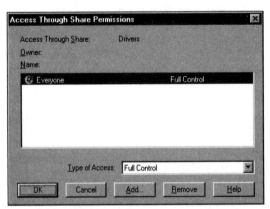

FIGURE 5-5   Setting user-level security by users
and groups in NT

4. The next step is to define the users, or groups of users to provide access to. Click the Permissions button to display the Access Through Share Permissions screen. (Shown in Figure 5-5.)

5. By default, Windows NT grants the group *Everyone* full control to a new shared resource. Full control enables any person to read, write, modify, and *delete* the files and sub-directories. Most of the time, this is not what you want. File deletions should be under the control of the owner of the files, or the Administrator. To change the Type of Access for any particular individual or group, highlight that individual user or group, and simply click the drop-down list to select one of the following:

- **No Access** (Excludes the individual or group from having access to files)
- **Read** (Enables the individual or group to review files only)
- **Change** (Enables the individual or group to read and write files, but not to delete files)
- **Full Control** (Grants the individual or group full control to files)

6. You can also click the Remove button to disallow a group or user from accessing the shared resources altogether.

7. To add other users or groups to the access list, click the Add button to display the Add Users and Groups screen. (Shown in Figure 5-6.)

8. In the Add Users and Groups screen, you begin to see the additional power of user-level security. Every valid user and group of users is displayed permitting you to select exactly who has access to this resource. Simply click on a user or group name from the list, and click Add. Not only can you add multiple users, but also you can choose on an *individual basis* what type of access they will have (read-only, change, or full). In other words, you can grant the group *Everyone* read access to this directory, and *add* other specific users to the list with Change or Full control access as well.

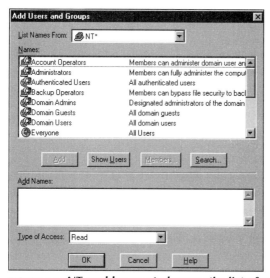

FIGURE 5-6 NT enables you to browse the list of users and groups for easy assignment of rights

In Windows NT, permissions are enforced for a resource as follows:

o If the user has explicit rights to the resource, those rights (such as granting change access to an individual user) are enforced.

o If the user does not have explicit rights to the resource, then the permissions are determined by the rights of each group to which the user belongs. For example, if a user's account does not have explicit rights to a particular folder, but that person belongs to a group that does have rights to that folder, the user is able to access the folder with the rights granted to the group.

o If none of the groups to which the user belongs has any rights to that resource, then the user is not granted access to the resource.

exam
preparation
pointer

User-level access is only available on NT servers that use the NT File System (NTFS). The File Allocation Table (FAT) format does not provide the advanced security features that NTFS does.

Internet Security Concepts

Because the Internet is becoming a mainstay of corporate networks, you need to take special care to secure the local network from intruders on the outside. The implementation of Internet security is normally done with a *firewall*. A firewall is any combination of software and hardware that prevents potentially dangerous packets from entering the local network. Many different techniques, which I discuss shortly, are employed to achieve the same security goal.

Most routers are capable of filtering packets and dropping certain packets based on where they originated. If a router does not pass packets onto the local network, no harm can come from them. The trick is to determine which packets are acceptable, and which are not. Many Internet attacks occur because of *spoofing*. Simply put, spoofing is a method of tricking a firewall into treating a dangerous packet as friendly. For example, a hacker may use a piece of software that overlays his or her sending IP address in order to gain illegal entry into a secure system.

Some of the basic techniques used to provide firewall protection include:

o **Packet filter:** Blocks traffic based on IP address and/or port numbers. Also known as a *screening router*. As I just discussed, screening packets is the basic function of the firewall.

o **Proxy server:** Among the advantages of a proxy server covered in Chapter 2, an Internet proxy server can be a relay between two networks, breaking the connection between the two. It creates a buffer between the internal and external networks, and if an attack occurs, it is possible to limit any damage to just the proxy server. When a proxy server is used on an IPX-based network, internal security is virtually guaranteed because all Internet traffic is only based on TCP/IP.

o **Network address translation (NAT):** This feature hides the IP addresses of client stations in an internal network by presenting only one IP address to the outside world. A firewall using NAT performs translations of internal IP addresses back and forth.

o **Stateful inspection:** At the high end (which also means more overhead), stateful inspection tracks transactions to verify that the destination of an inbound packet matches the source of a previous outbound request. Generally these firewalls can examine multiple layers of the protocol stack, including the data, if required, so blocking can be made at any layer or depth.

Data Encryption Usage

While firewalls are primarily used for Internet security, they can be very helpful for internal security as well. For example, a firewall might be used to provide high-level security for an accounting department, or for legal records maintained by a librarian in a law office.

Another security tool that provides a very high level of privacy is *data encryption*. Encryption is a method of applying a mathematical formula that scrambles readable data so any intruder is not able to make sense of it. Once the intended recipient possesses the information, the recipient applies a *decryption* algorithm to transform the data back into readable format.

The encryption algorithm uses a key, which is a binary number that is typically from 40 to 128 bits in length. The data is scrambled by mathematically combining the bits in the key with the data bits. The same key is used to unscramble the data, restoring it to its original binary form.

Many e-mail packages now provide encryption built into the software. You can also find a number of third-party encryption programs to protect any form of sensitive data. One of the best encryption programs available to the public is *Pretty Good Privacy,* which offers 128-bit keys, making it nearly impossible to crack. (It may be possible to decrypt a 128-bit code, but it would probably take many years and extremely powerful super-computer resources.) Appendix B lists a number of other good encryption programs and the Web site address where you can download them.

There are two basic methods of encryption: secret-key and public-key. With secret-key technology both the sender and the receiver use the same key. This is the fastest method, but the sender has to get the key to the receiver via some other secured means before decryption can occur. Depending on the method the sender uses to get the key to the receiver, overall security can be compromised.

Public-key technology uses a combination of a private key and a public key. Each recipient has a public key that is either published for others to use, or can be safely exchanged with someone over non-secured channels. The owner has a private key that is never shared with anyone. The public and private keys are mathematically related in a way that what is encoded with one is decodable with the other. Thus, the sender uses the known public key to encrypt the message and the recipient uses the private key to decrypt it.

When data privacy is a must, be it an e-mail message or documents stored on a local or network drive, data encryption is probably the only way to assure complete privacy.

EXAM PREPARATION SUMMARY

This chapter presented the fundamental concepts of network security. I first discussed the importance of defining a naming convention for users, and presented a number of suggestions for maintaining passwords. Next, I described the uses for and differences of share-level and user-level security models and how each is implemented within the Windows environment. I finished the chapter with a discussion of securing a network by using firewalls and data encryption.

I recommend you review the key concepts below to make sure you understand the material you just read.

It is crucial you implement good practices to ensure network security, including:

- Selecting a security model (user and share level)
- Maintaining standard password practices and procedures
- Employing data encryption to protect network data
- Using a firewall for Internet security

APPLYING WHAT YOU'VE LEARNED

The following review questions give you an opportunity to test your knowledge of the information presented in this chapter. The answers to the assessment questions are in Appendix A. If you miss questions, review the sections in this chapter that cover those topics before going further.

1. How many users can share the same user name on a network?

   A. It depends on the number of licensed connections

   B. As many as you need, provided only one person is logged in at a time

   C. Only one; each person must have a unique network name

   D. Two, provided each user has a unique password

2. What three practices will create a good password policy?

   A. Mix letters and numbers, use more than nine characters, and force changes yearly

   B. Mix letter and numbers, use no less than four characters, and no more than nine characters

   C. Use all uppercase letters, force changes quarterly, and write the passwords down

   D. Keep a written list of passwords, use easy to remember names, and do not enforce password use

3. If you require passwords be changed four times a year, how many unique changes are recommended before you allow a previously used password to be used again?

    A. Three

    B. Two

    C. One

    D. It doesn't matter

4. As a safeguard, an administrator should always:

    A. Create a *super-user* with administrator rights

    B. Keep a written list of all user passwords

    C. Remove the administrator account before the network goes *live*

    D. Make sure all password files are backed up on a regular basis

5. What security model provides the best control over shared resources?

    A. User-level security

    B. Share-level security

    C. User names and passwords

    D. Windows NT

6. User-level security requires:

    A. Administrator control for the directories to be shared

    B. Share-level security to be implemented first

    C. A dollar sign to be appended to each shared directory name

    D. A security provider service

7. In order to share folders in Windows 95, you must:

    A. Format the drive with NTFS

    B. Add File and Print Sharing services in the network configuration

    C. NL2Convert any FAT16 partitions to FAT32

8. Access types for share-level security consist of:

    A. Read-only, Full, and Depends on Password

    B. Read-only, Read/Write, and Create

    C. Read-only, Erase, and Browse

    D. Read-only and Read/Write

9. The number of users that can access a shared resource using user-level security on an NT server is:

    A. One

    B. Unlimited

    C. Limited to the number of licensed users

    D. Depends on available free disk space

10. Access types for printers using user-level security consist of:

    A. Read-only, Full, and Depends on Password

    B. Access or No Access

    C. Single copy or multiple copies

    D. Paper tray selection, full access, color

11. A _____ installed on an IPX-based network provides additional network security.

    A. Firewall

    B. Application server

    C. Web and e-mail server

    D. Proxy server

12. More advanced firewall products implement this protection technique:

    A. Network address translation (NAT)

    B. Stateful inspection

    C. Spoofing protocols

    D. Packet filtering

13. The most secure method of transmitting sensitive data is by using:

    A. Anti-virus software to assure data has not been infected

    B. Secret key encryption

    C. Public key encryption *(remember that the private key is never transferred!)*

    D. Through a corporate firewall

14. Public key encryption consists of:

    A. Two keys; one of which is published for anyone's use

    B. Two keys; neither of which should be published

    C. One key, which is shared between sender and receiver

    D. One key, which is transmitted via a separate method from the shared data.

15. First names are the best method of creating network account names.

A. True. It's easy for people to remember.

B. False. It may create too many duplicates.

Knowledge of Networking Practices

The chapters in Part I constitute 67 percent of the Network+ exam. Part II of this study guide, the remaining 33 percent, focuses on the *soft skills*, testing your ability to actually *use* the knowledge learned. It is a real-world, practical, hands-on section that prepares you for the scenario type of questions on the exam. These soft skills are just as important, if not more so, than the technical knowledge covered thus far. A network engineer needs to know how and when to apply technology as much as understand the technology itself.

In the following pages, I look closely at identifying potential problems when analyzing the site of a new installation, developing good documentation habits, fundamental troubleshooting practices, and scheduled network maintenance. Chapters 6–8 take you from preinstallation reviews to actually installing and configuring network devices, identifying and resolving network problems, and keeping the network safe.

In the real world, your customers, or your fellow employees, will look to you to solve computing problems and ensure that the network stays up and running. This is no easy task, and there will be many times when solutions are extremely difficult to find. Don't let this discourage you. As you'll see, by applying systematic approaches to problem solving, along with good preinstallation techniques and good documentation habits, most situations become easier to conquer. In my 20+ years in this business, I have learned (sometimes the hard way) that the best network projects consisted of doing 80 percent of the work up front and documenting everything!

Network Installation and Troubleshooting Practices

About Chapter 6

Part I constitutes 67 percent of the Network+ exam. The remainder of this study guide, the final 33 percent, focuses on *soft skills*, testing your ability to actually *use* the knowledge learned—the practical, hands-on stuff that prepares you for the scenario type of questions on the exam.

Chapter 6 begins with a brief description of the work a network engineer typically does. From there I take a look at the necessary steps involved with preparing a site for the installation of a network, and some problems that may occur during the installation process. Once the system is in place, I discuss the steps required to connect the client workstations to the server(s). The chapter concludes with a look at the tools available to help you create user accounts and prepare your security policies.

A CAREER AS A NETWORK ENGINEER

So what does a network engineer actually do? Depending on the type of organization you work for, you may find yourself administering the overall operations, performing new installations, upgrading existing systems, or actually designing large networks. Of course, many of these responsibilities require experience as well as textbook knowledge, but once you've passed the Network+ exam, you're well on your way!

In reality, network engineering takes two distinct paths. You may work for a single company and deal with the company network only, or you may work for a network integrator that supports a number of different businesses. The advantage to working *in-house* is that you have the ability to really learn the ins and outs of one system. The longer you work with a particular system, the easier it is to identify changes and act proactively. The disadvantage of working in-house is the slower pace at which new technology is introduced. Few companies can afford the expense of doing major upgrades to their systems just to keep up with technology. It's easy to stagnate if you don't make a concerted effort to keep up with changes. For example, a large school district recently upgraded from NetWare 3.12 to 4.11 at a great hardware expense, but failed to provide training for the network administrator. The administrator was very comfortable with the old system, and didn't feel that the new version would be that different. The school district had to increase their expense budget for the new system in order to compensate for the network integrator assistance required while the school's own administrator became knowledgeable with the new software.

The advantage to working with an integrator is the variety of products and businesses you're exposed to. It's easier to stay up-to-date because you are constantly working with the latest technologies. The downside, however, is the very fast pace, and the seeming endless problems. Because you rarely spend more than a few weeks on any one project, you don't have the time to learn the nuances of every system. You must judge the perceivable performance of the network based solely on what would be *normal* given the number of users and types of applications being used. This type of career requires a great deal of listening to the end users, relying on your experience, and possibly using expensive test and monitoring equipment to identify problems. Fortunately, these costly devices are easier to justify when they can be used on larger numbers of systems.

Beginning with this chapter, you will be rolling up your sleeves and applying the basic knowledge that you've learned. I cover fewer details, and introduce more practical applications. I go over the necessary steps for preparing a site for an installation, for performing the installation, for using troubleshooting techniques, and for practicing good documentation practices. When all is said and done, the documentation is often just as important as the installation itself. I can't stress enough how important it is to get in the habit of recording everything right from the start. This part of the business is not always emphasized, so I highlight the concept often.

One last point to raise is, although you won't find it on the Network+ exam, a large part of this business calls for *people skills*. I have met many people over the years who were far more technically adept than I, but were woefully unable to communicate in a business environment. If you're uncomfortable dealing with all types of people, or if you lack professional communication skills, both verbal and written, invest some time in developing these abilities further. Poor people skills will probably be more damaging to your career than poor computer skills. There are many good seminars, books, and videotapes to help you communicate clearly and professionally. Many local colleges have adult education classes to assist you in improving your verbal and writing skills. You may want to check if there is a local Toastmasters chapter in your area (www.Toastmaster.org). This is an international, non-profit organization that prepares its members to conduct meetings, give impromptu speeches, present prepared speeches, and generally deal clearly and effectively with people. A membership is inexpensive, and the teachings will compensate you many times during your career.

exam
preparation
pointer

The Network+ exam presents a number of scenarios and tests you on your ability to demonstrate an *awareness* that certain aspects to networking may only be applied. For example, a typical question may present a troubleshooting scenario where all of the proper steps have been accomplished. The question attempts to find out if you are aware that an administrative password was required in order for the process to have been performed. These *soft skills* are difficult to identify in a textbook, so pay special attention to the exam pointers that mention: *demonstrate awareness.*

UNDERSTANDING BASIC TROUBLESHOOTING PRACTICES

As with any other profession, you are often responsible for identifying and, hopefully, resolving problems. Network troubleshooting is not always a simple matter. It's not uncommon to find that a fix for one problem creates other problems. Oftentimes, the symptoms do not clearly identify what is really happening. Software vendors are not well known for providing useful error messages either. My all time favorite is the message: Keyboard failure. Press <F1> to continue. I often wonder what was going through the mind of that programmer!

caution

A word of caution about liability for data loss: Ideally the system you work on has been backed up recently. If you represent a network integrator, you may want your customer to sign a document stating that they are responsible for reliable backups to restore their data should it become necessary. Your liability should be limited to hardware issues only. One network integrator I worked for paid $10,000 to satisfy a customer whose data was lost. The integrator relied solely on verbal statements regarding liability. Even if you're an in-house administrator, you don't want to lose your job, or face possible civil actions for neglecting to take basic steps to safeguard the company's data. Backing-up concepts will be discussed later in this chapter.

The Troubleshooting Process

The troubleshooting processes can easily be divided into seven steps:

1. **Identify and document the problem.** It may seem self-evident, but often people spend more time trying to fix symptoms than correcting the actual cause of the problem. Identifying and documenting the problem is also the starting point for a *problem resolution document*. Many times you come up against problems that have occurred before, either with you or someone else. If you keep good records, you save countless hours of reinventing the wheel the next time. It is also important to remember that you may not be around the next time a problem arises. Knowing what you did, and the outcome of your findings, may be invaluable to the next person working on the system.

2. **Isolate variables causing the problem.** Suppose you have an Internet connection problem. If possible, try dialing in to a different service provider. Perhaps changing the modem to a different brand will yield different results. Does the problem continue if a different phone line is used? Some software problems can be isolated by removing other programs or drivers. If you have a possible hardware problem, you may want to remove any electrical devices near the PC. If you are troubleshooting a software error, find out if it only occurs on this one PC, or if the software error is department wide. The main goal is to eliminate as many outside influences as possible.

3. **Duplicate the problem.** If a user complains that a specific program causes a General Protection Fault, have the user run the program again and see if the problem reoccurs. If the program *always* fails at the same point, it is easier to diagnose. If the error is still intermittent, then other factors need to be examined. Perhaps a Windows .DLL (a common file to many Windows programs) is causing the problem. Perhaps the problem only occurs with a particular customer in an accounting program, or a specific row on a spreadsheet. The more you can duplicate the problem, the more likely it is a pattern will form.

4. **Develop a plan to correct the problem.** Once you identify the problem, outline in as much detail as is practical what steps you plan to take to correct the situation. If your plan requires exclusive use of the PC for any length of time, make sure the people who rely on that machine know in advance how long you estimate the repairs will take. If you'll be requiring outside assis-

tance, make sure you document who assists you, and what role he or she plays. If you have contacted a vendor's software support line and are instructed to download and apply a patch, make sure you write down whom you talked to, where the patch came from, its name, and what, if any, installation instructions accompanied the software.

in the real world

Your people skills are important here, especially if you are an integrator. As good as your intentions are, remember that you are an *intruder* in your customer's personal space. Something as simple as using the telephone on someone's desk without first asking can generate a complaint to your boss!

5. **Implement the corrective action**. Follow your implementation plan and document any deviations. If further assistance is required, note it in your problem resolution document.

6. **Test the results**. This is *extremely* important. Far too often, people fix a problem only to the point that the initial symptom is gone. It is very possible for new problems to occur while fixing another. In addition, depending on the type of problem, it may take a while to fully test the changes. For example, if your problem was with a payroll application, you may not be able to fully test the results until the next payroll period. This is a great example of why it's important to document what you do.

7. **Document the findings**. Now that the problem is resolved, complete the documentation. If you've followed the suggested outline, most of your work will already be done. Make sure you fill in any items undone from previous steps. If your fix required additional software, and it's practical, include a diskette with the software implemented. If outside help was required, make sure you note any important telephone numbers, e-mail addresses, or Web sites. You should develop some form of filing system so that this document, and other problem resolution documents, can easily be retrieved in the future. There are a number of electronic systems available, but a plain-old file cabinet works wonders too!

This entire process is really twofold. First you need to get at the root of the problem, and second you need to fully document the process from problem to resolution.

IMPLEMENTING THE NETWORK INSTALLATION

Long before the actual components of the data network are assembled and powered on, there are many factors that you need to review. In this first section, I discuss the checklist of items that should be accomplished prior to the physical installation of the hardware. Remember that it is easier to document everything from the beginning than to start the documentation process at the end!

The Preinstallation Site Inspection

Before you install network hardware, you should perform a physical site inspection. Specifically, you need to review the location where the file server(s), network components, (hubs, switches, and so forth), and workstations will be placed. There are a number of factors that can cause problems during and after the installation that can often be avoided by a proper preinspection. Some of the most important factors to look for are outlined below:

- **Room conditions**. Heat and humidity are probably the two greatest threats to computer equipment, especially servers. If room conditions are uncomfortably warm, odds are the computers will eventually develop problems. It is especially important to keep the season in mind. If the installation takes place during a time when air-conditioning is not required, you may not be thinking about the room temperature during the warmer times of the year. Rooms that house file servers should have adequate cooling and ventilation systems. Ideally, there is a separate air-conditioner powered by a dedicated electrical outlet. It is not uncommon for central air-conditioning to fail during peak heat spells, and while people can usually continue to function, computer equipment often cannot.

  - Humidity may even be more devastating than heat. As water content in the room increases, moisture can form on a computer's sensitive electrical components. This can (and often does) create electrical shorts that can permanently damage the equipment. Likewise, low humidity increases static electricity that is equally capable of causing critical hardware damage. In colder regions a typical humidity reading may be 17 percent. If you are in this type of climate, many manufacturers will simply tell you to install a humidifier before you call them back for further consultation. In addition to electrical discharge, static electricity greatly increases dust and dirt collection; this negatively impacts the performance and life expectancies of computer power supplies.

- While it may not be practical for small businesses to invest in large environmental testing equipment, smaller, hand-held units can be purchased or rented for a few hundred dollars. These devices should be used in the areas in question for a number of days in order to gather enough data to properly determine the average temperature and humidity levels. If heat, cold, or humidity is a problem, consider installing air-conditioning units, room heaters, humidifiers, or de-humidifiers as the needs dictate. Again, keep the seasons in mind. It may be necessary to retest room conditions quarterly for the first year.

- **Personal effects**. Workstations are usually set up where people spend the bulk of their day. For this reason, environmental conditions are not usually as much a concern as are the conditions for file servers, hubs, switches, and so on. However, many people have personal items that can cause problems with the PC. If you live in a cold-winter area, you probably know all about portable heating units. These little devices are often found scattered under every desk in the office. They do an excellent job of keeping one's feet and legs warm, but they are also responsible for creating intermittent power draws and surges. The heater thermostats turn the unit on and off to maintain a relative heat level. When the temperature drops and the heater kicks in, a momentary drop in the electrical source often occurs. If the heater is plugged into the same outlet with the workstation, the PC may experience power problems. Uneven power can corrupt data stored on hard drives or packets being transmitted on the network cable. Even if data corruption doesn't occur, the life expectancy of the PC's power supply can be greatly reduced. Other portable electronic devices can
be responsible for the same conditions. Radios, television sets, paper shredders, desktop calculators, postage machines, and other small devices should all be reviewed prior to the installation. These can cause phantom problems you can't easily get a handle on.

- Many offices undergo numerous floor plan changes. Desks can end up far away from the electrical outlets that were originally accessible. It is quite common to find that power strips and other extension cords are being used in order to accommodate all of the necessary electrical devices. While these strips and cords may be useful, they can contribute to electrical problems that sensitive computer equipment will be susceptible to. It is best to keep the PC components on separate outlets, thus isolating them from power fluctuations caused by other electrical items. If necessary, small *un-interruptable power supplies*, or UPSs, should be used. These small battery powered units regulate a constant level of power to devices plugged into them. If a power outage — even a momentary brownout occurs — the battery maintains a regulated current.

○ While it is necessary to visually inspect a work area, it is also important to discuss work area matters with the people using them. You need to find out if people often get shocks when touching items around desks, or if people notice the lights in the area dim frequently. Small A/C power monitors can be used whenever there is a question of electrical conditions. These devices monitor the flow of electricity from a wall outlet over a period of a few days. Clean power grounds are particularly important for digital equipment. A neutral to ground voltage of more than two volts is not desirable. The monitor records any line voltage changes, either high or low, and provides the data necessary to determine if dedicated outlets, surge protectors, or UPSs are warranted. You will often find that the printouts from a power monitor are invaluable; they'll help convince your customer or your boss to spend the extra money to fix identified power problems.

○ **Cabling issues**. Along with adequate electrical access, you should review the areas with access to telephone lines and data jacks. If a certain location will use a local modem, it is necessary to have an analog telephone jack within reach. Many businesses have an in-house telephone switching system known as a *Private Branch eXchange*, or PBX. The PBX interconnects telephone extensions to one another, as well as to the outside telephone network. Many PBXs use all-digital methods for switching and can damage analog modems. You cannot visually differentiate an analog jack from a digital one, so you must inquire about the telephone system, and test the jack if you're unsure. You can find a simple telephone line tester for a few dollars at any electronics store.

○ Likewise, many data cables use RJ-45 connectors, so it is not safe to assume that a wall data-jack is Ethernet or Token Ring simply by its appearance. When in doubt, these factors need to be verified either by someone who knows, or by using test equipment. (Another fine example of the importance of having good documentation.)

- Much like electrical outlets that are no longer near the desk, data jacks may be located some distance from the PC. If long patch cables are used, keep in mind that the patch cable contributes to the overall cable length.

   If the person who installed the cable measured the distance from the wiring closet to the wall jack and determined that the length was just within tolerance, the patch cable may cause the overall length to exceed the maximum limit. It is possible that additional cable has been coiled up behind the wall jack to allow for extension later on. If the distance from the workstation to the closet is questionable, it should be tested. Again, there are a number of testing devices, from Hubbell's simple UTP testers for about $60 (`www.hubbell.com`) to Microtest's Pentascanner for about $3,500 (`www.microtest.com`), and the many units in between.

- **Other computer equipment**. It's incredibly rare to find *brand-new* installs these days. Most projects are upgrades to existing systems; therefore, a preview of existing computer equipment is necessary. You need to know if the new hardware is compatible with the old hardware, if existing software will work on the new hardware, and if the networking components are compatible. Generally, end users expect existing programs to be migrated to the new computer with the expectation all existing programs will operate exactly as they did before the upgrade. The *only* way to assure this is to inventory all of the applications that user has, and verify with the vendor that the software will operate correctly on the new PC. Some software can simply be copied from one system to the next, but other applications may require a full reinstallation. In either case, you should make sure that the original media (diskettes, or CDs) are available, as well as any incremental upgrades that may have been added.

   - In addition to reviewing physical items, a personal review with an end user often uncovers existing problems and it may prevent many future headaches. If someone has been experiencing problems on the existing system, they are likely to think the problem will be resolved with the new computer. This may not be the case, and can lead to unsatisfied customers. All existing problems should be documented, and addressed *before* new installation begins. This not only clarifies an end user's expectations, but also provides the engineer with valuable information to assist in troubleshooting problems during and after the new system goes on-line.

- In your initial documentation package, include a list of all software applications that currently exist and will remain in use. Document the software name; version number; serial number, if appropriate; vendor support numbers; and Web page addresses. Identify the people who use the applications and briefly include a description of what the software is used for.

- Once you inspected all of the items discussed, and anything else pertinent to your specific installation, *document it*. The most important lesson I've learned in my more than twenty years of experience is to put *everything* in writing. No matter how good you think your memory is, or how insignificant an issue might seem, it is always best to have your notes on paper.

Identifying Network Devices

During your inspection, you need to pay special attention to which devices will be installed and whether you have the proper connections for these devices. You need to be able to identify visually, or by description, the following items (some of which I've covered in previous chapters):

Print servers

Network printing can be accomplished by sharing printers that are physically attached to workstations. However, the preferred method is to use a dedicated network-printing device. The most commonly used are the JetDirect products manufactured by Hewlett-Packard (see Figure 6-1), and Intel's NetPort line. Print servers have an Ethernet or Token Ring connector and one or more printer connections. The printer connections are either 25-pin parallel, 9-pin or 25-pin serial, depending on which options you need. The more printers a single device can serve, the more expensive the device. Typically, a single printer box costs between $150 and $200.

FIGURE 6-1 Hewlett-Packard JetDirect print server devices: front and back

Patch panels

There are many wire management devices used to organize the maze of cables that accumulate with a network. Typically, cables from the workstations are pulled into central locations known as *wiring closets*. These wiring closets are then connected together, usually with a high-speed backbone, such as a 100MB CAT5 or fiber optic cable, and terminated at the file server(s). A primary wire management device is the patch panel. All of the loose workstation wires are *punched down* to the backside of a central patch panel. From the front, short patch cables connect the panel to the switches, routers, and hubs. Figure 6-2 shows a patch panel.

24 port, 1 space patch panel

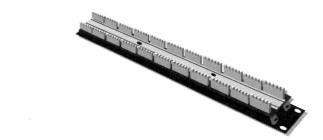

FIGURE 6-2 Front and rear view of a common patch panel

Uninterruptable power supplies

As stated previously, reliable power is necessary for file servers and network devices. An uninterruptable power supply (UPS) provides continuous reliable electricity. These units contain high-end batteries that assure the regulated flow of electricity during brownouts or surges. If the main power goes out, the battery automatically kicks in to continue the uninterrupted flow of electricity. Should the main power stay off longer than the battery life, special software can be used to send a signal to the NOS to initiate a safe shutdown. Figure 6-3 shows UPSs.

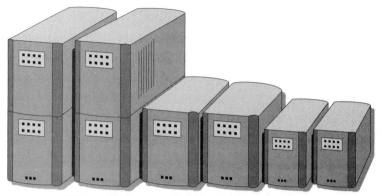

FIGURE 6-3 UPSs come in many sizes for just about any size device.

Hubs, routers, brouters, bridges, and NICs

As you know, these are all the devices that enable you to physically connect networks. With the exception of the NICs, all of these devices share a similar design. They all have an A/C outlet, and have one or more Ethernet or Token Ring connection(s), depending on the device. Hubs have the most connections; routers typically have one. NICs resemble most other internal PC cards and for the most part are either ISA- or PCI-based.

To complete the preinstallation inspection, you need to gather some additional administrative information:

o **Test accounts**: In order to test applications and assure that users are able to make the necessary connections to their data, a test user (account) is very useful. If you are working on an existing network, the network administrator should create this account for you; otherwise, you can create the account at the time you install the NOS.

o **Administrative accounts and passwords**: It may be necessary to obtain an administrator-level account and password, as well as user passwords, depending on the installation. Oftentimes you will need these accounts to perform administrative functions such as setting up other user accounts, printers, server services, or installing additional hardware. User accounts and passwords may be required to test access to important applications, or specific user needs. If you find this necessary, always take precautions to maintain the secrecy of the passwords, and inform the administrator when you no longer require the passwords so they may be changed. Attempt to limit any possible liability you may have by assuring that all access you are given is removed once you no longer require it.

- **IP configuration**: Many networks have existing IP addresses and addressing methods (static or dynamic). Before you add or move devices, obtain an IP list of every network component. This is especially important in a routed environment so you will know which addresses the routers use. If the network is all statically assigned, make sure you have sufficient unassigned IP addresses for any new devices you add.

- **Standard operating procedures**: Many organizations have formal policies in place that must be followed. Standard operating procedures, or SOPs, need to be identified and understood. The network engineer is responsible for identifying who has the relevant SOPs and assuring that all related policies in these documents are followed.

ADMINISTERING THE CHANGE CONTROL SYSTEM

Throughout installation, many changes affect equipment already in place. It is important to know what outcome these changes have, and be prepared to take appropriate actions to return a system to a usable condition. There is no faster way to lose a customer, or perhaps a job, than to have an unforeseen circumstance create serious downtime.

exam preparation pointer

The Network+ exam presents a number of scenarios and asks you to select a course of action. Understanding the importance of the items listed in the following section will greatly assist you in selecting the best action to take.

Preparing for Change

Before any changes occur, the state of the current system should be documented. This is known as establishing a *baseline*. Begin with simple things such as how a workstation boots up. Visually measure the average time it takes from power-on to the point where the user is logged in and able to work. Document any system errors or messages that happen during the power-up cycle, and listen for any unusual noise.

In addition to getting a feel for the hardware's performance, you need to examine all current configurations. You can't rely on the end users to remember how they initiated a particular program, or the telephone number their banking software dials up. The following list covers typical configuration settings that should be documented before making changes, but certainly the list can be added to ad infinitum. Common sense should dictate which settings are critical to any particular situation.

- **Identify all IP addresses and settings**. Especially in a statically assigned environment, make sure you document the workstation's IP address, the default gateway, DNS servers, and so on.

- **Document the settings of the network card**. Specifically note the make and model of the card, the IRQ and I/O address settings, and the software driver.

- **List the configured printers**. Identify the default printer, as well as other printers that the user may use. If these are network devices, note the capture settings (discussed a little later in this chapter), any special tray usage, defined physical memory, the ports the printer is associated with, and, if appropriate, which software drivers the printer(s) use.

- **Identify visible workstation icons and menu systems**. It may be necessary, especially for DOS applications, that each program's environment settings are noted, as are the path to the application, and any BATCH files that may be necessary to execute the program.

- **Document critical programs**. If you can't inventory all of the installed applications, get a list of those programs the user considers invaluable. A user can probably use another PC somewhere to zip off a quick letter in Word, but he or she may have the only computer with the banking software installed.

- **Locate hardware configuration information**. On Windows 95, 98, and NT workstations, you can get most of the hardware configuration information you're likely to need from the System applet in the control panel. Many other programs on the market provide similar reports.

Part of the reason for documenting all these items is to provide a method of returning a system to its original state if needed. If you don't know where the computer started from, you will not likely be able to restore it to the proper configuration should the upgrade(s) fail. During your documentation stage, it is advisable that you gather, or know how to quickly access, software drivers for critical components such as the NIC, printers, scanners, monitors, CD-ROMs, and tape drives.

For example, if your work on a PC leaves it in such a state that the only option is to reload Windows (and this *does* happen), you will need the DOS-based CD-ROM drivers in order to redo the installation.

Before you do anything that could negatively affect a system, you should take steps to *backup* the local hard drive(s). A backup is the method of copying important data to a different storage medium for safety. Should anything happen to cause the computer to become unusable, you can use your backup to restore the PC to its original condition. When selecting a backup method, it is important to think about how you'll get to the backup data if you need it. For example, if you use folder replication (discussed below), you assume that you can get to the network in an emergency. Some operations, for example, upgrading user applications, normally won't have an impact on the network connection, and folder replication may be best. On the other hand, if you're upgrading a PC from Windows 3.1 to Windows 95, you may very well find yourself without a connection to your backup folder. The main thing to consider is how safe your backup is, how much additional time it will take, and what resources are at your disposal. The following options are usually the most popular:

o **Tape backup**. Probably the easiest way to create a safe PC backup is to use a backup tape drive. Depending on the tape drive type and amount of data to save, the process is usually straightforward and enables easy restoration of the entire drive(s) or selected files. When you use a tape, make sure the backup software performs data verification at the end of the copy process. As an additional safety measure, you can restore a small amount of data to a temporary directory just to make sure the backup data is readable. Many a network administrator has been caught off guard in his or her time of need by a backup that is not usable. If you do a fair amount of workstation upgrades, you may be able to justify the cost of an external, portable tape backup unit. Many of these parallel port devices offer reasonable transfer rates and cost just a few hundred dollars. Although tape is a safe medium, it is usually not the fastest method. If you need to backup an entire 2GB hard drive, including a comparison afterward, the process might take three to five hours.

- **Folder replication to a network drive**. If a network drive has enough available space, you can *temporarily* copy the contents of the local drive to the network. I stress you copy contents temporarily, because you don't want to take up a lot of disk space (potentially a gigabyte or more) on the network. As soon as you're sure you no longer need the replicated data, get rid of it. For non-Unix systems, you can typically use the XCOPY utility to copy the data, but this should be done from DOS, and not from a DOS prompt within Windows. In order for this utility to work, you may need to configure a DOS-based connection to the network. Additionally, disk-cloning software is becoming very popular. Programs like Symantec's Ghost works by creating an exact image of a PC's hard drive, effectively taking a *snapshot* of all the files — hidden, visible, and active — that make up the operating system, applications, and configuration settings. These images can be stored on other local drives, network drives, or removable devices such as recordable CD-ROM, Zip, or Jazz drives. This method is typically much faster than tape, and enables you to easily restore selected files. The downside to folder replication is that you'll need a method of connecting to the network in order to restore the data. This may not be possible, depending on the problems you run into during the upgrade or repair.

- **Removable media**. As prices for writable CD-ROMs, Zip, and Jazz drives drop, and capacities increase, the external models of these devices make them very useful for on-site data archiving. These devices typically cost between $100 and $350, and plug into the serial or parallel ports, thus eliminating the need to open the computer case. As mentioned above, disk-cloning software can store mirror images of hard drives on these types of removable media, usually in a very short amount of time. Symantec's Ghost program can create a 2GB image-file in less than 20 minutes.

When protecting data with any of these methods, keep in mind that you may not need to backup *all* of the data. For example, if you're upgrading a particular application, you can probably cover your bases by simply copying the directory where the main application resides. However, don't forget that many Windows applications create support files in the Windows and/or Windows/System directory. It is always better to backup more data than not enough.

in the
real world **Whenever you work on a Windows 95/98 PC, it is a good idea to
backup the registry. The registry is the system database that contains many required settings, configurations, and parameters that
applications need in order to operate. The complete registry is contained in two files, SYSTEM.DAT and USER.DAT, located in the
\WINDOWS directory. To effectively backup these files, use a
backup software that will copy *in-use* files, or reboot the PC into
DOS mode (not a DOS box within Windows), and copy the files using one of the methods discussed above. Should any changes cause
the PC to fail to boot, you can replace the registry files to get the
system back up. (You can also use the Emergency Recovery Utility,
ERU.EXE, found in the Other\Misc subdirectory of the Windows 95
installation disk to backup the registry.)**

More backup principles

One of the most important aspects of maintaining a network's integrity is performing regular, verified backups. Most networks have a tape backup unit installed
in a file server, and use backup software that automatically begins late in the
evening when most users are gone for the day. These backup procedures are capable of performing workstation backups, but often they do not, due to the excessive
amount of data. (Assuming an average company with twenty PCs and one file
server, a corporate wide backup would require a tape system that could hold nearly
50GB or more of data. This is not usually practical.) Because workstations are not
typically backed up, users should be instructed to save their important information on the file server only. This not only ensures regular backups, but also uses
the NOS's security features to prevent unauthorized access to data. Two popular
backup applications are Seagate's BackupExec and Computer Associate's ArcServe.
These products, and others like them, support a wide range of backup drives, have
versions for all of the popular NOSs, and provide automation features desired in an
enterprise network

When designing a backup policy, you must take into account a number of
factors. Ideally, a backup occurs automatically every night of the week, and copies
every file on the server(s). This may not be practical, however, if the amount of
data exceeds the capacity of a single tape (and you would need someone to change
the tape very late at night, and again during the compare process). Large storage

media is available, but these devices often cost more than a company wants to spend. Therefore, if the amount of data that needs to be backed up exceeds the physical limits of the backup hardware, other options must be used.

Table 6-1 identifies the common multigenerational backup methods, starting with the complete backup concept. You should understand these options, and know when best to implement them.

TABLE 6-1 COMMON BACKUP METHODS

BACKUP TYPE	WHAT IT DOES AND WHEN TO USE IT
Full backup	Backs up all selected files. This is the preferred method if your backup system is capable of storing all the data on a single tape or other media (such as optical disks).
Differential backup	Backs up only selected files that have changed since the last time they were backed-up. This method is best in cases where a full backup is not practical, or when only the latest version of a file is required.
Incremental backup	As with the differential backup, this method backs up selected files that have been changed, but will *append* the current copy of the file to the end of the media (not replacing the old copy). This is used when each revision of a file must be maintained.
Delta backup	Similar to an incremental backup, but backs up only the actual data in the selected files that have changed and not the files themselves. This is rarely used except in large database applications where specific data changes can easily be restored.

Being aware of the stumbling blocks

Knowing what types of problems can occur during an upgrade or modification can save many hours of frustration. I wish I could present a table with all of the possible obstacles, but one truth about networking is that you never know how difficult something is going to be until the job is done. In all honesty, I can't count the number of times I've underestimated a project that for all intent and purposes should never have taken as long as it did. So before embarking on a new project, be prepared for the unexpected. Some of the problems you may run into are outlined below. Being aware of these things should help you avoid some of the common trouble spots.

It is very important you identify the possible adverse effects on the network caused by local changes. Many times, installing new software locally can introduce problems that prevent a workstation from accessing the network. Two common problems include software version conflicts and overwriting Windows DLL files.

Problems with software version conflicts Each workstation needs a network client component in order to attach to the network. If a client is installed or upgraded with a different version (newer or older) than the corresponding server component, the workstation *may not* be able to connect. Anytime you work on an upgrade that might make changes to the network components, you should read all of the supplied documentation to see if there are any known version conflict problems. This is especially true with updated NIC drivers. Although NIC manufacturers work closely with many popular NOS vendors, NOS clients can change faster than the NIC vendors can prepare for. And it is not uncommon for newer NIC drivers to conflict with older NOS client or server components. The safest way to avoid possible problems is to install the new software on a nonessential PC first and make sure you can connect to the network.

Even non-network programs can cause problems with software version differences. A recent example is the release of Microsoft Office 97. In order to achieve many of the new features, Office 97 was not made backward compatible with older versions of the Office product line. As new PCs were ordered, they often shipped with the newer Office 97 applications. If these versions were installed as a shared copy to the network, the older versions would fail. This was not always evident right away because workstations where the installation was done worked just fine. If the installer completed the upgrade and only tested that one computer, he or she was not aware that the majority of the other users were unable to use the applications. Even if the programs were not installed to the network, many problems occurred. When a user of the Office 97 software created new files, or opened existing files created by the older version, Office 97 would convert the files to the new format. When these files were saved back to the disk, users working with the older version were unable to read the data.

In order to avoid these kind of problems, a thorough investigation should be made to find out what changes the applications contain. At the very least, most vendors include either a file on the installation media, or in the supplied documentation that outlines the software changes; it should indicate any compatibility problems. If this information is missing, or not clear, you should make a telephone call to the vendor's technical support line. In order to avoid potential long hold times when calling the vendor, it often is better to call the vendor's sales department first. Generally, these lines are easier to get through to, and the sales staff can usually assist you in nontechnical issues of this nature.

Dynamic Link Library (DLL) conflicts   Software development is light-years ahead of where it was just a few years ago. One concept that greatly improved development time is Dynamic Link Libraries, or DLLs. A DLL is a collection of commonly used routines that any application program can use. This way, programmers do not need to constantly rewrite the same functions in their software. Another advantage of DLLs is the fact that they can be shared by more than one application at the same time. Windows provides a number of DLLs that are commonly stored in the \WINDOWS\SYSTEM directory. Almost all Windows-based programs use DLLs, either ones supplied by the Windows operating system or collections written specifically by third-party developers.

While DLLs conserve space, and simplify programming, they are inherently flawed. The reason for this is that although Microsoft has published guidelines for writing and using DLLs, there is no way to enforce them. Some applications overwrite an existing DLL with the one on their installation disks without ever notifying you. This installation disk DLL may be newer or it may be older. In either case, other programs that rely on routines contained in a DLL may (and often do) fail. It's not only third-party developers that do this, but Microsoft has also been known to replace older DLLs during an installation of their own software. This obviously can turn a relatively simple upgrade into a daunting troubleshooting nightmare!

There really isn't a clean way of preventing these problems. The best you can hope for is that the installation routine asks if you want to overwrite an existing DLL before replacing any existing files on your system. However, without knowing what changes have been made to a DLL, it is next to impossible to decide whether you should permit the program to replace the files or not. Again, be aware that these potential problems exist, but by using backup methods discussed earlier, you are prepared to recover from a DLL conflict problem.

Completing the installation

Once the installation or upgrade has been done, there are a few more steps to complete the project. First, you need to test your results. As you've seen before, you can't simply test the computer you are working with; you must also look at other things that may have been affected. If there is a shared directory on a PC, make sure others can still connect to it. If you install software that is used by others, even if the installation is local, make sure other users can still use their applications, and that they can access any data shared with the PC you worked on. Although you may not be able to test every application on the PC, you should make sure that any critical programs operate as expected. You may not be able to determine this yourself; have the person who uses the PC test the applications before you leave.

Once you are sure everything runs correctly, remove any outdated drivers and/or properties that are no longer needed. For example, if you replace a modem, remove the drivers for the old one. The same can be done for NICs, printers, hard drives, and other peripherals. If you update the network protocols, for example switch from IPX to IP, then make sure you remove any protocols that are no longer in use. Once you clean the drivers up, test things again, just to make sure a removed driver does not cause problems elsewhere.

Sometimes the install or upgrade entails simply moving a piece of equipment from one location to another. Perhaps you are replacing an existing PC with a new one, and the old machine needs to be moved for someone else to use. Make sure you test the equipment after it has been moved as well. It is possible that moving the PC to another part of the building affects the network connection, and the PC is now located on a different segment. The PC may connect to the server properly, but users who need access to a printer shared on that machine may no longer have access. The main thing to take into consideration is which resources this PC shares with others, and which resources the PC needs itself. Check all of the connections to these resources before you leave. If you move an existing PC from desk to desk, find out what, if any, applications need to be removed before the new user has access to the computer. You don't want to leave a payroll program on a PC once it leaves the payroll department!

Connecting to Network Resources

Throughout this book, logging on to the network, connecting to network drives and printers, and setting up network users and passwords has come up often. In this section, I look at *how* to make and maintain these connections. I focus primarily on NT and NetWare because these are the two most prevalent NOSs, and the NOSs that will be covered in the Network+ exam.

To quickly review, logging on to the network is the method of establishing a physical connection from the workstation to the server, and requesting access to the server via a security method. When you log into a server, you will be presented with a login dialog box (which is visibly different depending on which NOS and client you use). This box requires you to enter a user name, password, and either a server name or network domain. (NetWare Version 4.x and higher provides an option for a *NetWare Directory Services,* or NDS, tree. In these versions, you can log in to the entire *network* and not just a single server on the network. In NT and older versions of NetWare, you must log in to each server that you need resources from.) If the user name is valid, and the password is correct, the NOS grants you access to the server (or network in NetWare 4.x and higher). At this point, you are an authenticated user but don't have any direct connections to the server's drives, printers, or other resources.

Hard drives on network servers are often called *volumes*. A *volume set* is a logical storage area on a network server that physically spans multiple hard drives (such as in a RAID 5 configuration). The act of connecting to a volume, or a directory on a volume, that it is accessible from the local workstation is known as *mapping*. You map network drives and/or directories to an available drive letter on your local PC. For example, most PCs have a C: drive that is the primary hard drive. If you have a second hard drive installed, it is accessed as the D: drive. Furthermore, if you have a CD-ROM drive, it is usually assigned the E: drive. When you map to a network volume, you assign it a letter *higher* than the last physical local drive in the PC. When NetWare was first introduced (long before NT was available), it was very uncommon to have more than two hard drives in a workstation. To be on the safe side, Novell defined drive letters A: through E: as local drives (A: and B: as the floppy drives); this left F: as the first *network* drive. This standard is still in effect today. Normally, when you connect to a network, drive F: is the *root* of the primary server. There are no official *rules* pertaining to which network resources are mapped to which drive letters, but some combinations are generally accepted. For example, the drive letter M: is usually reserved for users' e-mail folders (M for mail). S: is commonly used for a directory that contains commonly (S)hared data. By default, Z: is mapped to a *public* directory on a NetWare network, and Y: is used to map to a shared version of DOS on DOS-based PCs.

Drive mapping in NetWare

NetWare uses the command MAP to associate a letter to a network drive or directory. The following commands are samples used in NetWare to manage drive mappings:

- `MAP G:=SYS:\OFFICE` This command associates the drive letter G: with the directory named OFFICE on NetWare's SYS volume (the primary volume on every NetWare server is named SYS:). After issuing this command from a logged in workstation, if you look in My Computer on a Windows 95/98 PC, you will see drive G:. Clicking on this drive letter displays the contents of the OFFICE folder on the NetWare server.

- `MAP N SYS:\OFFICE` The N option tells NetWare to use the next available drive letter to map the directory to. For example, if drives F:, G:, and H: are already assigned to network directories, this command maps drive I: to the OFFICE folder.

- `MAP S1:=SYS:\OFFICE` The S# parameter tells NetWare to map the specified directory to the drive letter as a search drive. A search drive is similar in function to the DOS PATH command. When a drive is added as a search drive, it is actually added to the search path for executables. In other words, if you are at a DOS command line prompt, and type in WP in order to run a word processing program called WP.EXE, DOS searches through all directories listed in the PATH for that program. If DOS fails to locate it, NetWare then searches through all of its search drives in the exact same way. Without search drives, you must explicitly tell NetWare the volume and directory location of the program in order to run it.

- `MAP DEL G` This command completely removes the drive mapping to G:.

- `MAP` When used by itself, the MAP command displays a list of all current drive mappings with their drive letter and network path.

 There are a number of other options available with the MAP command, but they are seldom used. For a complete list, you can type `MAP /?` **from the command line of a NetWare workstation.**

Drive mapping with NT

NT uses the command `NET USE` to map network volumes. NT also uses *Universal Naming Convention,* or UNC, to identify network locations. A UNC path uses double backslashes to precede the name of the computer. The path (disk and directories) within the computer are separated with a single backslash. For example, the following commands are used in NT (and UNIX) to manage drive mappings:

- `NET USE G: \\SERVER\OFFICE` As with the first MAP command above, this command assigns the drive letter G: to the OFFICE folder on primary volume of the server named SERVER.

- `NET USE * \\SERVER\OFFICE` The * is used to assign the next available drive letter to the specified directory; it's just like NetWare's N parameter.

- `NET USE /DELETE X` The /DELETE parameter releases the mapping associated with the specified drive letter.

- `NET USE` When used by itself, the `NET USE` command displays a list of all current drive mappings with their drive letter and network path.

 There are a number of other options available with the `NET USE`. **For a complete list, type** `NET USE /?` **at the command line of an NT server, NT workstation, or Windows 9x PC.**

Network printing

Printing is the second most often used service for a network. (Sharing files is the first.) It is also the single largest service that consumes bandwidth. Rather than have a printer attached to every computer, a few strategically placed printers can service many people. This not only saves money on hardware, but also reduces support costs. Before a workstation can use a network printer, however, you must define a connection to it. The concepts are similar to drive mappings, but the commands differ between the NOS you are using.

Network printing consists of a number of components. First, you need a *print server*. A file server may run printing services (thereby being a print server), or you may have an external device, such as the JetDirect box discussed in the beginning of this chapter. An external print server does not necessarily need to be a box; it may also be incorporated into the printer itself. If this is the case, the printer is equipped with a card that closely resembles a NIC. The network cable connects to this card just as it does to a PC. If you use the file server as the print server, the printers are physically attached to the parallel port(s) of the file server computer. While this is less expensive, it also means that users need to access the printers near the file server, and this may not be desirable from a security standpoint.

When using external print servers, you need to configure them to use at least one protocol that is running on your network, that is TCP/IP, IPX, or NetBEUI. The configuration methods for these devices vary between brands and manufacturers. Just be aware that they need to be setup properly on your network before they will function.

The next component in network printing is a print *queue* or print *spooler*, depending on which NOS you use. Although there are subtle differences, these two components provide the same basic service. When a workstation sends a print job to a network printer, the print server software intercepts the job and places the job into the queue/spooler. Once the job is ready to print, the print server takes the data in the queue/spooler and sends it to the physical printer.

in the real world
In NT, a printer is defined as the *print server software,* and the physical printer hardware is called the *printing device.* Should you ever take a Microsoft Certification Exam, it is important you remember this terminology.

Connecting to network printers in 32-bit Windows clients

Windows 95/98 and NT make connecting to network printers straightforward. You define and manage the printers through the Printers icon in My Computer, or in Control Panel. Use the Add Printer icon in the Printers folder to create a new printer. Clicking on Add Printer initiates the set of dialog boxes listed here:

TO CREATE A NEW PRINTER IN WINDOWS 98/98/NT, FOLLOW THESE STEPS:

1. You are first asked in Add Printer Wizard how the printer is attached: local or network. Select Network and click Next.

2. The next dialog box asks you for the Network path or queue name. This is the location of the print server (or the print queue defined on a NetWare print server). It is usually best to use the Browse button and navigate to the proper path as shown in Figure 6-4. If you prefer, you can type the proper path in the dialog box using the UNC format (as discussed before with drive mapping).

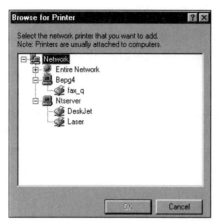

FIGURE 6-4 **Browsing for a network printer**
in the Add Printer Wizard in
Windows 98

3. This same dialog box has a radio button that asks if you will use this printer from DOS mode. If this is a possibility, you need to check Yes as Windows adds additional support to print jobs initiated from DOS programs. Because DOS applications usually require sending print jobs to a specific local printer port (such as LPT1 or LPT2) you need to create a *Capture* filter that redirects all printing from a local physical printer port to the network print queue/ spooler.

4. If you elect to install DOS printing support, the next dialog box sets up the proper Capturing filters (as shown in Figure 6-5). Simply select a printer port from the drop down box. For example, if you choose LPT1, then all DOS programs that print to the physical LPT1 port will have the print job intercepted by Windows and sent to the printer that you define here.

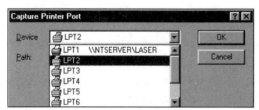

FIGURE 6-5 **Select the local printer port for DOS**
applications to print to.

5. Next you provide a name for this printer. (See Figure 6-6.) The name you enter is displayed to users when they select this printer for use. You might use a name to describe the actual printer, for example, *HP LaserJet III*, or you can use the printer's location, as in *Payroll Dept. Laser Printer*.

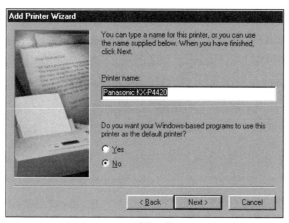

FIGURE 6-6 Assign a *user-friendly* name to the printer.

6. You can also set this printer to be the default for the workstation. If you choose Yes, the printer is selected each time a user prints a job, unless the user selects a different one.

7. Finally, after the printer is installed, you have the option to print a test page. This is always a good idea; this way you are certain the printing components are all defined properly.

■ ■ ■

Manually connecting a NetWare printer

NetWare uses a `Capture` command from DOS to connect network printers. In order to send DOS-based print jobs to a network printer, you need to assign a print queue to a physical printer port. The following command sets up a connection between a NetWare print queue, named *LaserJet*, and printer port LPT1.

```
CAPTURE LPT1 Q=LaserJet
```

After issuing this command, all data sent by DOS programs to LPT1 is intercepted by NetWare and redirected to the print queue, LaserJet. The print server then sends the data from the LaserJet queue to the actual printer defined by the print server. There are a number of additional options that can be included on the `CAPTURE` command line. For a complete list, type `CAPTURE /?` at the command line. Table 6-2 lists some of the most common options.

TABLE 6-2 COMMON SWITCHES USED WITH THE NETWARE **CAPTURE** COMMAND

NFF	No Form Feed. This option suppresses the form feed that normally is sent at the end of the print job. A form feed is only useful on dot matrix printers.
NB	No Banner. By default, before the first page of every print job, NetWare prints a *banner* page; this is a single page that indicates, among other things, which user sent the job to the printer.
TI=#	Time Out. A NetWare print queue remains *open*, accepting data until the program sends a command to close the printer, or the program ends. Many DOS programs fail to send this close command, so the print jobs are not sent to the printer until the program exits. This is usually undesirable, and the Time Out option can be used. The value after the equal sign tells NetWare to automatically close the print queue, thus releasing the data to the printer, after so many seconds (indicated by the value) elapse without any data coming into the queue.
NT	No Tabs. To conserve memory, NetWare passes the TAB character to the printer unmodified. Many laser printers do not interpret the TAB character properly and the output gets garbled. The NT parameter instructs the NetWare print server to convert all tabs embedded in documents to spaces before sending the data to the printer.

Manually connecting an NT printer

NT (and Unix) use the NET USE command to connect printers outside of Windows. Similar to mapping drives, the following command connects the workstation to the printer device called *Laser* for any data that is sent to the device LPT1.

```
NET USE LPT1: \\NTSERVER\Laser
```

To remove the redirection, follow the above line with: /DELETE

The command NET PRINT enables you to control all aspects of the print server, such as viewing, pausing, resuming, and deleting print jobs in the spooler.

Automating the connections

If you thought ahead a little bit, you probably think that it takes a lot of work to re-connect all the drives and printers each time a user logs in to the network. In or-der to automate the process, the NOSs provide a process called a *login script* to execute each time the user is authenticated. The login script differs somewhat from NOS to NOS, but the concept is the same. All of the commands that you can run manually can also be contained in the script. In NetWare, the login script is built into the operating system. That is, you create and edit it with tools supplied by NetWare. If you don't create a script, a default script is run that maps essential drives for all users. In NT, the script is optional. NT's login script is nothing more than a standard batch file, and if one exists for the user, it will be executed. Below are examples of a NetWare login script and an NT login script/batch file. They both map two drives and connect LPT1 to a printer called Laser. Lines that start with rem are comments describing the actions of the next line.

Simple NetWare login script

```
rem Displays drive mappings during execution of the script
MAP DISPLAY ON
rem Maps a drive to the corporate mail directory
MAP M:=SYS:\MAIL
rem Maps a drive to a shared directory
MAP S:=SYS:\SHARE
rem redirect all DOS printing to the Laser printer
CAPTURE LPT1 Q=LASER /NFF /NB /TI=5
```

Simple NT login script/batch file

```
rem Display each command as it is executed
Echo ON
rem Maps a drive to the corporate mail directory
NET USE M: \\NTSERVER\MAIL
rem Maps a drive to a shared directory
NET USE S: \\NTSERVER\SHARED
rem redirect all DOS printing to the Laser printer
NET USE LPT1: \\NTSERVER\LASER
```

User Administration Concepts

Small networks with less than ten or fifteen users are relatively easy to maintain. Security can be assigned on a per-user basis, scripts can be customized for the few exceptions that exist, and printer assignments are generally easy to maintain. However, as the network grows, or on large networks to begin with, there may be hundreds of users, printers, and possibly thousands of data directories (folders). Keeping track of which users should have access to which directories, who needs rights to which printers, and how to enforce password policies can be very time consuming at best. Unix, NT, and NetWare all provide built-in methods to assist with these administration problems. Although each NOS implements these tools a bit differently, the basic concepts are the same across all three platforms.

Policies

Policies provide a standard set of *rules* that can be applied to many aspects of a network. The various policy configurations available are listed below.

Account policies   Account policies enable you to set global definitions for all user accounts. Specifically, the account policy feature enables you to set password restrictions (as discussed in Chapter 5), and lockout parameters. Password policies provide for minimum and maximum password lengths, expiration time, and password uniqueness. The lockout feature enables you to set a maximum number of times a user can enter an incorrect password before the user account is locked out from network access. If an account is locked out, there is also a setting for the duration for the lockout. (The account can be automatically unlocked after a predetermined amount of time.) Account policies in NetWare are maintained in the NWAdmin program. Policies are created by means of defining a *template* for users, groups, or other manageable objects, such as printers, in NetWare.

▼ ▼ ▼

TO CREATE A DEFAULT TEMPLATE, FOLLOW THESE STEPS:

1. Start the NWAdmin program from the Novell program group.

2. Right-click the object (user, group, etc.) where you want to create the template, and then choose Create.

3. In Class of new object, choose Template, and then choose OK.

4. In Name, type a name for the new object.

5. (Optional) To base the template on an existing template or user, check Use template or user, and then choose the browse button to choose the Template or User.

6. Choose Create.

■ ■ ■

▼ ▼ ▼

TO DEFINE ACCOUNT POLICIES IN WINDOWS NT, FOLLOW THESE STEPS:

1. Click the Policies option on the menu bar.

2. The Policy dialog box will be displayed providing all of the options necessary to define the base policy for all new accounts.

■ ■ ■

User policies   User policies can be created by the network administrator to enforce a specific environment for a user, such as which wallpaper is displayed, which color schemes appear, which options to include or remove from the Start button, and more. As the name implies, these policies are unique to individual users, however, a *default user policy* can be defined whose properties will apply to all new users. User policies in NetWare are defined by right clicking a user object and selecting Details in the NWAdmin program. For NT, user policies are created and maintained by using the System Policy Editor program located on the Administrator Tools menu.

Group policies   Group policies provide the same features as the user policy, but apply to members of a specific group. Whatever definitions are supplied to the group policy are inherited by the individual members of that group (groups are discussed later in this chapter). Group policies are maintained in NWAdmin for NetWare, and the System Policy Editor in NT.

Computer policies   Computer policies are, as the name implies, policies that affect a specific computer. Some of the policies that can be set for a workstation include policies for disabling the browsing of locally attached printers, the creation of custom desktop icons, start menu items, shared program folders, customized login banners, and security password strings for the *Simple Network Management Protocol* (SNMP). Computer profiles are available in the System Policy Editor in NT, and through the ZenWorks package for NetWare.

System policies   System policies are the collection of the above policies in any combination. For example, if you implement User and Computer policies, this combination is considered a custom system policy.

Policy hierarchy   It is important to understand the method with which various policies are applied. Users may be affected by numerous rules depending on which groups they belong to, or what computer they log in from. The basic hierarchy of applying policy rules is as follows (note that there may be differences between various NOSs, but the common formula is virtually the same):

- If a user policy exists, it is applied to the user first. If no specific user policy exists but a default user policy exists, it is applied.

- If the user is a member of a group that has a group policy defined, the rules for the group are applied to this user. If the user is a member of multiple groups, each of the group policies is applied in order.

concept link

NetWare's group security model grants the most restrictive rights first, whereas NT applies the least restrictive rights first. In other words, when a user or group is created in NetWare, that object has minimum rights, and the administrator *adds* additional rights. In NT, the user or group is initially given full rights and the Administrator *removes* rights that are not required. This is a fundamental difference between the two NOS security policy functions, and it is a very important concept to understand when dealing with a mixed NT and NetWare environment.

- If a computer policy exists for the PC being used, then the computer policy is applied next. If there is no specific computer policy but a default computer policy exists, it is applied.

Generally speaking, when a new policy rule is applied that conflicts with an existing policy, the more restrictive policy takes precedence. For example, if a user has a user policy that removes the RUN command from the Windows 95 Start button, but also has a group policy that supports the RUN command, the user will not have access to the RUN command because the user policy takes precedence.

The main point to remember is that policies, regardless of which category they fall under, are useful administrative tools that enable you to enforce certain rules on the network. Whenever you need to enable or disable certain functions of the network, or workstations, for more than a single individual, consider deploying a policy rather than explicitly defining properties for each user. It is important to keep good documentation of your policy use, however. When troubleshooting access problems for a user, it is very inconvenient to have to display all groups' memberships when you are only looking for one individual's membership. The more policies that can impact a user, the more difficult it is to trace down the *effective* rights of that user.

User

User profiles are the collection of settings and options that define a given user's working environment. For example, a user profile may define specific settings for applications such as NotePad, Clock, or the Calculator, and desktop settings, such as screen savers, backgrounds, and wallpaper. Network and printing connections can also be defined in User Profiles. Windows NT uses User Profiles more than the other NOSs do, but NetWare's add-on ZenWorks product provides the same functionality.

User rights

The term *user rights* is different in NetWare and NT. In NetWare, user rights define which resources (disk and printers) the user has access to. For NT, user rights authorize the user to perform specific *tasks*, such as conducting a system backup, or creating new users within a group. NT uses the term *permissions* to describe resource access rights.

Groups

The group function is one of the basic tools for managing large numbers of users. A group is nothing more than a single identity that contains a number of other users. Suppose, for example, that you have a payroll directory on the server, and there are 25 people in the payroll department that need access to that data. Obviously, you don't want nonpayroll people to have access to these files, and you really don't want to manually assign rights individually to every person in the payroll department. You can create a *payroll group* and assign the necessary access rights to the group. Any user that is a member of this payroll group is granted the rights that have been assigned to the group object.

Practical Knowledge Application

Following are three real-world situations you may face. I outline applying newly learned concepts as you solve the problems at hand.

1. A new employee joins your organization and you are charged with setting this person up with a new PC. Your company's network consists of a NetWare LAN with Internet access. The default login script provides drive mappings to the company's primary applications, the e-mail directory, and all NetWare specific utilities. You need to provide this user with:

   a. A new user name and password

   b. Access to the Human Resources data located on the SYS: volume in a directory called HR

   c. Access to a shared printer with a queue name, HR_Laser

   The first step is to consult your company's SOP (standard operating procedure) to determine how user names are formed, and what the password policies are. Assume that the SOP calls for user names comprised of *first name* and *last name initials*, with enough characters to make the name unique. The MIS department assigns passwords and, if you recall, they should be at least five characters long but no more than seven characters long, and, ideally, they should include both letters and numbers.

   Next, you need to log in to the network using an account name that has administrator rights in order to create the new user and assign access rights.

   In this case, your new user's name is John Smith. When you look at the existing users, you see a JohnS already exists; therefore, you create a new user account, JohnSM; and assign it the password *klw54op*.

   When you look at the company's groups, you find that there is an existing group for all employees of the HR department, so you add JohnSM as a member of the HR_Group.

   When you check the login script, you see that the members of the HR_Group have drive L: mapped to SYS:\HR so you don't need to do anything else to provide John access to the applications he needs. (The default for everyone gives John access to the common applications, and because he is a member of the HR group, he inherits rights to the HR directory as well.)

You can provide John access to the HR_LASER printer one of two ways. You can modify the login script like this (the `%login_name` option enables you to uniquely identify the person logging in):

a. `IF %LOGIN_NAME=="JohnSM" THEN CAPTURE LPT1:`
`Q=HR_Laser`

b. You can create the connection from John's PC using the Windows 95 printer wizard.

2. A user in sales complains that she can't access her e-mail after lunch. You need to analyze the problem and find a solution.

First, verify that she could access her e-mail before lunch. You find out that she could.

Then, check that the physical connections (the modem, phone line, connectors, and so on) do not reveal any obvious problems. Because her e-mail was accessible before lunch, it is reasonable to assume your visual inspection of the hardware is sufficient for now.

You watch as the user attempts to retrieve e-mail. As expected, the program fails, and an error message indicates that the e-mail program is not found. But when the user logs in to the network from another computer, she can successfully get her e-mail.

When you check the drive mappings on her computer, you see that drive M: is mapped to `\\NTSERVER\SALES` and not to the mail directory. By having the user log out and back in again, you find that drive M: is correctly mapped to `\\NTSERVER\MAIL` and she can successfully access her e-mail.

The next step is to have the user recreate everything she did on the computer from the moment she returned from lunch. The first thing she did was run a DOS program to print a list of sales leads, and then she checked for e-mail. You check the Properties of the DOS program and find that it executes a BATCH file on the local drive. Using NotePad you open the BATCH file and see the following line:

```
NET USE M: \\NTSERVER\SALES /YES
```

By typing **Net Use /?** from DOS, you see that the `/YES` option forces the execution of the `NET USE` command without prompting for confirmations. In this case, the Batch file was re-mapping the M: drive without stopping to inform you that the drive was already mapped. By modifying the Batch file to use drive N: the user can now access her e-mail after lunch.

The same employee calls back the next day and says that now she can't run her spreadsheet application in the afternoon *after* she checks e-mail!

What went wrong? You didn't do a proper job of testing our results. If you had spent a little more time, you would have found out that drive N: was used by the spreadsheet program, so by modifying the BATCH file, you solved one problem, but caused another.

3. A customer's business is rapidly growing, and has outgrown the current location. The customer has purchased a new building and has already moved the NT server, networking components, and most of the workstations to this location. In this course of the transition, the customer has encountered a number of problems and needs your assistance to get things back to normal as quickly as possible.

The first step is to create a project documentation file. This is to both document all of your findings and actions for billing purposes and record the *baseline* of the computers you work on.

Next, you talk to the principle contact to gather the list of problems. You determine that the file server is fine, and most users experience no problem at all. You also gather all company SOPs to assure you stay within required company guidelines.

With the list of problems, you work with the customer to identify the most critical issues, and to prioritize the items.

It turns out that the top critical issue has to do with the user, Mary; she performs all on-line banking transactions. Prior to the move, she was able to connect to the bank's computers via a direct dial-in. Since the move, however, the software errors out with a message that there is no response from the modem. The modem's power light is on, as is the TX light. The modem is connected directly into the wall jack and does not connect to the telephone on Mary's desk.

Visual inspection does not reveal any physical problems. There is a FAX machine within easy reach of Mary's desk so you reroute the modem line to the wall jack used by the FAX machine and have Mary test the application again. The same error occurs. You also notice that none of the lights on the modem changed.

You replace the modem with a known-good unit from your stock. Because the modems are different, you install the proper drivers and test the local loopback connection using Windows built-in diagnostics. Because you know the FAX machine is on an analog connection, you use that line for testing. This time, when Mary tries the application, it works. You check with the office manager and discover that the telephone system is completely digital; therefore, you can safely assume that the modem was damaged when plugged into this wall jack.

You add a Y adapter into the analog FAX jack, and leave the modem and FAX machine connected to the same line until the telephone company can bring a new dedicated analog line in for Mary.

The next day the customer calls to complain that Mary's PC intermittently locks up.

What's wrong? First, you should have removed the drivers for the original modem. Because this modem is not going to be used, there is no reason to leave the drivers installed. It is very possible that the two modem drivers are not compatible with each other, but the symptoms will not be apparent until the PC is rebooted.

Second, because Windows did not identify that the original modem was bad, it reserved an IRQ for the device. The Plug and Play installation of the new modem selected an IRQ for the new modem that conflicted with other hardware in Mary's PC. Depending on which hardware was used, the IRQ conflict caused Mary's PC to lock up. You should have deleted the modem in Windows, then physically removed the modem from the PC. Then you could install the second modem and Windows would correctly assign non-conflicting resources to it.

The other item listed on our critical list has to do with the user, Tom; he cannot log in to the network. When the PC boots up, he receives the message that *No Domain Controller could be found.* Tom works at the rear end of the building, and there are no other computers in this area.

You know that Tom's user name and password are correct and that he has been added to the NT user database. The network client that appears when booting up is the proper Windows Client for Microsoft Networks.

The only protocols the user's LAN is running are TCP/IP and NetBEUI. You check Tom's IP settings and they match the IP address that the SOP documentation says his PC should have.

A visual review of the hardware indicates that the link light on the NIC is not on. The hub does not indicate a link either, so you replace the patch cable from the NIC to the wall plate. With the new patch cable, the link lights come on, and you are able to connect.

Exam Preparation Summary

Chapter 6 presents a key section of the Network+ exam. The material covered in this section will count for about 25 percent of the final exam. Most of the discussion focuses on practical, hands-on networking information. These are more of the *soft skills* side of the exam. From the knowledge you've acquired thus far, you should be comfortable addressing a scenario and explaining the necessary steps to achieve a desired result.

I began this chapter with the importance of understanding basic troubleshooting processes, and the need to document everything done on a network. Before implementing the network, you should perform a preinstallation checklist to check environmental conditions, the placement and impact of personal items, cable issues, and compatibility with existing computer equipment.

I discuss the need to be able to identify, visually and by their descriptions, common network components such as print servers, patch panels, uninterruptable power supplies, hubs, routers, bridges, and NICs. You also need to be aware of various administrative factors, such as obtaining an administrator-level account and password, IP configuration information, and following a company's standard operating procedure.

When it is time to administer the change control system, it is extremely important to prepare for the changes. You should document the current state of the system (baseline). It is important to understand how the system is currently configured and to be prepared to restore the system to its original state, if necessary. Part of preparing for problems involves making a safe backup of the existing data, and making sure you are able to retrieve the backup data if need be. It is also important to understand the various backup methods such as full, differential, incremental, and delta. I also note that there is simply no guarantee catastrophic problems won't occur, especially with software version conflicts and changes made to DLL files.

Once you complete installation, the testing phase begins. Many times changes and modifications appear to work as expected, only to cause problems in other areas. It is necessary to fully test every aspect of the network that may be affected, and to document all of the changes made.

I outlined the methods used to connect network resources such as drives and printers. NetWare uses the MAP and CAPTURE commands, while NT and UNIX use NET USE commands and *Universal Naming Conventions* (UNC). To automate the connection process, these commands may be included in the *login script*.

To make administration easier, the NOS provides policies and profiles. These configurations furnish a standard set of *rules* that can be applied to groups of users who share common needs.

Finally, I examined several real world situations that required you to use the knowledge you have gained thus far. These examples point out some common oversights that you can avoid by using a basic troubleshooting checklist.

I recommend you review the key concepts below:

o Understanding basic troubleshooting concepts, including:

  o Identifying and documenting the problem

  o Isolating variables causing the problem

  o Duplicating the problem

  o Developing a plan to correct the problem

  o Implementing the corrective action

  o Testing the results

  o Documenting the findings

o Preparing for a basic local area network installation:

  o Check the physical location for proper power, communication outlets, network cabling jacks, and patch cables

o Understanding the impact of environmental factors on computer networks, including:

  o Room conditions (humidity, heat, and so on)

  o Building content and personal effects configurations (space heaters, TVs, radios, and so on)

  o Other computer equipment

- o Identifying connectivity incompatibilities (such as analog modem vs. PBX connections, RJ-45 Token Ring vs. RJ-45 Ethernet) that may arise during network installation
- o Administering the change control system:
  - o Determining a baseline prior to making any changes
  - o Knowing the importance of returning a system to baseline configuration
  - o Selecting an appropriate backup technique such as tape backup technologies, folder replication to a network drive, and other removable media
- o Finalizing a successful upgrade
- o Identifying the possible adverse effects on the network caused by local changes
- o Mapping drives and recognizing mapping problems:
  - o Connecting by using Universal Naming Convention (UNC)
- o Capturing printer ports
- o Verifying the functionality of the network and critical applications after additions, changes, and moves
- o Identifying the purpose and function of common networking elements:
  - o User profiles
  - o Rights
  - o Administrative utilities
  - o Login accounts, groups, and passwords

APPLYING WHAT YOU'VE LEARNED

The following review questions give you an opportunity to test your knowledge of the information presented in this chapter. The answers to the assessment questions are in Appendix A. If you miss questions, review the sections in this chapter that cover those topics before going further.

1. List, in order, the seven items that define the basic troubleshooting model.

2. Which two environmental conditions need to be checked before installing network servers and connectivity devices?

3. If the environmental conditions of a room are questionable, you should:

    A. Not worry about it until the summer, then check the heat one more time

    B. Use specialized testing equipment to verify the heat and humidity over a period of days or weeks

    C. Carpet the floors to increase the insulation of the room

    D. Purchase servers with higher heat and humidity tolerance levels

4. If a workstation is located in an area where many small electrical devices are used, how should power to the computer equipment be obtained?

    A. Daisy-chain a power-strip on an existing strip to assure you have enough outlets

    B. Make sure the office has a 220v power source available

    C. Place the computer on a separate outlet, and use a UPS if electrical drops or surges are identified

    D. Make sure all extension cords are UA approved

5. Before connecting modems to the telephone system, always:

    A. Verify that the wall jack is within 15 feet of the modem

    B. Verify that the wall jack supports dual lines if a telephone will also be used

    C. Use a Y splitter on a remote FAX line

    D. Verify that the wall connection for the modem line is analog

6. When upgrading a workstation, existing applications:

    A. Should be inventoried and a plan to migrate them be documented before the upgrade

    B. Must be removed from the existing PC for security reasons

    C. Must be reinstalled from the original CDs or diskettes

    D. Should be moved to the network so they will be backed-up nightly

7. What devices are commonly used to organize the cabling system in a wire closet?

    A. External parallel print servers

    B. Plastic twist ties

    C. Color coded RJ-45 ends

    D. Patch panels

8. What is a major advantage to using an uninterruptable power supply on file servers?

A. Most UPSs have software to initiate a safe shutdown before the power is exhausted

B. UPSs provide power to the server until the electrical company can fix the problem

C. UPSs provide regulated power that prevents the power fans from getting too hot

D. A UPS can convert a 220v outlet to 110v for rack-mount servers

9. What two items are necessary before you can create new users on a network?

A. An IP address and an administrator account

B. The user's first and last name

C. Knowledge of the company's SOP and IP addressing scheme

D. An administrative account, and knowledge of the company's SOP

10. Specifically, what hardware settings need to be documented before making changes to a workstation?

A. The NICs, IRQ, I/O address, and software driver

B. The settings (size, number of sectors, and landing zone) of all SCSI hard drives

C. The IP settings for the NIC, default gateway, and DNS servers

D. The color coding of the patch cables used to connect to the hub

11. What two DOS-related settings should be documented before making changes to a workstation?

A. Amount of physical RAM and disk space

B. Number and size of logical DOS partitions on the hard drive

C. Printer captures and batch file settings

D. The contents of the PATH command and environment size

12. What is the best method of saving the original state of a PC before making changes?

A. Use a parallel tape backup unit

B. Replicate the data to the network if space exists and you can easily get to the network from DOS, if necessary

C. Replicate the data to a network-based tape backup unit

D. Use a disk-cloning utility to store an image of the hard drive on a network folder

13. Assume a company needs to backup data stored on local workstations as well as the file server. There is not enough space on a single tape to backup all of the data. Which backup method minimizes the amount of tape space needed?

A. Full backup

B. Differential backup

C. Incremental backup

D. Delta backup

14. What two things are commonly known to cause adverse effects during an upgrade?

A. Faulty power supplies and space heaters

B. Outdated software drivers and DOS programs running on Windows 95/98

C. Cascaded hubs that cause large collision domains, and duplicate IP addresses

D. Different versions of application software and DLL files

15. What are file server hard drives typically called?

A. Volume sets

B. SCSI

C. EIDE/DMA devices

D. Volumes

16. Assume you have a workstation with two hard drives, and you map a network drive using the command CAPTURE N SYS:\OFFICE. Which drive letter is used?

A. E:

B. F:

C. Z:

D. This command won't work because the UNC name is used incorrectly

17. Using NT, what is the UNC path for the subdirectory DOCS in the OFFICE directory on the file server NTSERVER?

    A. \\DOCS\OFFICE\NTSERVER

    B. \\NTSERVER\\OFFICE\DOCS

    C. \\NTSERVE\OFFICE/DOCS

    D. \\ntserver\office\docs

18. Which command correctly sets up printer redirection to the primary printer port in DOS on a Windows NT network? Assume the server name is NTSERVER and the printer queue is Laser.

    A. NET USE LPT1: \\NTSERVER\Laser

    B. CAPTURE LPT1: Q=Laser

    C. CAPTURE LPT1: \\NTSERVER\Laser

    D. NET USE LPT1: \\NTSERVER\Q=Laser

19. Reconnecting drives and printers can be automated in NT or NetWare using:

    A. Computer policies

    B. User rights

    C. Login scripts

    D. Batch files

20. Profiles and policies are most useful as:

    A. Automation tools

    B. Security tools

    C. Human Resource tools

    D. Administration tools

21. User Profiles can be used to store user parameters for some applications:

    A. True

    B. False

22. In an NT environment, user rights:

    A. Provide access to disks and printers

    B. Provide access to disks only

    C. Grant a user the capability to backup the system

    A. Enable administrators the capability to set password restrictions

23. NT uses this applet to create and maintain most policy features:

    A. NWAdmin

    B. ZenWorks

    C. System Policy Editor

    D. Batch files

24. NT maintains profiles in _____, where NetWare Version 4 and higher uses _____.

    A. Encrypted text files, RAM

    B. Floppy disks for safety, encrypted text files

    C. Encrypted text files, NDS

    D. User Manager, ZenWorks

25. User policies always take precedence over group policies:

    A. True

    B. False

Maintaining and Supporting the Network

About Chapter 7

The previous chapters provide you with a great deal of PC networking knowledge and skills. Chapter 7 continues to build on the practical skills. Once the network is in place, keeping it up and running presents a whole new set of problems, and requires further expertise.

In the early days of PC Networking, when Novell was the only game in town, customers were sold on the idea that they would build the server, stick it in a corner, and then forget about it. For the most part this was true. NOS technology was pretty stable once the software was installed, configured, and tuned. Account maintenance and other day to day administration tasks, including backing up the server, could all be accomplished from a workstation. In fact, when it was necessary to work on the server itself, many times the administrator had to think for a moment to remember where the box actually was!

Nowadays, however, things are different. Although the operating systems are, for the most part, stable, much more server maintenance is required. As technology races forward and prices drop, network administrators are faced with many more network tasks. Tape backups have been moved to the server, many of the administration tools that once were used from a workstation are now server based, and hardware additions, moves, and changes occur much more frequently.

Today's hardware and software is much more complex than in days past, and compatibility issues can cause many a long night. In this chapter, I discuss the importance of identifying the types of vendor support available, knowing where to find it, and what tools you need to support the network.

In addition to getting you acquainted with the proper support tools, Chapter 7 explores many network maintenance issues. The issues covered include the importance of network maintenance, types of maintenance, network backup, and protecting the system from viruses.

USING DOCUMENTATION

There has been a long-standing joke in the IT field that *real techs don't read documentation*. This may be a throw back to the early days when technical documentation was rare and overly confusing at best. Today, however, companies employ highly trained people to write detailed documentation to assist engineers in maintaining their products. In addition, almost all hardware and software vendors offer some form of a *knowledge base,* a searchable database of technical issues, usually available over the Internet. Telephone support is normally provided for a fee, and popular products typically have plenty of third-party books written for them. The key to supporting the network is to be aware of what documentation is available, where to obtain the proper information, and how to implement the knowledge gained.

Identifying the Types of Documentation Available Through Vendors

The vast majority of hardware and software vendors provide a plethora of documentation to assist in implementing their products. And because vendors focus their attention on providing cutting-edge technology, most rely on third-party providers to actually incorporate their products in the field. Therefore, it is in the best interest of the manufacturers to supply as much assistance to the network engineer as they can.

Documentation usually accompanies a product. However, it is important to realize that the physical package may have been sitting on a warehouse shelf for a number of months. The included documentation may not be the most current. Depending on which devices or software you deal with, some of the important items to collect *before* implementation are:

o **Frequently Asked Questions (FAQs):** Most vendors compile a list of the most common support issues into a single *question and answer* document called a FAQ file. These FAQ files often prepare you to deal with compatibility issues that others have already encountered.

o **Hardware compatibility lists (HCLs):** Before you recommend, install, or replace any network component, you should consult the vendor's HCL to verify the component's compatibility with other equipment. In particular, NT is known to have many hardware incompatibilities so hardware manufacturers go to great lengths to test their products with NT in order to be listed in a product's HCL.

in the real world   **Be aware that individual products listed in a *hardware compatibility list* may not have been tested for compatibility in combinations with other products. For example, a specific SCSI controller and a spe-**

cific SCSI hard drive manufactured by different companies may each be listed on the HCL, but this does not guarantee that they are compatible with each other. When in doubt, check the HCL for the NOS, *and* verify with each vendor that the products are compatible when used together.

- **Installation and/or migration tools***:* Data migration is the process of moving existing user data, system configurations (printers, NIC drivers, and so on), and security information (such as users and passwords) from one system to another. Although installing the new software may not present a big challenge, migrating existing data probably will. This is especially true if you change from one NOS to another, or upgrading the same NOS from one major version to the next. Although common backup and restore methods may provide a solution, many companies develop special migration tools for these tasks. Even if a migration tool does not exist, the vendor has probably published a *recommended migration* document.

- **White papers**: A white paper is an authoritative report on a specific topic, usually written by vendors, research firms, or consultants. These documents may contain narratives on how a product is implemented or how a product is used in a real world situation. White papers exist for just about any technology subject imaginable and can provide a wealth of information not easily located in other sources.

- **Release notes**: Before installing new hardware or software, a good engineer reviews the release notes for the product. This document outlines the history of the product, and identifies any changes, fixes, and improvements for specific product versions. It is important to verify that the version of the product you plan to use is the most current release.

- **README files***:* Almost all software products contain a *readme* document on electronic media (floppy disk or CD-ROM). These files contain important information that has been updated, changed, or corrected since hardcopy documents were printed. Because the cost of updating printed documentation is quite high, companies often update the electronically stored information until enough has changed to warrant a reprinting of the formal manuals.

Locating the Necessary Documentation

Now that you've seen which documents are important to obtain, you need to know *how and where* to look for them. As stated above, the documentation that is provided with the product may be incomplete or out-dated. Therefore, you need to turn to other resources as well to assure that the information you need is current and pertains to your specific situations.

Product supplied documentation

Although you will need other sources as well, the first place to look for documentation is within the product packaging itself. Most vendors supply user manuals, installation guides, and other forms of documentation with their products. More and more companies are opting to replace the printed manuals with electronic versions, mostly manuals stored on CD-ROMs. Before you install new software or hardware, take the time to review the documentation that accompanies the products. You should not take the *minimum requirements* for granted either. Look for the vendor's recommendations regarding hardware and software requirements before introducing the product into the network. The included documentation should also contain specific information regarding the company's on-line, e-mail, and/or pay-per-incident support. Make sure you know how to contact the vendor and what information you will need to provide, such as product serial numbers, product version numbers, and end-user customer information.

Use the Internet

Probably the best source for product documentation is the Internet. Before I even use a product, I go to the Internet and see what support, if any, the vendor provides. Because the Internet is *open* 24 hours a day, seven days a week (assuming my ISP is up!), I know I can count on the assistance no matter what time of the day or night my network needs attention. If the on-line support documents are sparse, or if the site makes it too difficult to locate the needed information, I look at competitive products where I might have a better chance at getting the technical information I need. Although the Internet is relatively new, most vendors have made great strides in moving their support documentation there, and making it easily assessable. In Appendix B, I list a number Web addresses for vendor support sites that you may find useful.

Web searching techniques   The more information available on the Internet, the harder it is to locate. Fine tuning your skills searching the Internet and a vendor's Web site saves you many hours of time and frustration. Although each site uses different search methods, there are common basic techniques. Keyword searches, using words related to what you seek, is the primary search method. Many utilities use special characters to designate how keywords are used, such as the plus (+) or minus (-) signs. Also, using quotation marks makes a difference. For example, if you perform a search at Yahoo with the keywords **NetWare Printing**, you will find all sites containing the words NetWare *or* Printing. However, if you look only for sites that contain *both* words as in *Printing with NetWare*, place the phrase between quotation marks: "NetWare Printing". The plus sign specifies that the keywords ***must all appear*** in the results, and a minus sign tells the search engine that the specified word ***must not appear*** in the results. For example, a search with keywords: **NetWare +Printing** locates sites pertaining to NetWare that *also* contain the word *Printing*. Likewise, a search with **NetWare –Printing** results in a list of NetWare sites that *do not* contain the word *Printing*.

Locating the proper sites.   Before you are able to find the documentation you need, you need the proper Web site. Most of the time, you can find a vendor's Web address listed somewhere in their printed documentation. If this fails, you can try simply using the company name. For example, Compaq computer's URL is `www.compaq.com,` and Novell's is `www.novell.com`. Some sites are not quite as easy to find so you'll need to do a little more work (discussed next). Also, there are many *non-vendor* sites that offer support, and they are sometimes better than the vendor's own offering. Many on-line user groups exist to share problems and solutions that happen *in the real world*. Often you can find a solution to a problem from one of these places by reading about someone who as already experienced the same problem.

If you can't easily find the type of sites you need, try using an Internet search engine. Yahoo, Excite, and Hotbot are some of the better-known engines, but many more exist. As I discuss above, these sites enable you to enter a word or phrase (known as *keywords)* that describes the type of site or information you are looking for, and then they display a list of Internet sites that match. Although the basic search functions are fine most of the time, knowing how to perform *advanced* searches may be necessary to locate the information you need. There are many good books on Internet search techniques, and most of the popular search sites offer on-line help, so I won't go into detail on this subject here. The important thing to remember is that searching the Internet is somewhat of an *art*, and the better adept you are at using search techniques, the easier it is locate what you're looking for.

The capabilities you gain from the Internet search tools also assist you once you locate the intended site. Unfortunately, neither standards for Web page organization nor for the methods of searching a site for specific information exist. Each site is a bit different, but the concept is usually the same. First, look for specific links that take you to the information you're searching for. Many sites have *support* or *help desk* pages with links directly from the main page. If not, look for *site maps* that index all of the pages within the company's Web site. In addition, most sites offer some form of internal search tool. Most tools are *Java* based, so be sure you use a Web browser that supports Java. Java is a common HTML programming language incorporated into HTML pages. Netscape Version 2 and higher and Internet Explorer Version 3.02 and higher support Java.

Subscription CDs

An excellent source of information that can be overlooked is the subscription CD programs many vendors offer customers and engineers. Typically, these programs provide a monthly CD set that contains all of the patches, updates, FAQs, knowledge base articles, and useful utilities released for the specific product you subscribe to. For example, Microsoft's TechNet and Novell's Support Connection programs provide monthly CDs packed with information and software patches for their entire product lines. SCO UNIX and other UNIX vendors also offer monthly CD subscriptions. The prices for these programs vary, but they normally cost less than $300 per year. If you elect to purchase a subscription yourself, don't forget to check with your tax advisor to see if the cost can be deducted from your taxes.

 tip

If you continue your professional certification program and complete the Microsoft Certified Systems Engineer (MCSE) or Certified NetWare Engineer (CNE) program(s), you can obtain discounts up to one half off the normal price of the corresponding vendor subscriptions.

Third-party reference books

With very few exceptions, most products used on a network have at least one book written about it. There may not be a book about a specific piece of hardware, but many books incorporate hardware components of similar products. For software, both network systems and user applications, the third-party book market is vast. You can usually find plenty of additional support from books written by people who actually use and deploy the products. There are literally hundreds of books for topics such as NT, NetWare, and Unix. Likewise, books on hardware products such as routers, switches, and other components fill many a bookstore's shelves. There are large bookstores in most major cities, or you can order directly from a publisher or Internet site such as www.barnesandnoble.com, or www.amazon.com. Book clubs are also a great discount source for books. Avail yourself to as many reference books as you can. There is certainly no shortage of knowledge in this business! You should also keep a record of your book purchases because you may be able to deduct the cost from your taxes as an educational expense (make sure you consult an accountant before doing so). Also, many employers will reimburse a portion of educational expenses to their employees.

NETWORK MAINTENANCE

In this chapter's introduction I reminisce a bit about the days when once the server was installed it could be pretty much forgotten. While this may seem better than today's systems, you must also understand that back in those days networks did little more than share files and printers. Today, companies rely on the network more than ever. Very often an entire corporation's records are stored on the network. While this provides extra convenience, and typically more security, it also places more responsibility on network administrators to perform regularly scheduled maintenance of critical functions. Three of the most important tasks that must be performed on a regular basis are backups, virus protection, and staying current with software patches and upgrades.

Proper Backup Methodology

I have discussed the importance of backing up user data, but because this is such an important aspect of the network, it warrants a more detailed discussion.

Many devices can be used to do backups, but tape is still most common. Tape drivers are reliable, less expensive per megabyte, and widely supported. The best method is server based although backing up from a workstation can be done. Problems with workstation backups lie in its inability to backup critical system files, such as NetWare's NDS database, and the overall lower quality of hardware used in these devices. Its not a bad idea to have at least one workstation equipped with a tape unit to be used in the event that the server unit fails, but the workstation tape unit should not be relied upon for daily backups.

The most common backup formats are QIC, Travan, DAT, and DLT, which are shown in Figure 7-1. You should understand the advantages and disadvantages of each type.

- **QIC**: Quarter-inch cartridge. This is an older tape technology based on the *quarter inch* width of the original tape. QIC comes in two form factors: 3.5-inch mini-cartridges and 5.25-inch data cartridges. Mini-cartridges have been enhanced with wider and longer tapes (QIC-Wide, QIC-EX). While the technology for the QIC format is very seasoned, they are giving way to newer formats. The capacity of the standard QIC tapes is typically less than 1GB, although it can be up to 25GB with the 5.25–inch QIC-5210.

FIGURE 7-1 QIC–80, Travan TR–4, and DAT DDS–1 tape cartridges

- **Travan**: Imation Enterprises Corporation developed this format as an evolution from the QIC tapes. Travan uses wider tape, different tape guides, and improved magnetic media to yield higher capacities. Some drives known as the Network Series (NS) drives, provide hardware compression and read-while-write features for better overall performance. Travan technology is most appropriately used in small peer-to-peer workgroup backup. Tape capacity varies with the type of drive and tape used. The different formats are:

- TR-1 - 400MB
- TR-2 - 800MB
- TR-3 - 1.6GB
- HP 5GB (TR-4 with less tape) 2.5GB
- Travan 8GB (TR-4) 4GB
- Travan NS 8 4GB
- Travan 20GB (TR-5) 10GB
- Travan NS 20 10GB

- **DAT** (Digital Audio Tape): These smaller magnetic tapes use 4mm cartridges that conform to the *Digital Data Storage,* or DDS, standard. Originally they were designed as a CD-quality audio format to replace analog audio tapes, but in 1988, Sony and HP defined the DDS format and the quality level for computer storage. Among products in its class, DAT tape has become popular due to its high reliability, speed, and low cost. Special DAT tape libraries can hold several hundreds of cassettes and provide enough on-line storage to meet almost any need. The DAT format uses *helical scan* recording, which is similar to the way videotapes record. The helical scan method uses a rotating head and diagonal tracks, which enable a slow-traveling tape to provide a very fast transfer rate. The tape is pulled out of the cartridge and wrapped around the read/write head. The capacities of typical DAT cassettes without compression are:
  - DDS1: 2GB
  - DDS2: 4GB
  - DDS3: 12GB

- **DLT**: Digital Linear Tape is a magnetic tape technology that uses half-inch, single-hub cartridges. It writes 128 or 208 linear tracks, depending on the model, and provides capacities from 10 to 35GB. The use of DLT has grown rapidly since 1995, and the technology is widely used on medium to large-scale LANs.

Regardless of the type of drive you use, your backup process methodology is equally as important. Backups must be automated and require minimal operator intervention. Backup software supplied with the basic NOS rarely offer the type of features required for a proper enterprise system. While there are numerous backup software packages commercially available, Seagate's BackupExec and Computer Associate's ArcServe are among the most popular. It is critically important that backup media use is rotated, and that at least one copy is taken off-site. A common backup practice is to use a different tape for each day of the week, taking the prior night's tape home each day. The following section describes in detail some common tape rotation methods.

Tape Rotation Strategies

The key to proper backup strategies is to deploy a systematic schedule that ensures you can restore selected files or an entire disk as needed. In order to minimize the reliance of a single tape, and to extend the life expectancy of the media, a proper tape rotation system should be used. Ideally, the backup system should allow for a full backup on a single tape every night. This method provides the easiest way to fully restore a system with a maximum data loss of 24 hours. Likewise, by using a separate tape each day, the previous day's tape can be taken off-site; this greatly reduces the chance of total data loss due to disaster or theft. When this backup method is used, label tapes with the beginning date of service, and replace them according to the manufacturer's recommendations. If the full backup method is not possible, then a tape rotation system described below should be implemented.

Three- tape rotation

The three-tape rotation method, shown in Figure 7-2, is best suited for situations where less than 25 percent of the user data changes from day to day. Table 7-1 explains how to rotate the tapes, assuming your workday starts on Monday.

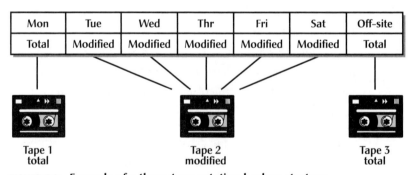

Mon	Tue	Wed	Thr	Fri	Sat	Off–site
Total	Modified	Modified	Modified	Modified	Modified	Total

Tape 1
total

Tape 2
modified

Tape 3
total

FIGURE 7-2: Example of a three–tape rotation backup strategy

TABLE 7-1 SCHEDULE FOR A THREE–TAPE ROTATION BACKUP SYSTEM			
	TAPE #	*DAY OF WEEK*	*WHAT TO COPY*
Week #1	1	Monday	Full backup.
	2	Remainder of the week	Backup only modifies files, *appending* the data to the end of the tape. Use the same tape each night.
Week #2	3	Monday	Full backup. (Tape 1 from week 1 is taken off–site)
	2	Remainder of the week	Erase Tape 2 before using it on Tuesday; then perform modified only backups daily, *appending* the data to the end of the tape. Alternate Tape 1 and 3 off–site

Six-tape rotation

The six-tape rotation method, shown in Figure 7-3, uses a different tape each workday and has one tape to keep off-site. This method is best suited to networks where data files change frequently, that is, more than 25 percent of the files change. The method is as follows:

1. Label the tapes Monday through Friday and *Off-Site*.

2. Perform two full backups on Monday using the Monday and Off-Site tapes.

3. Perform a modified copy only on Tuesdays through Fridays, over writing the existing data on the tape.

4. Alternate tapes 1 and 6 as the Off-site tape.

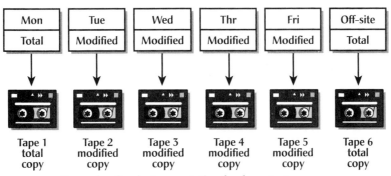

FIGURE 7-3 Example of a six-tape rotation backup strategy

Using this method, you can restore the whole system by first restoring the full copy from Monday, then sequentially restoring each day's backup to the point of the system crash. (Make sure you permit the tape backup software to overwrite existing data on the disk or your subsequent restores will not replace the older versions of the data.)

Other tape considerations

The vast majority of networks today use some form of tape backup system as their primary disaster recovery tool. To ensure your backups are current and well protected, I highly recommended you follow these precautions:

1. Make sure a full backup is performed *at least* weekly, and before any major changes are made to the system. If a major upgrade takes place on the file server, make *two* full and verified backups before proceeding.

2. Label your tapes clearly and log each day that they are used.

3. Rotate new tapes regularly. Never exceed the maximum number of hourly use recommended by the manufacturer.

4. Store tapes in their protective cases and keep them away from magnetic fields, power supplies, telephones, and monitors.

5. Always use the *compare* option of your software after each backup.

6. Periodically perform a tape restore on a non-production computer to assure that the data on the tapes is reliable.

7. On a monthly basis, retention your tapes using backup software.

PROTECTING THE NETWORK FROM VIRUSES

Computer viruses are defined as programs that cause damage to computer files and have the capability to replicate among computers. No doubt, viruses are nasty beasts that will not be eliminated any time soon. According to the Security Research Alliance, more than 40,000 viruses exist today. While it's impossible to prevent every virus from infecting your network, you can minimize the impact. If you work proactively, you can take steps to limit virus access to your computers, and you will be prepared to deal with viruses should the need arise. There are many myths about computer viruses along with many truths, but to completely ignore the possibility that one can infect the network is irresponsible. The cost of protecting a network is minimal compared to the cost of repairing virus damage after the fact.

The first step is to choose an anti-virus program. There are literally hundreds of packages to choose from, and they all perform basically the same tasks. Anti-virus programs focus on scanning computer programs as they are saved on disk, and, optionally, scanning computer programs when they are accessed. If a program appears to have been tampered with, the virus software usually issues a warning to the network administrator.

Where to Implement the Scanning Process

The two primary issues to resolve before implementing a protection program are deciding where to place the scanning process and how the virus detection updates are obtained and applied.

In a network environment, two main areas can be reviewed for anti-virus protection: the server alone, or the server and the workstations. Due to cost and administrative issues, many companies implement the anti-virus protection only at the file server level. This reduces administrative time, and protects the critical data. With this arrangement, you are assured a virus will not enter the server from a workstation, nor will a workstation become infected from the server. However, this method does not prevent the possibility that a virus infects a workstation from a local floppy disk, the Internet, or another dial-up connection. If users store critical data on the server, and the process of restoring workstation applications is not overly costly, this method may be the best choice.

Anti-virus software can be deployed not only on the server, but also out to the workstations. While this is a more complete solution, it does create additional administrative time to install and maintain the anti-virus software, and, depending on which product is used, it may create a small performance overhead on daily operations. If the network uses some peer-to-peer services, it may be worth the extra cost and effort to deploy anti-virus software on the workstations.

Anti-Virus Signatures Files

The most critical issue with an anti-virus policy is keeping the virus *signatures* up-to-date. Virus signature files are the updates issued by the anti-virus software vendor that are used by the application to identify new virus patterns. Each month, hundreds of viruses, or variations of old viruses, are identified. If the signature files are out of date, even by as little as 45 days, the anti-virus system is practically worthless. When selecting an anti-virus software program, the most important factor to look for is the vendor's ability to provide signature updates *at least* every 30 to 60 days. You can find this information simply by logging on to the company's Web site and seeing how often previous signature files have been posted. Most commercial anti-virus vendors permit you to freely download their signature files.

The last point to consider when you choose an anti-virus solution is how the vendor supplies their signature updates. As I mentioned, most vendors permit free downloads from their Web sites, but this does place increased responsibilities on the network administrator. Under most circumstances, companies can justify the cost of yearly subscription fees to have the anti-virus signatures delivered to them electronically. Many vendors automatically e-mail signature files to subscribers, and others incorporate *push* technologies. The push technology is a method of utilizing the Internet to automatically send files and notices to subscribers. Backweb (www.backweb.com) and Pointcast (www.pointcast.com) are examples of push products. By using push technologies it is possible to not only to receive virus signature files automatically, but in some cases, to actually automate the installation process to the server as well. As these technologies become increasingly sophisticated, the administrative overhead of running anti-virus software on all devices within the network may become a non-issue.

KEEPING THE SOFTWARE CURRENT

You don't have to be in this business long to learn that software changes faster than the proverbial *speeding bullet*. It often feels like you just get things stabilized when the vendor issues a patch or update. While it may not be necessary to apply every patch that is released, you do need to be aware of what updates are available, and what issues they address. If you subscribe to monthly vendor CD programs, this information will be available to you. If you don't use one of these programs, you either need to visit the company's Web site, or subscribe to their e-mail list. All of the major software vendors send out, at least quarterly, reports of what patches and fixes have been issued.

Its important to remember that your network is composed of many different products, probably by an equally disperse number of vendors. Most hardware components, NICs, routers, switches, and even motherboards have software components that also need to be reviewed for updates from time to time. You're probably beginning to see why I stress the importance of good documentation. Suppose for example, that you find a problem that an update to your NOS will fix. After reviewing the documentation you find that there are a number of know issues with various hardware drivers. Before you can install the update to solve the problem, you have to make sure your controller software is at a certain revision level. If you have maintained good documentation, this is probably not a major problem. However, if your documentation doesn't include hardware driver information, you likely have a long night in front of you bringing your documentation up to date.

Along the same lines, it's important to make sure your user applications are up-to-date as well. For example, Microsoft Office 97 has already released two large service packs (Microsoft's term for a major patch). These service packs fix many known bugs and generally offer some usability improvements. Again, your documentation should be complete enough for you to quickly identify what application *patch* levels are installed on your workstations.

The bottom line here is to have a common organization sense and awareness. You need to develop a feasible reoccurring schedule to scan the Web sites of the vendors whose products you use, and to completely document the system(s) you're responsible for. With these two practices, you should have all the tools you need to keep your network(s) running as trouble free as possible.

IDENTIFYING THE PURPOSE OF COMMON NETWORK TOOLS

As with any craftsperson, the longer you work in the IT field, the more tools you'll collect. Tools are not limited to physical products such as screwdrivers and cable crimpers; they include software tools that provide information not visible by other means. I've already discussed many of the software items you'll need, such as the *ping*, *tracert*, and *ipconfig* utilities, but there are other equally important tools you'll want to collect. The rest of this chapter addresses which items you should be familiar with, and when you should apply them.

Essential Software Tools

Probably the most valuable software tool you can ever have is an Internet connection. If you do a lot of fieldwork, an investment in a good laptop computer is easily justified. Rather than carrying around hundreds of diskettes, or CDs with software drivers, configuration charts, and other important documentation, you should be able to access the Internet for such items. Not only is this easier, but it ensures that you can access all possible information you may need, and that the information is current. If you travel to locations outside of your local ISP's dialing area, ask the ISP if they can give you a toll free number. Many ISP make such provision for a modest additional charge.

Since the time I bought my first PC, I've felt that all PC owners should have a copy of the Norton Utilities. This collection supports the whole Windows product line and offers all of the functions you're ever likely to need. Just remember that this is a commercial product. Read and follow the licensing agreements!

You should always have a clean *write protected*, bootable floppy disk. A *clean* diskette is one you are certain *does not* contain a virus. Don't count on being able to make one when you need it—all of your potential sources may be infected! I normally carry a number of bootable diskettes, one for each operating system that I support. Specifically, you should have a DOS disk and a disk for each of the common Windows platforms: 95, 98, and NT. In addition to bootable diskettes, you should have an anti-virus disk that at least has the virus detection software, and preferably the detection *and* removal programs.

Because many problems can be fixed from DOS, I keep two special DOS diskettes with me. One is simply an identical copy just in case the first one fails. On this disk, I have the programs listed in Table 7-2.

TABLE 7-2 IMPORTANT DOS FILES TO KEEP HANDY

DOS Version 6.22	This is the last Microsoft release and offers the best memory management capabilities.
FDISK from DOS *v*6.22	It is sometimes necessary to reload everything from scratch.
FORMAT from DOS *v*6.22	If you have to repartition the drive with FDISK, you'll need to format the partition as well.
A DOS-based text editor	I personally use a shareware program called Qedit (www.semware.com). It's small (70K) and only requires 96K of RAM.
A few generic CD-ROM drivers	It depends on what products you support the most, but the Mitsumi drivers seem to cover a lot of drives.
McAfee's SCAN and CLEAN anti-virus programs	Choose whichever anti-virus software you prefer, but make sure there is a small DOS-based version available and *keep the signatures up-to-date.*

There are, of course, many more items that you can have on your boot disk(s), but I find the ones listed in Table 7-2 to be the basics. Remember to keep more than one copy on hand, and *use the write-protect tab* to eliminate the possibility of infecting the files with a virus.

Even with my laptop nearby, I carry disk copies of the diagnostic software for the hardware I support most often. For example, most of my customer's use 3COM NICs, hubs, switches and routers, so I keep copies of 3COM's diagnostics handy. I could download them as needed, but these applications don't change very often, and they can be quite large to download over a 56K modem.

If you work on NetWare systems, you should also get a copy of the Novell Consulting Toolkit. The Toolkit contains a variety of useful tools and links for Novell software users. It is perhaps the best-kept secret on Novell's Web site. The web address for this item is `http://consulting.novell.com/toolkit/tkhome.html`. Specifically, you should get a copy of the NetWare Ram Estimator, which helps calculate the amount of RAM required in a server, and the NetWare Config reader, which provides detailed documentation about the devices and services on your servers.

Essential Hardware Tools

Nothing beats a good old fashion screwdriver, but for networks you'll need a few specialty items. As with the software recommendations, *your mileage may vary*. In other words, what tools you choose to keep on hand will differ greatly based on the type of system(s) you work with, and the level of service you provide. The following list, however, includes items I recommend you have readily available when troubleshooting systems:

1. **Crossover cable**: If you ever need to cascade two hubs together, or test communications specifically between two devices, you will need a crossover cable. I carry two with me: a three-foot and a ten-foot cable.

2. **CAT 5 patch cable**: I normally carry a variety of lengths, from three to fifteen feet.

3. **Coax connectors**: If you work on LANs that use COAX cabling, keep a few share *T* connectors, barrel connectors, and a 50 ohm terminator on hand.

4. **Known good NIC**: When basic testing leads you to believe the NIC is bad, it's normally more cost effective to simply replace the questionable card with

one you're certain works. Make sure you have good drivers, and *backup* the drivers for the NIC you replace in case it turns out not to be the culprit.

5. **Spare hub**: A simple four-port hub can be purchased for less than $50, and even less if you locate a used model. There are just too many times that you find yourself searching for an available port to plug into; this way you know you have room for a couple of devices.

6. **ISA video card**: Many Windows problems can be traced to the video drivers. A basic 16-bit ISA video card can often be used to remove the possibility of a PCI video driver problem. Again, this is used to remove variables in the troubleshooting process.

7. **Hardware loopback plugs**: There are a number of loopback devices useful in the troubleshooting process. Serial and parallel plugs should be familiar to you from your A+ training. Network cards also have loopback plugs that can be used to determine if communication problems extend beyond the NIC. Most NIC manufacturers supply diagnostic software but the number of tests is limited unless you use a loopback plug. (Refer back to Chapter 1 for instructions on making a loopback plug.)

8. **Tone generators**: Faulty cabling causes many communication problems. In environments where cables are poorly labeled, if labeled at all, it may be next to impossible to identify the specific cable suspected of being faulty. A tone generator sends a signal on the wire, and a receiver piece emits an audible tone when connected to the same wire. This greatly reduces the time it takes to locate wire ends between rooms, floors, or buildings.

EXAM PREPARATION SUMMARY

This chapter prepared you to think about the on-going maintenance required for a network. The Network+ exam focuses in on a number of issues covered in Chapter 7. Specifically, you should be able to identify the types of documentation that vendors make available regarding patches, fixes, and updates. You should understand how and where to locate this documentation, and, especially, become familiar with documentation available in product packaging, the Internet, and vendor subscription CD programs.

Two major concerns of maintaining and supporting the network are regular systematic backups and virus protection. You should understand the various backup methods and procedures, and be aware that virus signature files must be kept up-to-date. Policies and procedures for both of these functions should be well thought-out, documented, and followed.

There are a number of software and hardware tools commonly used to assist in diagnosing problems with the network. Many software programs are included with the network operating system, and others are commercial packages that can make your job as an engineer easier. You should keep some simple hardware items, such as patch cables, loopback products, and tone generators readily available, and you should understand how and when to use them. I recommend you review the key concepts in this chapter to make sure you understand the material that you just read. You should be able to:

- Identify common network troubleshooting resources, including:
  - Knowledge bases on the World Wide Web
  - Telephone technical support
  - Vendor CD subscription programs
- Given a network maintenance scenario, demonstrate an awareness of the following issues:
  - Standard backup procedures and backup media storage practices
  - The need for periodic application of software patches and other fixes to the network
  - The need to install anti-virus software on the server and workstations
  - The need to frequently update virus signatures.
- Specify the tools that are commonly used to resolve network equipment problems. Identify the purpose and function of common network tools, including:
  - Crossover cables
  - Hardware loopback products
  - Tone generators

Applying What You've Learned

The following review questions give you an opportunity to test your knowledge of the information presented in this chapter. The answers to these assessment questions can be found in Appendix A. If you miss questions, review the sections in this chapter that cover those topics before going further.

1. A common file that discusses common issues published by vendors on their Web site is:

    A. Frequently Asked Questions (FAQ)

    B. Hardware compatibility list (HCL)

    C. Minimum requirements list (MRL)

    D. Subscription CD program (SCDP)

2. If two or more hardware components are listed on a vendor's hardware compatibility list, you can be assured that the hardware will perform as expected in the server?

    A. True

    B. False

3. When replacing a server or workstation, _____ is probably required, and the best approach is to check the vendor's recommended method.

    A. Adding more RAM

    B. Defragmenting the hard drive

    C. Migrating data and applications

    D. Reconfiguring the NIC

4. Before installing new hardware or software, the _____ file should be consulted to see what changes have occurred since the last printing of the documentation.

    A. Update

    B. Readme

    C. Changes

    D. FAQ

5. Why is it necessary to look for product documentation on the Web or from other sources when the product includes printed documentation?

   A. The product may have been packaged for resale because newer versions have been released or problems have been identified.

   B. Product supplied documentation rarely covers installation instructions.

   C. Product supplied documentation is too difficult to understand

   D. The product requirements may not be identified in the supplied documentation.

6. The best place to locate free technical information is:

   A. Monthly CD subscription programs

   B. Local user groups

   C. The vendor's Internet site

   D. Third-party books

7. When searching for an Internet site using popular search engines, what two special characters can be used to include or exclude specific words?

   A. Place the words between double quotation marks

   B. The plus (+) and minus (-) signs

   C. A single (\) and double (\\) backslash

   D. The words Include and Exclude preceding the keyword

8. What name does Microsoft use for their monthly CD subscription service?

   A. MSN

   B. TechNet

   C. MSCDROM

   D. TechROM

9. What name does Novell use for their monthly CD subscription service?

   A. TechNet

   B. Brainshare

   C. NetWare Connect

   D. NetWare Support Connection

10. Under normal circumstances, the preferred backup method is:

    A. Three-tape rotation

    B. Full backup with one tape taken off-site weekly

    C. Six-tape rotation

    D. Daily full backup with previous night's tape taken off-site

11. A three-tape rotation backup method is best suited:

    A. For companies with less than two file servers

    B. When a single tape is not large enough for a daily full backup, and less than 25 percent of the data changes daily

    C. When a single tape is not large enough for a daily full backup, and more than 25 percent of the data changes daily

    D. When the backup system is based on the QIC tape format

12. What four common tape formats are currently in use?

    A. QIC, DAT, DLT, and Travan

    B. QIC, DSS, Travan, and Scottch

    C. Travan, Linear, TR1, and Audio

    D. DAT, DDS, TR3, and TR4

13. Digital Audio Tape (DAT) uses _____ recording method, similar to VCR recording.

    A. Servo scan

    B. Reel-to-reel

    C. Helical scan

    D. Laser

14. On a monthly basis, tapes should be:

    A. Taken off-site

    B. Retentioned

    C. Replaced

    D. Scanned for viruses

15. Complete virus protection consists of:

    A. Anti-virus software on the workstations to prevent entry to the network

    B. Anti-virus software on users' floppy diskettes

    C. A bootable diskette that is write-protected that contains anti-virus software

D. Anti-virus software on the server and on the workstations

16. Updates to anti-virus software are commonly known as:

A. V-Files

B. Update patches

C. Push files

D. Signatures

17. Two methods of obtaining updates for anti-virus programs are:

A. Manually download from the Internet

B. Internet Push technology

C. A monthly TechNet subscription

D. Retail outlets

18. A bootable floppy disk used for troubleshooting should contain these files:

A. FDISK, FORMAT, SCAN, and GWBASIC

B. EDIT, TSE, and FORMAT

C. MSAV, FORMAT, CDROM, and SCAN

D. FORMAT, FDISK, and a text Editor

19. A proper toolkit will likely include these hardware items:

A. Patch cable, screws, NIC, and modem

B. Crossover cable, screwdriver, modem, and a tone generator

C. Normal and crossover cables, screwdriver, video card, and loopback plugs

D. Loopback plugs, CAT 5 cable, CDROM drive, and tone generator

20. A tone generator is useful to detect:

A. Faulty hub connections

B. Faulty wiring

C. Faulty termination

D. STP category level

Troubleshooting the Network

About Chapter 8

I n past chapters, I have discussed the systematic approach to troubleshooting. In addition to these steps, how you approach and handle the problem is equally important. Chapter 8 looks deeper into the troubleshooting process, developing the skills to identify network problems based on initial symptoms, and working though the elimination of variables until the problem is resolved. In the real world, network problems rarely happen one at a time. A successful network engineer develops the skills to effectively prioritize multiple problems. Likewise, you'll need the ability to determine if a given situation requires technical services, information transfer, or user handholding.

This chapter presents a number of scenarios and guides you through the thought process of approaching the troubleshooting process. I also look at and define the steps of troubleshooting that will serve as your troubleshooting checklist.

TROUBLESHOOTING THE NETWORK

Most of the time you are alerted to potential network problems by the end-user. Sometimes the problems are obvious, other times they may not be. The first steps you need to take when a possible problem occurs are to identify the issue, determine whether it is truly a network problem, and respond to it. Additionally, you need to examine the nature of the problem, and decide what action to take.

Prioritizing problems may appear to be a simple matter, but in reality, there are many other factors to consider. Obviously serious network problems, such as downed file servers, are usually placed at the top of the list, but other less obvious factors may necessitate escalating a problem call. For example, under normal circumstances your crashed file server takes precedence because it directly effects all users. However, if you suspect that repairs will take some time, it may be more important to first restore payroll information on a standalone PC so that employees can be paid on time.

 in the real world **Rule number 1: Payroll problems usually take precedence over all other items. People need to be paid, and paid on time. The fastest way to make a lot of enemies really fast is to do anything that disrupts the processing of their paychecks!**

Every organization has its own criteria for determining which network problems are most important. The job of the network engineer is to understand these objectives and work to restore the systems in an efficient manner. For example, attorneys often require documents for court dates. Making sure that the word processing department is up and running first may be more important than the accounting department. If you work for a network integrator, where you support many different companies, you need to discuss the ramifications of the required repairs with the people in charge. The network administrator may be most concerned with getting the printers up and running, but the president of the company may care more about e-mail than printing. As with any profession, politics plays a big role in success.

BEING AWARE OF PHYSICAL AND LOGICAL INDICATORS OF NETWORK PROBLEMS

The Network+ exam defines seven specific actions that can reveal network problems:

1. Checking the validity of account names and passwords

2. Rechecking operator logon procedures

3. Checking the status of the server(s)

4. Checking configuration problems with DNS, WINS, and HOST files.

5. Recognizing abnormal physical conditions

6. Isolating and correcting problems with faulty physical media (patch cables)

7. Checking for viruses

When you analyze network client problems, they usually fall under one or more of these areas.

IDENTIFYING, ASSESSING, AND RESPONDING TO PROBLEMS – A SCENARIO APPROACH

Scenario 1: Problems Accessing Application Programs

You are the network administrator of a LAN consisting of 200 computers. Tom calls your help desk to report that he is receiving an error message when he tries to access the company calendar program. The program is located on the NT file server. The proper method of addressing this call is to:

1. Create a problem ticket, or follow the problem tracking procedures established by your company's standard operating procedures (SOPs).

2. Ask Tom for specific error information. If the error is no longer on the screen, have him try to duplicate the steps and record any messages displayed. For this example, assume that the error message indicates that the network resource is not available.

3. Identify the four likely causes:

    A. Is this is a network problem (has a server or a router failed)?

    B. Is this a security issue (does Tom actually have rights to the program)?

    C. Is this an operator error (is Tom properly logged on to the network)?

    D. Is this a software problem (has newly installed software created a conflict somewhere)?

4. To test for network problems, you can either physically look to see if the server(s) is active, checking your own connections and other user connections or if you use network management software and can see if it reports any problems.

5. You can verify that Tom's has rights to the application by using your network administration tools. Additionally, you can log on from your PC using Tom's user name and password to test the connection. If you can successfully access the application, you may ask Tom to try other network applications. If these programs fail as well, having Tom reboot his PC and logging in again may solve the problem. If you suspect there is a login problem, make sure that Tom describes each step he performs, and informs you of any errors or problems that may occur.

6. Software problems may be a bit more difficult to determine. If your network is properly documented, you should be able to determine if any changes or upgrades have been done that may effect Tom's user account, or this particular PC. Compare the client software version to yours (assuming you have been successful at accessing the application). If they differ, you may need to reinstall or upgrade Tom's client software. If everything appears to be correct, it is quite possible that a virus has infected the workstation, and a virus scan would be in order.

For this example, suppose first that the problem was due to the fact that Tom did not log into the network properly. Rather than reading the initial error message that would have identified the login problem, Tom ignored it and proceeded on. Given these circumstances, the solution would have been a *knowledge transfer*. That is to say that you would instruct Tom on how to properly log in to the network, and the types of messages that may be displayed if a login error occurs.

Scenario 2: Misconfigured Network Resources

Danielle works in the advertising department using a Windows NT workstation attached to both an NT server, and a NetWare server. The network protocol is TCP/IP and IPX. The topology is all CAT5, shared 10Mbps Ethernet. One morning Danielle calls your help desk to report that she cannot log in to the network although she successfully connected the previous day. Before beginning your troubleshooting process, you check the problem history log and it shows that Danielle has experienced this problem intermittently before, but no specific problem has been deduced.

According to the Network+ guidelines listed above, the first thing you do is check to see if Danielle's user name and password are still valid. You may have to check both the NT domain account, and the NetWare account. If both accounts have been disabled, and there is no security reason for the disabling, you can re-enable the account and have her try again.

If the accounts are good, you next verify that Danielle is using the proper procedure to log in to the network. Either visually, or by having her describe her actions step-by-step, you instruct Danielle to reenter her user name and password. You remind her that passwords are case sensitive and, therefore, she should make sure the caps-lock key on her keyboard is not activated. (This is a very common cause for rejected passwords, as often passwords are all lower case letters or a mix of upper and lower case.) In order to verify that the login process is not simply an account name/password issue, you have Danielle try logging on as another user. Preferably, you use an administrative account because an administrator's account would not be denied access. (Of course you immediately delete this account, or change the password after the test to avoid breaching security!)

If Danielle still is unable to connect, we check the status of the server(s). Not only do you need to verify that the server(s) are up and running, but that other users are actively connected. If the server is up, but nobody is attached, you can turn your attention to a potential physical problem with the server.

in the real world **If some users are unable to connect to a NetWare server, you should check the total number of licensed connections in use. Once all licensed connections are active, NetWare simply ignores all additional requests to log in. Neither the user nor the administrator will receive messages stating that logins are failing due to maximum license issues. This may manifest itself during the login process if Windows reports that the NetWare server is unknown or unavailable.**

You can safely assume that the problem is not associated with DNS, WINS, or HOST file configurations because Danielle is unable to connect to the NT and the NetWare server, and the network is not configured for TCP/IP on the NetWare side.

Your next step is to check the physical condition of the workstation, and possibly the network. A visual inspection shows that there is a link light on the workstation's NIC that indicates the cable connections are probably okay, and that there is a physical connection from the NIC to the HUB. You cannot be completely certain that the cable system is not causing the problem, but initial indications make it a less likely cause. Noting this, you move on to the next possibility

Because you have maintained a well-documented system (right?), a quick review of recent changes indicates that no new software has been added or updated since the problems began. It is possible, therefore, that a virus has infected this PC. To effectively scan for viruses at the local workstation, you have created a bootable floppy diskette with your anti-virus software. You have also been very diligent in keeping the virus signature files up-to-date. Booting the workstation with this diskette and running the anti-virus software produces no results. Because the workstation behavior otherwise does not indicate typical virus infections, you do not bother running a second virus detection program on this PC.

At this point it makes sense to revisit the cable issue. Begin by replacing the patch cable from the workstation to the wall jack with a known-good patch cable and try logging in again. Because you still are unable to make a connection, you return the original cable and head to the wire closet. Using a laptop computer, you connect to the same port that Danielle's workstation is connected to and find you can successfully connect using her account name and password. This leaves two possibilities: either the cable from the hub to the wall jack is faulty, or the overall length of the cable from PC to server exceeds the Ethernet guideline. Because both of these situations can cause intermittent problems, you decide to call in the cable experts to verify the condition of the cable, and check its point-to-point length.

To wrap this scenario up, the problem was caused by a cable fault at the wall jack. A replacement jack is installed and the problem is solved. All of your testing needs to be documented, including the outcome of the cable tests, and don't forget to follow up the problem ticket documentation.

Scenario 3: Problems Caused by Environmental Issues

Mike Welling, a coworker of mine, tells of this situation:

At approximately 5:00 PM all workstations on a NetWare *v*4.10 LAN loose connection to the server. The network includes a secondary NetWare server that contains a read/write replica of the NetWare Directory. This is a shared Ethernet system with 10BaseT cabling.

After creating the necessary paperwork, Mike first checks the patch cables, the status of the hub, and the LAN driver statistics on both servers. The NICs in both servers are actively passing packets. Utilization on the primary server is noted to be at 99 percent and at 50 percent on the secondary server.

Mike tries logging in with an administrative account, but fails on both servers. On each server, the command Display Servers only identifies itself. (This is a NetWare command used to identify all known servers on the LAN.) Mike then resets both servers and checks the symptoms again. Even though communication between the two servers momentarily occur, utilization quickly returns to 99 percent and to 50 percent respectively, and the Display Servers command again fails to identify each other.

Suspecting a hub or cable problem, Mike removes the cable from the server to the hub and connects his laptop directly into the server via a crossover cable. Using this process, Mike is able to log in and everything appears to be normal. The same setup is equally successful on the secondary server.

At this point, Mike is certain that the problem is a physical one within the cable infrastructure. With all wires back in their original places, Mike begins disconnecting one patch cable at a time and using a DOS workstation to attempt to gain access. Mike selects the DOS station because it was easy to reset if needed, and relatively fast in determining a failed login.

Finally this trial and error process identifies a specific cable that when removed enables the workstation access to the server. It also brings the utilization of the servers back to normal numbers. When reconnected, server utilization again jumps up and workstation connections are lost. A discussion with the customer indicates that the workstation connected on this cable had been added to the network about a week prior. Mike inspects the workstation and finds that a flat, satin, four-pair patch cable connects this PC to the wall jack. The room where this particular PC is located houses mostly telephone equipment (the customer is a local telephone company), and the patch cable was placed over numerous pieces of communication devices. The electrical interference generated by the equipment in this room is causing data packets from this PC to become corrupted and flood the cable system, preventing good data to get through. The problem is finally resolved by replacing the lesser grade cable with CAT 5 and carefully routing the cable away from electrical devices.

Scenario 4: Problems Caused by IP Address Conflicts

Figure 8-1 illustrates this scenario. A network has just been installed and all of the cabling has been tested and certified. Only the Admin user name has been assigned. TCP/IP is the only protocol loaded on a network using DHCP to assign IP addresses to the Windows 9x workstations. Although all configurations appear to be correct, none of the workstations are able to access the file server or the Internet.

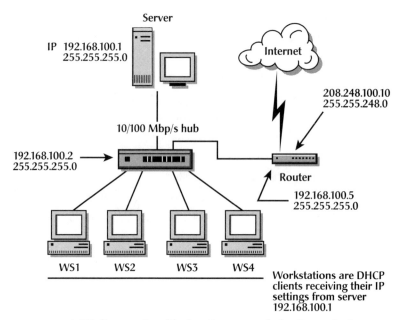

FIGURE 8-1 LAN diagram troubleshooting example for Scenario 4

Because no communication takes place, the first thing you need to test are the physical connections. You start by running the manufacturer's diagnostics on the file server's NIC. This test passes, so we can assume the NIC itself is functioning properly. Next you try removing the hub from the equation by attaching one of the workstations directly into the server using a crossover cable. This test fails, so you can be relatively sure the problem is not a physical one. Your next step is to review the TCP/IP settings. By running the winipcfg utility, you find that the DHCP server assigned this workstation the IP address 192.168.100.100 with a subnet mask of 255.255.255.248. From this information, you should see that the subnet mask defines a separate network for the workstations that prevents you from seeing the rest of the network

By changing the settings on the DHCP server to assign the proper subnet mask of 255.255.255.0, the workstations are finally able to connect to the server. However, none of the PCs are able to access the Internet.

By re-running the winipcfg utility, you see that there is no default gateway defined on the workstation. Again, you modify the values in the DHCP server to also assign a default gateway of 192.168.100.5, and reboot the workstation. With these changes, the workstations can reach the Internet as well as the local LAN.

When you deal with an IP network, it is extremely important to document addressing methods carefully. Improper IP address issues come up again and again in the real world of networking, and although dynamic addressing can make life easier, small mistakes or omissions can cause serious communication problems. The network engineer must remember to double-check all dynamic addresses, subnet masks, default gateways, and WINS and DNS server addresses.

Scenario 5: Hardware Conflict Issues

Refer to Figure 8-2 for the scenario. This NetWare LAN uses the file server configured with two network cards to route between two separate IPX network segments. Occasionally, users on segment B cannot connect to the server or lose their connections for no apparent reason. The network includes two shared 10Mbps hubs, one for each network segment. Assume that your Network Integrator has recently performed a network analysis with a protocol analyzer (discussed later) that indicated that network traffic is within a normal range.

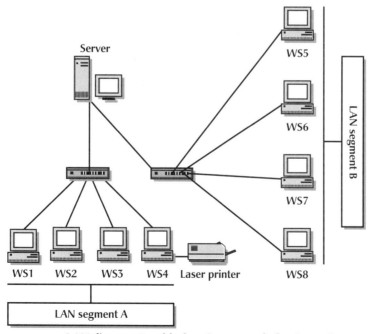

FIGURE 8-2 LAN diagram troubleshooting example for Scenario 5

First you create the proper problem documentation paperwork. Symptoms for dropped connections generally lead you to the physical cable system, or network traffic problems. Because the recent network analysis showed there was no abnormal traffic patterns, you can safely assume for now that the problem is not caused by the cabling system. Therefore, you eliminate the first two items from your troubleshooting checklist: abnormal physical conditions and faulty physical media.

Our next step is to examine the file server. Using NetWare's Monitor utility, you can see that both network cards are active and are passing packets. You also note that utilization is less than 20 percent and only 7 of 100 licensed connections are active. On the surface, none of these items indicate a problematic situation.

The next item on the list is to check configuration problems with DNS, WINS, and HOST files. Because this is a pure IPX network, none of these items are implemented.

A virus could very well cause the type of symptoms described. Our server-based virus software does not report any infections; however, this is not proof that a virus has not infected the network. The first task is to verify that your virus signatures are up-to-date. Your quick check of the vendor's Web site indicates that a newer signature file is available, so you download and install this file. Rescanning the server with the updated virus software still fails to identify an infection. Because there are only eight workstations on this network, and they are all in the same building, you elect to scan each workstation as well, but the results still don't indicate a virus problem.

The next two items on the checklist deal with account names, passwords, and login procedures. Because users are able to connect to the server sometimes, you can generally be sure that these items do not cause the problems. Therefore, you have narrowed down the possibilities to something within the routing mechanism, or the connection components between the server and network segment B.

You then try to duplicate the problem with the minimal number of components possible. First you shut down all workstations and restart the server. Once the server is back up, you check the NIC statistics to be sure the protocols have bound properly to the cards, and that the packets are being transmitted. Noting that these things are within expected ranges, you bring up one PC on LAN A.

WS1 on LAN A successfully connects to the network. Next, you bring up workstation WS5 on LAN B. This station, too, connects properly. Your review of the hubs indicates that connections exist, and packet traffic is present. From both workstations, you perform a number of large file transfers to the server. Neither workstation loses connection.

When you examine your network diagram, and think through the daily communications processes that normally occur, you see that WS4 has a printer connected to it that is shared using a Windows 9x file and print sharing. You also see that all workstations on LAN B have access to this printer. To eliminate as many variables as possible, you shut down WS1 and boot up WS4. WS4 connects properly to the network and you see that WS5 remains attached as well. Now you try sending a print job from WS5 to the laser printer on WS4. The first page prints just fine, but before the job finishes, WS5 loses its connection to the server. Now that you have duplicated the problem, you must review the communications leading to the failure.

On the surface, the problem appears to be related to the printing process. The most common explanation would be either a corrupted print queue (file), or, possibly, that there is not enough disk space to spool the print job. However, a less obvious factor here is, in fact, the more likely possibility. From your trials, it appears that the connections remain active as long as no routing occurs between the two segments. Once you sent a print job to WS4, the server had to route the packets from segment B to segment A. Because printing is an intermittent activity, this process may explain the randomness of our disconnects.

When you review the settings on your server's network cards, you see that the NIC connected to segment A is using IRQ 2, and the NIC connected to segment B uses IRQ 9. As you may remember from Chapter 4, IRQ 2 and IRQ 9 actually share a single physical interrupt. While the cards initialize properly, and work independently without a problem, once you attempt to use both cards simultaneously across the two segments, the interrupts cause a conflict that causes one side of the internal router to fail. By reconfiguring your NICs to use IRQ 10 and 11, the problem is resolved and you can now cross segments without losing connections.

Additionally, it is important to understand that, by coincidence, the users on LAN A always log in to the network before users on LAN B. If, however, someone on LAN B were to connect first, symptoms would not have been limited to LAN B, but rather would have shown up on either segment depending on the login order.

Scenario 6: Dealing with Protocol Problems

A special thank you to Dave Schueller, my technical editor, for supplying this real situation, as well as Scenario 7:

A large medical facility calls you, the network integrator, stating that no one can print using one particular print server. This customer operates 24 hours a day, 7 days a week, and for the most part, this account maintains and alters it own network. The network consists of an NT 4 server, many Windows 95 workstations, and UTP media. It was installed by your company over a year ago and has worked fine for months. The network uses TCP/IP and NetBEUI.

Upon arrival you examine the Print Server node. It appears to be in a normal idle state waiting for a print job. When you try to print from a workstation, you get an error message with reference to not being able to find the print server on the network. When you examine the Properties dialog box for this printer, it shows that you are attempting to print to the port \\Fiery\Print. You also note that the printer icon is grayed out. Upon rebooting the print server, the printer icon at the workstation becomes solid again and you can print without a problem. However in about ten minutes, the print server drops off the network and the printer icon on the workstation grays out. The print server appears to be normal. You print out a configuration page from the print server and everything seems in order. You decide to ping the print server from the workstation and it pings fine. Yet you can not print to it. After rebooting the print server, everything is back up and operational for about ten minutes until, once again, the print server drops off the network. The printer icon grays out but you can still ping the print server. The medical facilities technician insists the problem is the print server that you sold them, and that nothing has changed on the network. To assist in the troubleshooting process, you replace the print server with a new one.

However, this print server also uses the NetBEUI protocol and appears to operate properly when first booted up. But in ten minutes the print server drops off the network. Now it dawns on you that this ten minute time span points to the amount of time NetBIOS name resolution is kept in cache on any work station. Upon rebooting the print server, a broadcast is made, the cache is updated, and then your workstation can resolve the NetBIOS name of \\Fiery\Print. Yet after the cache is flushed, the name can no longer be resolved. Why? You confidently and respectfully inform the customer that they have a NetBIOS name resolution problem and something must have changed on the network. You review the documentation for the network and discover that a PC was added and assigned the same IP address as the print server. It so happens that this took place on the same afternoon the print server started dropping off the network.

Assigning duplicate IP address is a fairly common error; you can never be sure what results will appear on the network. Typically your routers and servers are statically assigned an address. In a large organization your documentation is key to keeping the right hand informed as to what the left hand is doing.

Scenario 7: When All Else Fails . . .

You have been asked to setup a small NetWare 4.11 network on your show floor to demonstrate a new print server your company is selling. The LAN consists of a file server, a workstation, the print server box, and a five-port hub. The UTP cables are all within Ethernet specifications and they are in good condition. The LAN is configured for the IPX 802.3 frame type. You create your print queue object, printer object, and print server object via NWADMIN.

Next you get on the print server box and begin the procedures to configure it. You have the MONITOR.NLM utility running on the file server so you can see your print server log on to the network. You are in configuration mode on the print server, and you scan the tree on the file server to get your print server's name and queue name loaded into your new print server box. You finish configuring the print server, exit the configuration utility, and reboot. The print server comes up ready but does not log in to the file server. You have enough user licenses because the print server box does indeed require a license to log on to the file server. The configuration of the print server appears to be in order. The question is why does it log on to the network during configuration but not when you want to run it as a print server? You can see the frames passing through the hub.

Most packets on a NetWare network are IPX, but when reliable communication is required, SPX is used. You find that communication with a print server is one of those SPX situations. You walk over to your five-port hub, unplug the AC power adapter and plug it back into the wall (reset the hub). Next you reboot your print server box and it logs in to the network. For some reason the hub was not passing SPX packets until the unit was reset. The point in this scenario is that no matter what NOS you work with, hardware restarts, reboots, and reinitializations may cure a multitude of problems.

ADVANCED NETWORK DIAGNOSTICS USING A PROTOCOL ANALYZER

I've discussed a number of troubleshooting processes and tools, but have only briefly mentioned the *protocol analyzer*. Using this advanced diagnostic tool is sometimes the only way to truly identify critical network conditions. A protocol analyzer, sometimes called a *network analyzer*, or a *sniffer*, can be either a dedicated hardware solution, or a software component loaded on a PC or laptop computer. The analyzer *sees* every data packet that passes along the cable and has the capability to present hundreds of statistical analysis. Many modern network cards increase their performance by dropping all erroneous data packets. For normal day-to-day processes, you don't want the network card passing bad packets up the protocol stack only to be discarded at a higher level. However, if you use an analyzer to locate and identify problems on the cable system, you want to see all packets, good and bad. In order to accomplish this, the NIC used by the analyzer must be capable of running in a mode termed *promiscuous*. A promiscuous mode NIC passes every single packet up through the application layer so that the protocol analyzer software can decode and examine the data packets.

A primary function of the analyzer is to capture and display data packets. A network engineer must fully understand how the protocol is analyzed to properly decipher the data packets. This calls for an advanced understanding of how a data packet is formed, and what each bit of the packet represents. This is typically a specialty and not something most engineers in the field use. If this area is of interest to you, I list several good resource recommendations in Appendix B.

However, many analyzers examine the data and present very useful statistics that do not require in-depth understanding of packet formation. For example, most analyzers display a table showing the number of broadcasts, multicasts, errors, fragments, and other malformed packets by MAC and/or IP address. Using this information, an engineer can quickly identify situations where broadcast floods are degrading network performance. Likewise, if a NIC driver becomes corrupt, it may start *jabbering*. This simply means that the card is constantly sending out bad data bits on the cable without regard to the rules of the protocol. For example, on an Ethernet LAN, the NIC driver may not perform the back-off algorithm rule of the CSMA/CD protocol. The result is that a single NIC saturates the cable and prevents all other devices from communicating.

The analyzer software is also able to show statistics such as the top ten *talkers*. (See Figure 8-3.) Logic tells you that the devices sending the most data should be file servers because they are communicating with many devices on the LAN. If this report indicates that the workstations are talking more than the servers are, you can do further analysis to find out why. This may lead you to problems that might otherwise go undetected.

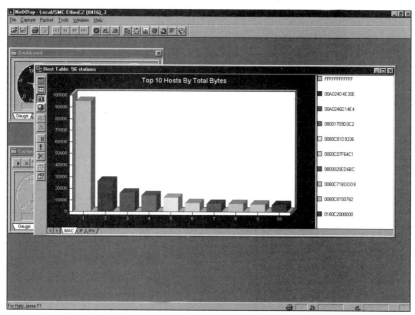

FIGURE 8-3　Top ten talkers as seen by a protocol analyzer

Figure 8-4 is another example taken from a protocol analyzer that graphically displays data communications between end nodes on the network. In a true client/server environment, this graphic shows nearly all of the traffic crossing the sphere horizontally toward file servers. If however, you see many connections running vertically, you can quickly determine that many nodes are running peer-to-peer services. This type of information is critical when evaluating performance and security issues.

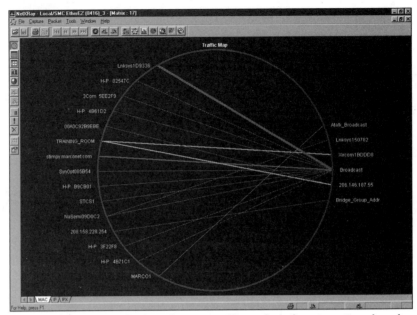

FIGURE 8-4 **A graphic display of a LAN traffic analysis from a protocol analyzer**

There are a number of analyzers available on the market, priced from a thousand dollars for software only solutions to twenty or thirty thousand for very sophisticated hardware products. One analyzer that provides the most useful features, priced in the one thousand-dollar range is Network Associate's Sniffer Basic (formerly known as NetXRay) A 30-day evaluation copy can be downloaded from Network Associate's web page (www.nai.com).

Although quite a bit of learning is required before an analyzer is truly beneficial, it's a tool that should be evaluated when serious troubleshooting requirements arise. Even if you choose not to use this product yourself, at least be aware of the information it can provide. If you suspect you have a network problem that may be easier to isolate with an analyzer, you can often purchase this service on a contract basis.

DEVELOPING A LOGICAL APPROACH TO PROBLEM SOLVING

Throughout this book, I've discussed troubleshooting methods using a structured approach. Your skills will become refined as you gain experience. When you approach any network problem, be aware that often the solution is subtle, and difficult to uncover. Whenever possible, draw out a diagram of the suspect components. Much like the figures in this book demonstrate, it is sometimes necessary to step back and look at the big picture.

When a problem arises that you are unable to quickly identify (such as a broken communication link, a bad login, a wrong password, and so on), you need to develop a logical thought process. Your first mental step is to take the available information and draw a conclusion pointing to the most likely causes of the problem. Remember, however, symptoms can be deceiving. You've seen a number of cases throughout this book where the obvious solution may fix a symptom but leaves the root problem unresolved. It is crucially important to eliminate as many variables surrounding a problem as possible. You've reviewed some of these processes already. For example, when workstations have problems connecting to the server, even though the physical links appear to be operating properly, you can eliminate certain components by testing the connections directly with a crossover cable. When you use vendor-supplied diagnostics, you can eliminate many hardware problems. And by maintaining detailed installation and change records, you are much more likely to identify software-related conflicts. The main point to consider when you approach a problem is to gather all available information and narrow down the probable causes through a detailed process of elimination. The remaining data will provide a reasonable starting point to draw some basic conclusions, formulate a theory, and test that theory.

PARTING THOUGHTS

A successful network engineer avails him or herself to all available resources. Remember that your toolkits should contain more than a couple feet of wire, a few screwdrivers, and some loopback plugs. You also need to keep your vendor CD subscriptions current, stay up-to-date with changing technologies, network with other engineers, and constantly continue your education. As I mention at the beginning of this book, this field changes rapidly. It is inconceivable to think that you will one day understand *all* aspects of the business. The Network+ program is an excellent starting point for beginning a career in computer networking, but it is only a beginning. While there is no substitute for experience and on-the-job training, you individually need to constantly pursue continuing education and self-improvement.

EXAM PREPARATION SUMMARY

This chapter wraps up your study for the Network+ exam, and network basics in general. From the very beginning, my goal has been not only to teach you what you need to know for the exam, but, to equally, give you necessary knowledge to start your career. This final chapter discussed many issues regarding the troubleshooting process and identified many of the real world pitfalls you're likely to run into. Remember to keep your documentation current, and include visual diagrams whenever possible. When looking at a network problem, remember the goal is to eliminate as many variables as possible, and to start with a logical conclusion based on all available information. Always remain aware of physical and logical indicators, and, specifically, follow these seven steps of action:

1. Check the validity of account names and passwords

2. Recheck operator logon procedures

3. Check the status of the server(s)

4. Check configuration problems with DNS, WINS, and HOST files.

5. Recognize abnormal physical conditions

6. Isolate and correct problems with faulty physical media (patch cables)

7. Check for viruses

If you think through your problems in a logical manner, and try to visualize what should be happening on your network, you will find the troubleshooting process to be more effective and less time-consuming. When necessary, or as available, use a protocol analyzer to see precisely what is actually taking place.

Lastly, remember that networking is an ever-changing technology. The tools and procedures you practice so religiously today may very well be outdated next year. There is no substitute for experience, but continuing education is the key to keeping your skills sharp and guaranteeing your continued success in the networking field.

APPLYING WHAT YOU'VE LEARNED

The following review questions give you an opportunity to test your knowledge of the information presented in this chapter. The answers to these assessment questions can be found in Appendix A. If you miss questions, review the sections in this chapter that cover those topics before going further.

1. When a problem is first called in, the first step in the troubleshooting process is to:

   A. Check the status of the server(s)

   B. Check the user's login account name and password

   C. Document the problem request

   D. Scan for viruses

2. When a communication problem exists in a shared Ethernet network, the way to eliminate the largest variable is to:

   A. Replace all hubs with switches

   B. Connect directly to the server using a crossover cable

   C. Remove network cables one at a time until the problem goes away

   D. Reboot the servers and try connecting again

3. If a user complains that the server is rejecting his or her login, and you have verified that the account name is valid and active, a likely cause for this may be:

   A. The user has their caps-lock key on and the password contains lower case letters

   B. The user has attempted to login more times than the network permits

   C. The DHCP addresses are improperly configured

   D. The default gateway is missing

4. When you suspect a virus has infected a workstation on your network, the best way to initiate a virus scan is to:

   A. Run the virus software from the network if the network is continually monitored for viruses

   B. Run the virus software from another workstation

   C. Run the virus software from a known virus-free workstation

   D. Boot the workstation with a write-protected diskette that contains the anti-virus software.

5. When prioritizing multiple problems, the most important issue is:

    A. Understanding the politics of the organization and following the companies priorities for the specific situation

    B. Getting the primary file servers back on line first because nothing else on the network can function without the server

    C. Making sure the payroll department is able to process checks even if it means installing their applications on a standalone PC

    D. Asking the president of the company if she or he has any urgent e-mail that needs to be processed before starting on other aspects of the network

6. If you suspect that serious communication problems are not due to physical components, but none of your other tests identify a problem, you might look for these conditions using a protocol analyzer:

    A. Workstations that are *talking* more that servers

    B. Jabber, excessive broadcasts, and/or excessive multicasts

    C. Unusual high occurrence of peer-to-peer communications on a basically client/server network

    D. All of the above

7. A user calls the help desk complaining that he is not able to log in to the server. The Ethernet network consists of 20 PCs running only TCP/IP. IP addresses are statically assigned. The results from the winipcfg utility appear to be correct and all required addresses (IP, subnet, DNS, default, and default gateway) are present. What else is a logical item to check?

    A. If a router has failed

    B. If the IP address that was statically assigned to this PC is already used by another device on the network

    C. If a NIC is jabbering, which causes so much traffic on the cable system that no other PCs can communicate

    D. All of the above

8. A user calls the help desk complaining that she is not able to reach the Internet. The network consists of 200 PCs running both IPX and TCP/IP. IP addresses are dynamically assigned with a DHCP server on every segment. The results from the winipcfg utility appear to be correct and all required addresses (IP, subnet, DNS, and default gateway) are present. What else is a logical item to check?

A. If the NetWare server has reached its maximum number of licensed connections

B. If the server has failed

C. If other users are able to get to the Internet

D. If this workstation's IP address has been assigned to another device on the network

9. Users complain that the network performance is sluggish. There are only ten users on this LAN and NetBIOS is the only protocol in use. What service can be added to this network to increase performance?

A. WINS to resolve NetBIOS names without resorting to broadcasts

B. DNS or HOST files to resolve names without resorting to broadcasts

C. 100Mbps network cards and switches

D. Add TCP/IP because this protocol is more efficient

10. Users suddenly start to loose connections to the file server. Your documentation indicates that nothing new has been added or changed on the network for almost a week. You have updated virus software running on the server and each workstation, and there are no indications that a virus has invaded the system. All cabling is certified as within distance limits and is made from high quality material. A visual inspection does not indicate problems with the physical cabling. None of the normal tests locate any abnormalities. Your boss gives you the authority to *do what it takes* to identify and correct the problem. Which of these options is a logical next step? (Select two answers.)

A. Replace all of the NICs with new 32-bit cards

B. Purchase a Protocol Analyzer and take a three-day class to learn how to use it

C. Hire a senior systems engineer to analyze the network with a protocol analyzer

D. Install a promiscuous mode NIC, and then download an evaluation copy of a protocol analyzer and use it to see if it detects any unusual traffic patters or network errors

Answers to Chapter Review Questions

CHAPTER 1: THE BASICS OF NETWORKING TECHNOLOGIES

1. Define a LAN:

A local area network (LAN) is a communication system that shares data between devices.

2. Define a WAN:

A wide area network (WAN) is a communication system that connects two or more LANs over a large geographic area.

3. What type of network is composed of a number of computers that connect to a central computer for file storage, printing, and shared applications?

Client/server

4. What type of network topology is depicted by a single cable where devices connect using *T* connectors?

B. Bus

5. What type of network topology is usually depicted when a hub is used with Ethernet?

A. Star

6. Name the three most popular network operating systems used today:

- Netware (Novell Corporation)
- NT (Microsoft)
- Unix (various vendors)

7. Which operating system uses IPX as its default protocol?

Netware

8. Which operating systems use TCP/IP as their default protocols?

o NT

o UNIX

9. Why is disk redundancy important, and what characteristics are common to all RAID levels?

Redundancy provides on-line protection of data and reduces the amount of time a network is unavailable for use due to hard disk failures. All RAID systems use at least two hard drives.

10. What level of RAID is defined by using three or more disk drives where the data is stripped across all drives in the array?

RAID 5

11. What RAID level offers the greatest performance?

RAID 0

12. What RAID level offers the least fault tolerance?

RAID 0. It is the only RAID technology that does not provide fault tolerance

13. What happens when a device is disconnected from the middle of a BUS network?

All other devices lose their network connections

14. What type of cable is used on a 100BaseT network?

Category 5: Unshielded twisted-pair

15. Name the maximum distances of 10Base2, 100BaseTx, and 10Base5:

10Base2	200 meters
100BaseTx	150 meters
10Base5	500 meters

16. What is a crossover cable typically used for?

It is typically used to directly connect two devices together. These devices can be a combination of hubs or switches, or two PCs.

17. If your Ethernet LAN contains a large number of devices and performance is poor, what type of device can you install to create more collision domains?

A bridge

18. What kind of device might you need if you wanted to connect your corporate LAN to the Internet?

A router

19. A modem would be normally used in:

B. Broadband communications

20. What are some advantages of a client/server network over a peer-to-peer network?

Client/server architecture can scale to hundreds or thousands of connected devices; it provides a central location for all data storage; it can share peripherals without causing performance problems on an end-user computer; and it can incorporate extremely high levels of data security.

CHAPTER 2: THE OSI MODEL AND NETWORK DEVICES

1. What is the OSI model, and why is it important?

The OSI model is a generally accepted standard for facilitating data communications between devices on a network. It is important because in a multi-vender environment, manufacturers and programmers need some guidance as to what their products must be capable of in order to fit into a network comprised of various other products.

2. Name the seven layers of the OSI model:

1. Application
2. Presentation
3. Session
4. Network
5. Transport
6. Data-Link
7. Physical

3. At which layer are hardware addresses maintained?

The Data-Link Layer (Layer 2)

4. Which layer of the OSI model is responsible for packaging and transmitting data on the physical media?

The Physical Layer (Layer 1)

5. Which layer of the OSI model is responsible for creating, maintaining, and tearing down of the data transportation connections?

The Transport Layer (Layer 4)

6. Which layer of the OSI model is concerned with network applications such as Telnet and FTP?

The Application Layer (Layer 7)

7. What layer of the OSI model is concerned with user applications such as word processing and spreadsheets?

None. This level of functionality is not addressed within the OSI model.

8. At which layer of the OSI model are the functions of TCP and IP defined?

The Transport Layer (Layer 4)

9. How many categories are defined by the IEEE 802 committee?

12

10. What networking system is described by the 802.2 standard?

Ethernet

11. What networking system is described by the 802.5 standard?

Token Ring

12. Name four physical layer devices:

1. Hubs

2. Transceivers

3. MAUs

4. Repeaters

13. What are two types of Ethernet hubs?

o Passive

o Active

14. What is a transceiver typically used for?

To convert the physical connection from one Ethernet type to another

15. How many Ethernet collision domains are created when you connect two active hubs together?

One

16. When is a repeater useful to extend cable length signals?

It is useful in areas that contain large amounts of electrical interference because the signal is regenerated — not simply amplified.

17. Why is there a limit to the number of MAUs that can be connected together in a standard Token Ring network?

If there are too many devices connected into a stack of MAUs, the time it takes for any one device to gain control of the token in order to communicate may be unacceptable.

18. How many devices can communicate simultaneously within a Token Ring LAN?

One

19. What are three common items that must be configured correctly when installing a Network Interface Card (NIC)?

- IRQ
- DMA
- I/O Address

20. When you troubleshoot connection problems, you can confirm that physical layer devices are communicating by visually inspecting _____ on the NIC and hub.

The link light

21. What is the name of a common test performed on a NIC with vendor supplied diagnostic software?

A loopback test

22. Name two driver interfaces that enable a NIC to communicate on more than one protocol:

- NDIS
- ODI

23. Bridges operate at the _____ OSI level.

Data-Link Layer

24. Which bridging method is commonly used in an Ethernet with only one bridge?

Transparent bridging

25. Where are bridging address tables maintained when using source-route bridging?

On each PC on the network

26. What bridging protocol can be used to prevent bridge looping when more than one physical path exists between two or more network segments?

The spanning tree protocol

27. Which two methods do switching hubs use to transport data between devices?

- Cut-through
- Store-and-forward

28. Which method of transporting data with a switch is fastest?

Cut-through

29. Can switching hubs propagate broadcast packets on the network?

Yes

30. How many physical addresses can be assigned to a NIC?

One

31. What are the two types of routing connections?

- Connectionless
- Connection orientated

32. Which type of routing connection would typically fragment data packets?

Connectionless

33. Which types of connections are usually established across the layers of a WAN?

Connectionless

34. When would a brouter be useful?

In environments where both routable and non-routable protocols exist

35. Which type of device is used to connect an external digital signal to an in-house line?

Digital (or Data) Service Unit/Channel Service Unit or DSU/CSU

36. Name two routing protocols and the characteristics they use to determine routes:

- Routing Information Protocol (RIP) performs route discovery based on hops
- Open Shortest Path First (OSPF) performs route discovery based on the available bandwidth

37. Which device is required to connect networks using different protocols, such as IPX and TCP/IP?

A gateway

38. What can be defined within a router to assure that packets addressed to networks the router is unaware of can be forwarded on?

The default gateway

39. At which layer of the OSI model does routing occur?

The Network Layer

40. What type of routing table is used when routers are not configured to share address tables?

Static

CHAPTER 3: THE FUNDAMENTALS OF TCP/IP

1. What are devices connected on a TCP/IP network commonly referred to as?

Hosts

2. Name two protocols in the TCP/IP suite that function at the Transport Layer of the OSI model:

- TCP
- UDP

3. IP is responsible for sorting and _____ packets.

Delivering

4. What is the first octet range for a Class A IP address?

1–126

5. What is the first octet range for a Class B IP address?

128–191

6. What is the first octet range for a Class C IP address?

192–223

7. What is the reserved *loopback* IP address that can be used to test the configuration of the local IP device?

127.0.0.1

8. Is the IP address 132.10.0.15 valid?

Yes

9. Is the IP address 192.168.10.0 valid?

No, hosts cannot be 0

10. What is the *maximum* number of host IDs available on a Class C address?

254 (0 and 255 are invalid IDs)

11. How many network addresses are needed when routers connect two LANs?

One for each LAN, and a third for the path between the routers

12. If two devices on a LAN are unable to communicate, what two common IP addressing problems should be investigated first?

- The possibility that the IP addresses contain different network numbers
- The possibility that two devices have the same IP address configured

13. What is the default subnet mask for a Class A address?

255.0.0.0

14. What is the default subnet mask for a Class B address?

255.255.0.0

15. What is the default subnet mask for a Class C address?

255.255.255.0

16. When is a subnet required?

Anytime you assign an IP address to a device

17. How many bits are subnets comprised of?

32

18. The process of subnetting can be useful to create additional _____.

Networks

19. What are the two methods used to assign IP addresses?

- Static
- Dynamic

20. What is DHCP used for?

To dynamically assign IP addresses

21. In addition to IP addresses, what information can a DHCP server assign?

- Subnet Mask
- Default gateway
- DNS server address

22. What does a host do first to request a dynamic IP address?

It issues a broadcast requesting a DHCP server on the local network segment.

23. What is the default lease life of a dynamically assigned IP address?

C. 72 hours

24. How many network segments can a single DHCP server provide services to?

One

25. Describe the basic concept of name resolution:

It is the method of associating a host name to its IP or MAC address.

26. What is the primary protocol used for name resolution?

ARP

27. Which type of address does ARP resolve?

A MAC (hardware) address

28. What is the first thing ARP does when attempting to resolve a host name?

It looks for a matching entry in its cache (ARP cache).

29. By default, ARP entries are retained in memory for:

A. Two minutes unless they have been reused, then they are retained up to 10 minutes

30. What is the file name that resides locally on a host, and contains host names and their IP addresses?

Host files

31. What name resolution protocol is most commonly used in large environments, including the Internet?

DNS

32. Name four popular top-level domain names: (Six possible answers are listed.)

- COM
- ORG
- EDU
- GOV
- MIL
- NET

33. What is the primary DNS server known as?

The root server

34. What is the order in which a server named `rocky.bullwinkle@cartoon.com` is located in a typical DNS request?

Root ⇒ COM servers ⇒ Cartoon servers ⇒ Bullwinkle servers ⇒ Rocky server

35. In which operating systems would you typically find NetBIOS?

Microsoft Windows

36. NetBIOS is routable:

A. Never

37. What are the five methods NetBIOS uses to resolve names to addresses?

- By looking up in cache
- From a WINS server
- By local broadcast
- From a local hosts file
- From a DNS server

38. What is the order that a router uses to search for a path in the routing table?

B. Host, subnet, network, default

39. What is the difference between a multicast and a broadcast?

A broadcast is sent to and reviewed by every host on the segment; a multicast is sent only to a specific group of hosts.

40. TCP is:

C. Connection-orientated and reliable

41. What are the commonly used port numbers known as:

Well-known ports

42. When a unique IP address *and* port number are used to identify a specific connection between two hosts, a _____ is created.

Socket

43. UDP is:

B. Connectionless and unreliable

44. Name two services that use UDP as their transport protocol: (Four possible answers are listed.)

- TFTP
- SNMP
- DNS
- NFS

45. What is the function of the FTP protocol?

To transport files between two hosts on a TCP/IP network

46. What is the difference between FTP and TFTP?

FTP uses TCP for reliable transfers and offers basic security such as user names and passwords. TFTP uses UDP and does not offer security features.

47. Where are you most likely to see the Hypertext Transport Protocol (HTTP) used?

On the Internet to display Hypertext Markup Language (HTML) pages.

48. What is the basic message handling method of the POP3 protocol?

Store and forward. All mail received at a POP3 server is held until a client requests the information, and then all of the messages are forwarded to the client at once.

49. What protocol is used between e-mail servers?

Simple Mail Transport Protocol (SMTP)

50. What is the standard protocol for network management features?

Simple Network Management Protocol (SNMP)

51. When a managed threshold is exceeded, a management agent issues a:

    B. Trap

52. What are two main benefits of a proxy server?

    - It removes the need for multiple registered IP addresses for Internet access

    - It removes the need to run IP on the network to gain access to the Internet

53. What is the first recommended check when troubleshooting connectivity problems across a WAN link?

    Verify that the host has a valid default gateway assigned

54. What simple utility can you use to see if a TCP/IP device is active?

    Ping

55. What is an easy method to use to see if name resolution is functioning on a TCP/IP network?

    Ping a known good host by its device name instead of its IP address

56. What information does TRACERT provide that ping does not?

    The number of hops taken for the test packet to reach the destination, and the round trip time

57. What utility can you use to see the local IP address, subnet mask, and default gateway of every NIC in your host?

    Ipconfig (winipcfg in Windows 9.x)

58. What utility provides you with current TCP/IP network connection statistics?

    Netstat

59. What utility could you use to access a router or a UNIX server using a text-based connection?

    Telnet

60. What utility provides a list of NetBIOS names and IP address that have been resolved on the network?

    NBTSTAT

CHAPTER 4: REMOTE ACCESS TECHNOLOGIES

1. Your customer has a number of salespeople that need access to the company inventory files. The data is accessed through a spreadsheet program that is loaded on each of their laptops. Which is the best remote access method to deploy?

   B. Remote node

2. The key payroll person at a company will be on maternity leave for three months. During this time, she needs to process payroll from home. For security reasons, the payroll applications are only installed on her office PC. Which method of remote access is best?

   A. Remote control

3. A company plans to upgrade a major piece of software that requires training 100 people. Rather than sending the instructor to six different cities over five months, the company would like to use technology to make training more efficient. What remote technology can you suggest to help train large numbers of dispersed employees?

   A. Remote control

4. A company opens a small branch office within the local dialing zone. The office needs three people to have access to the main computer to run the 32-bit Windows version of Microsoft Office suite. It is not important that users are connected at all times, but they may need simultaneous access. The company's network hardware is centrally located with easy access to the company's PBX telephone system. Which remote solution would best suit these needs?

   C. WinFrame or Terminal Server

5. When designing a remote access solution, the main requirement is easy access for remote users who may need access from many different locations. What connectivity method would be best to implement?

   B. POTS

6. How many channels are required for an ISDN line to operate?

   C. At least three; two *B* channels for data, and one *D* channel for signaling

7. What is the major roadblock to providing full digital service over POTS?

    A. The *last mile* of telephone cable is still copper

8. Name two advantages of xDSL technology:

    A. It runs on fiber optic cables and has increased bandwidth

9. What dial-up protocol is capable of passing multiple LAN protocols across the link?

    B. PPP

10. Which dial-up protocol is considered self-configuring?

    B. PPP

11. Which dial-up protocol requires that devices on each end know the other's address?

    A. SLIP

12. What protocol provides an encrypted connection between devices using Virtual Private Networking?

    A. PPTP

13. What three configurations must be checked in order to avoid conflicts that could cause a modem to fail?

    B. Serial COM ports, I/O addresses, and IRQ settings

14. Where do you disable a COM port in order to install an internal modem on COM2?

    C. The system BIOS/CMOS

15. What is the standard IRQ for COM1 and COM3?

    B. 4

16. What would happen if you installed an external modem on COM2 with an I/O address of 0F8-0FF?

    A. The modem would probably fail since this is a common I/O range for the math co-processor

17. A customer calls to say that the new modem he or she just installed is not connecting to his or her Internet Service Provider. A dial tone and the other modem answering can be heard, but the connection is dropped within a few seconds. What might be a logical reason for this?

D. The customer checked the *only connect at this speed* option and the ISP's modems are not as fast as the customer's are.

18. Where would you look to find what IRQs are already assigned on a Windows 95/98 PC?

B. Computer Properties in the Device Manager under Control Panel

19. Your customer calls to complain that their modem randomly disconnects from the Internet even though they have disabled all auto-disconnect features. The telephone company has tested the lines and is certain that there is no unusual noise. What option should you look at first when troubleshooting this problem?

B. Enter the code to disable call waiting in the modem's property screen

20. Remote node technology is a good solution when remote users need data from their personal PC in the office as long as they have applications loaded on their laptops?

B. False

CHAPTER 5: NETWORK SECURITY

1. How many users can share the same user name on a network?

C. Only one; each person must have a unique network name.

2. What three practices will create a good password policy?

B. Mix letter and numbers, use no less than four characters, and no more than nine characters

3. If you require passwords be changed four times a year, how many unique changes are recommended before you allow a previously used password to be used again?

A. Three

4. As a safeguard, an administrator should always:

    A. Create a *super-user* with administrator rights

5. What security model provides the best control over shared resources?

    A. User-level security

6. User-level security requires:

    D. A security provider service

7. In order to share folders in Windows 95, you must:

    B. Add File and Print Sharing services in the network configuration

8. Access types for share-level security consist of:

    A. Read-only, Full, and Depends on Password

9. The number of users that can access a shared resource using user-level security on an NT server is:

    C. Limited to the number of licensed users

10. Access types for printers using user-level security consist of:

    B. Access or No Access

11. A _____ installed on an IPX-based network provides additional network security.

    D. Proxy server

12. More advanced firewall products implement this protection technique:

    B. Stateful inspection

13. The most secure method of transmitting sensitive data is by using:

    C. Public key encryption *(remember that the private key is never transferred!)*

14. Public key encryption consists of:

    A. Two keys; one of which is published for anyone's use

15. First names are the best method of creating network account names.

    Neither True nor False. There really isn't a *best* method for all situations.

CHAPTER 6: NETWORK INSTALLATION & TROUBLESHOOTING PRACTICES

1. List, in order, the seven items that define the basic troubleshooting model.

   1. Identify and document the problem

   2. Isolate variables causing the problem

   3. Duplicate the problem

   4. Develop a plan to correct the problem

   5. Implement the corrective action

   6. Test the results

   7. Document the findings

2. Which two environmental conditions need to be checked before installing network servers and connectivity devices?

   o Heat

   o Humidity

3. If the environmental conditions of a room are questionable, you should:

   B. Use specialized testing equipment to verify the heat and humidity over a period of days or weeks

4. If a workstation is located in an area where many small electrical devices are used, how should power to the computer equipment be obtained?

   C. Place the computer on a separate outlet, and use a UPS if electrical drops or surges are identified

5. Before connecting modems to the telephone system, always:

   D. Verify that the wall connection for the modem line is analog

6. When upgrading a workstation, existing applications:

   A. Should be inventoried and a plan to migrate them be documented before the upgrade

7. What devices are commonly used to organize the cabling system in a wire closet?

   D. Patch panels

8. What is a major advantage to using an uninterruptable power supply on file servers?

　A. Most UPSs have software to initiate a safe shutdown before the power is exhausted.

9. What two items are necessary before you can create new users on a network?

　D. An administrative account and knowledge of the company's SOP

10. Specifically, what hardware settings need to be documented before making changes to a workstation?

　A. The NICs, IRQ, I/O address, and software driver

11. What two DOS-related settings should be documented before making changes to a workstation?

　C. Printer captures and batch file settings

12. What is the best method of saving the original state of a PC before making changes?

　B. Replicate the data to the network if space exists and you can easily get to the network from DOS, if necessary

13. Assume a company needs to backup data stored on local workstations as well as the file server. There is not enough space on a single tape to backup all of the data. Which backup method minimizes the amount of tape space needed?

　B. Differential backup

14. What two things are commonly known to cause adverse effects during an upgrade?

　D. Different versions of application software and DLL files

15. What are file server hard drives typically called?

　D. Volumes

16. Assume you have a workstation with two hard drives, and you map a network drive using the command `CAPTURE N SYS:\OFFICE`. Which drive letter is used?

B. F:

17. Using NT, what is the UNC path for the subdirectory DOCS in the OFFICE directory on the file server NTSERVER?

B. `\\NTSERVER\\OFFICE\DOCS`

18. Which command correctly sets up printer redirection to the primary printer port in DOS on a Windows NT network? Assume the server name is NTSERVER and the printer queue is Laser.

A. NET USE LPT1: \\NTSERVER\Laser

19. Reconnecting drives and printers can be automated in NT or NetWare using:

C. Login scripts

20. Profiles and policies are most useful as:

D. Administration tools

21. User Profiles can be used to store user specific settings for some applications.

B. False

22. In an NT environment, user rights:

C. Grant a user the capability to backup the system

23. NT uses this applet to create and maintain most policy features:

C. System Policy Editor

24. NT maintains profiles in _____, where NetWare Version 4 and higher uses _____.

C. Encrypted text files, NDS

25. User policies always take precedence over group policies:

B. False

Chapter 7: Maintaining and Supporting the Network

1. A common file that discusses common issues published by vendors on their Web site is:

A. Frequently Asked Questions (FAQ)

2. If two or more hardware components are listed on a vendor's hardware compatibility list, you can be assured that the hardware will perform as expected in the server?

B. False

3. When replacing a server or workstation, _____ is probably required, and the best approach is to check the vendor's recommended method.

C. Migrating data and applications

4. Before installing new hardware or software, the _____ file should be consulted to see what changes have occurred since the last printing of the documentation.

B. Readme

5. Why is it necessary to look for product documentation on the Web or from other sources when the product includes printed documentation?

A. The product may have been packaged for resale because newer versions have been released or problems have been identified.

6. The best place to locate free technical information is:

C. The vendor's Internet site

7. When searching for an Internet site using popular search engines, what two special characters can be used to include or exclude specific words?

B. The plus (+) and minus (-) signs

8. What name does Microsoft use for their monthly CD subscription service?

B. TechNet

9. What name does Novell use for their monthly CD subscription service?

   D. NetWare Support Connection

10. Under normal circumstances, the preferred backup method is:

    D. Daily full backup with previous night's tape taken off-site

11. A three-tape rotation backup method is best suited:

    B. When a single tape is not large enough for a daily full backup, and less than 25 percent of the data changes daily

12. What four common tape formats are currently in use?

    A. QIC, DAT, DLT, and Travan

13. Digital Audio Tape (DAT) uses _____ recording method, similar to VCR recording.

    C. Helical scan

14. On a monthly basis, tapes should be:

    B. Retentioned

15. Complete virus protection consists of:

    D. Anti-virus software on the server and on the workstations

16. Updates to anti-virus software are commonly known as:

    D. Signatures

17. Two methods of obtaining updates for anti-virus programs are:

    A. Manually download from the Internet

    B. Internet Push technology

18. A bootable floppy disk used for troubleshooting should contain these files:

    D. FORMAT, FDISK, and a text Editor

19. A proper toolkit will likely include these hardware items:

    C. Normal and crossover cables, screwdriver, video card, and loopback plugs

20. A tone generator is useful to detect:

    B. Faulty wiring

CHAPTER 8: TROUBLESHOOTING THE NETWORK

1. When a problem is first called in, the first step in the troubleshooting process is to:

   C. Document the problem request

2. When a communication problem exists in a shared Ethernet network, the way to eliminate the largest variable is to:

   B. Connect directly to the server using a crossover cable

3. If a user complains that the server is rejecting his or her login, and you have verified that the account name is valid and active, a likely cause for this may be:

   A. The user has their caps-lock key on and the password contains lower case letters

4. When you suspect a virus has infected a workstation on your network, the best way to initiate a virus scan is to:

   D. Boot the workstation with a write-protected diskette that contains the anti-virus software

5. When prioritizing multiple problems, the most important issue is:

   A. Understanding the politics of the organization and following the company's priorities for the specific situation

6. If you suspect that serious communication problems are not due to physical components, but none of your other tests identify a problem, you might look for these conditions using a protocol analyzer:

   D. All of the above

7. A user calls the help desk complaining that he is not able to log in to the server. The Ethernet network consists of 20 PCs running only TCP/IP. IP addresses are statically assigned. The results from the winipcfg utility appear to be correct and all required addresses (IP, subnet, DNS, default, and default gateway) are present. What else is a logical item to check?

   B. If the IP address that was statically assigned to this PC is already used by another device on the network

8. A user calls the help desk complaining that she is not able to reach the Internet. The network consists of 200 PCs running both IPX and TCP/IP. IP addresses are dynamically assigned with a DHCP server on every segment. The results from the winipcfg utility appear to be correct and all required addresses (IP, subnet, DNS, and default gateway) are present. What else is a logical item to check?

C. If other users are able to get to the Internet

9. Users complain that the network performance is sluggish. There are only ten users on this LAN and NetBIOS is the only protocol in use. What service can be added to this network to increase performance?

A. WINS to resolve NetBIOS names without resorting to broadcasts

10. Users suddenly start to loose connections to the file server. Your documentation indicates that nothing new has been added or changed on the network for almost a week. You have updated virus software running on the server and each workstation, and there are no indications that a virus has invaded the system. All cabling is certified as within distance limits and is made from high quality material. A visual inspection does not indicate problems with the physical cabling. None of the normal tests locate any abnormalities. Your boss gives you the authority to *do what it takes* to identify and correct the problem. Which of these options is a logical next step? (Select two answers.)

C. Hire a senior systems engineer to analyze the network with a protocol analyzer

D. Install a promiscuous mode NIC, and then download an evaluation copy of a protocol analyzer and use it to see if it detects any unusual traffic patters or network errors

Additional Resources

O ne point that I've tried to drive home is the fact that networking is an ever-changing business. There is no single source for all of the information available on any given topic. The good news, however, is that there are many, many informational sources to tap into. The Internet is by far the largest depository of information to exist, and it will continue to be the largest for the foreseeable future. In this appendix I list a number of Web sites that I find invaluable. As dynamic as the Internet is, please be aware that sites move often; I cannot guarantee how long these addresses will be current.

NETWORKING CONCEPTS, DESIGNS, AND THEORIES

I've created a Web site dedicated to all network professionals, both experienced and beginning. It is a noncommercial site with the sole purpose of helping advance the professionalism of computer networking, and it is a forum to share resources and knowledge with you, my fellow colleagues.

`http://www.Net-Engineer.com`

Here are several other sites I recommend:

o Network Computing online Network Design Manual:

`http://www.networkcomputing.com/netdesign/series.htm`

- Intel's On-line Learning Center (OLC) site enables you to download interactive courses and complete them at your own pace:

  `http://www.intel.com/network/learning_ctr/index.htm`

- The Network Module Underground Map site is a good resource to see how all the protocols fit together.

  `http://www.cne.gmu.edu/modules/network/map-graph.html`

- Microsoft Windows Hardware Compatibility List (HCL) is a compilation of computers and computer hardware that have been extensively tested with Windows operating systems:

  `http://www.microsoft.com/HWTEST/HCL/`

- Cisco System's site is a resource for IP Protocols, White Papers, and other useful information:

  `http://cio-europe.cisco.com/warp/public/732/IP/index.html`

- Daryl's TCP/IP Primer online document gives readers a reasonable working knowledge of TCP/IP subnetting, addressing, and routing:

  `http://ipprimer.2ndlevel.net/section.cfm/2.htm?SectionID=2`

- Hardware Central's Ultimate Guide to Networking is a very good multi-part tutorial on PC networking:

  `http://www.hardwarecentral.com/features/reports/`
  `networking1/?nl`

- Novell's Consulting Toolkit is a must site if you work with NetWare:

  `http://www.consulting.novell.com/toolkit/tkhome.html`

- Homepclan.com is a Web site dedicated to helping you install your own network at home or in the small office:

  `http://www.homepclan.com/`

WINDOWS ADD-ONS, UPDATES, AND TRIAL SOFTWARE

o Microsoft's Windows Update helps you download and install updates:

    `http://www.microsoft.com/windows/downloads/default.asp`

PUBLIC KEY ENCRYPTION PROGRAMS

o Network Associates PGP (Pretty Good Privacy) freeware:

    `http://www.nai.com/products/security/freeware.asp`

o RSA provides a directory of secure products created by their customers:

    `http://www.rsa.com/solutions/`

The Network+ Examination Blueprint

The Network+ exam consists of approximately 75 items, divided into two distinct groups: Knowledge of Networking Technology, and Knowledge of Networking Practices. Appendix C outlines the exam, identifying the test objectives for each category, and closely representing the percentage of the overall test that each section, and each item, weighs on the final exam. The percentages are current as of March 1999.

NETWORK+ EXAM OBJECTIVES

The following table summarizes the categories for each group. The detailed breakdown follows the summary.

I. KNOWLEDGE OF NETWORKING TECHNOLOGY	67%
1. Basic knowledge	16%
2. Physical Layer	6%
3. Data Link Layer	5%
4. Network Layer	5%
5. Transport Layer	4%
6. TCP/IP fundamentals	12%
7. TCP/IP suite: utilities	8%
8. Remote connectivity	5%
9. Security	6%

II. KNOWLEDGE OF NETWORKING PRACTICES	33%
1. Implementing the installation of the network	6%
2. Administering the change control system	4%
3. Maintaining and supporting the network	6%
4. Identifying, assessing, and responding to problems	6%
5. Troubleshooting the network	11%

I. Knowledge of Networking Technology (67%)

I.1 Basic knowledge (16%)

I.1.1 Demonstrate understanding of basic network structure, including:

- The characteristics of star, bus, mesh, and ring topologies, and the advantages and disadvantages to each
- The characteristics of segments and backbones

I.1.2 Identify the following:

- The major network operating systems, including Microsoft Windows NT, Novell NetWare, and Unix
- The clients that best serve specific network operating systems and their resources
- The directory services of the major network operating systems

I.1.3 Associate IPX, IP, and NetBEUI with their functions

I.1.4 Define the following terms and explain how each relates to fault tolerance or high availability:

- Mirroring
- Duplexing

- Stripping (with and without parity)
- Volumes
- Tape backup

1.1.5 Define the layers of the OSI model and identify the protocols, services, and functions that pertain to each layer

1.1.6 Recognize and describe the following characteristics of networking media and connectors:

- The advantages and disadvantages of coax, Cat 3, Cat 5, fiber optic, UTP, and STP, and the conditions under which each is appropriate
- The length and speed of 10Base2, 10BaseT, and 100BaseT
- The length and speed of 10Base5, 100Base VGAnyLan, 100Base TX
- The visual appearances of RJ 24 and BNC, and how each is crimped

1.1.7 Identify the basic attributes, purpose, and function of the following network elements:

- Full- and half-duplexing
- WAN and LAN
- Server, workstation, and host
- Server-based networking and peer-to-peer networking
- Cable, NIC, and router
- Broadband and baseband
- Gateway, as both a default IP router and as a method to connect dissimilar systems or protocols

1.2 Physical Layer (6%)

1.2.1 Given an installation, configuration, or troubleshooting scenario, select an appropriate course of action if a client workstation does not connect to the network after installing or replacing a network interface

card. Explain why a given action is warranted. The following issues may be covered:

o Knowing how the network card is usually configured, including EPROM, jumpers, and Plug and Play software

o Using network card diagnostics, including the loopback test and vendor-supplied diagnostics

o Resolving hardware resource conflicts, including IRQ, DMA, and I/O base address

1.2.2 Identify what the following network components are used for and the differences among them:

o Hubs

o MAUs

o Switching hubs

o Repeaters

o Transceivers

1.3 Data-Link Layer (5%)

1.3.1 Describe the following Data-Link Layer concepts:

o Bridges, what they are and why they are used

o The 802 specs, including the topics covered in 802.2, 802.3, and 802.5

o MAC addresses, their function and characteristics

1.4 Network Layer (5%)

1.4.1 Explain the following routing and Network Layer concepts, including:

o The fact that routing occurs at the Network Layer

o The difference between a router and a brouter

o The difference between routable and nonroutable protocols

o The concept of default gateways and subnetworks

o The reason for employing unique network IDs

o The difference between static and dynamic routing

1.5 Transport Layer (4%)

1.5.1 Explain the following Transport Layer concepts:

o The distinction between connectionless and connection transport

o The purpose of name resolution, either to an IP/IPX address or a network protocol

1.6 TCP/IP fundamentals (12%)

1.6.1 Demonstrate knowledge of the following TCP/IP fundamentals:

o The concept of IP default gateways

o The purpose and use of DHCP, DNS, WINS, and HOST files

o The identity of the main protocols that make up the TCP/IP suite, including TCP, UDP, POP3, SMTP, SNMP, FTP, HTTP, and IP

o The idea that TCP/IP is supported by every operating system and millions of hosts worldwide

o The purpose and function of Internet domain name server hierarchies (how e-mail arrives in another country)

1.6.2 Demonstrate knowledge of the fundamental concepts of TCP/IP addressing, including:

o The A, B, and C classes of IP addresses, and their default subnet mask numbers

o The use of port number (HTTP, FTP, SMTP), and port numbers commonly assigned to a given service

I.6.3 Demonstrate knowledge of TCP/IP configuration concepts, including:

o The definition of IP proxy and why it is used

o The identity of the normal configuration parameters for a workstation,
   including IP address, DNS, default gateway, IP proxy configuration, WINS,
   DHCP, host name, and Internet domain name

I.7 TCP/IP suite: utilities (8%)

I.7.1 Explain how and when to use the following TCP/IP utilities to test, validate, and troubleshoot IP connectivity:

o ARP

o Telnet

o NBTSTAT

o Tracert

o NETSTAT

o ipconfig/winipcfg

o FTP

o ping

I.8 Remote connectivity (5%)

I.8.1 Explain the following remote connectivity concepts:

o The distinction between PPP and SLIP

o The purpose and function of PPTP, and the conditions under which it is useful

o The attributes, advantages, and disadvantages of ISDN and PSTN (POTS)

I.8.2 Specify the following elements of dial-up networking:

o The modem configuration parameters that must be set, including serial
   port IRQ, I/O address, and maximum port speed

o The requirements for a remote connection

I.9 Security (6%)

I.9.1 Identify good practices to ensure network security, including:

- The selection of a security model (user and share level)
- The implementation of standard password practices and procedures
- The need to employ data encryption to protect network data
- The use of a firewall

II. Knowledge of Networking Practices (33%)

II.1 Implementing the installation of the network (6%)

II.1.1 Demonstrate awareness that administrative and test accounts, passwords, IP addresses, IP configurations, relevant sops, and so on must be obtained prior to network implementation.

II.1.2 Explain the impact of environmental factors on computer networks. Given a network installation scenario, identify unexpected or atypical conditions that could either cause problems for the network or signify that a problem condition exists, including:

- Room conditions (for example, humidity, heat, and so forth)
- Building content and personal effects placement (such as space heaters, TVs, radios, and so on)
- Computer equipment
- Error messages

II.1.3 Recognize visually, or by description, common peripheral ports, external SCSI (especially DB-25 connectors), and common network components, including:

- Print servers
- Peripherals

- Hubs
- Routers
- Brouters

II.1.4 Given an installation scenario, demonstrate an awareness of the following compatibility and cabling issues:

- The consequences of trying to install an analog modem in a digital jack
- The uses for RJ-45 connectors that may differ greatly depending on cabling
- The contribution patch cables make to the overall length of the cabling segment

II.2 Administering the change control system (4%)

II.2.1 Demonstrate an awareness of the need to document the current status and configuration of the workstation (such as providing a baseline) prior to making any changes.

II.2.2 Given a configuration scenario, select a course of action that enables the system to return to its original state.

II.2.3 Given a scenario involving workstation backups, select the appropriate backup technique from the following:

- Tape backup
- Folder replication to a network drive
- Removable media
- Multigeneration

II.2.4 Demonstrate an awareness of the need to remove outdated or unused drivers, properties, and so forth when an upgrade is successfully completed.

II.2.5 Identify possible adverse effects on a network caused by local changes (for example, version conflicts, overwritten Dlls, and so on).

II.2.6 Explain the purpose of drive mapping and, given a scenario, identify the mapping that will produce the desired results using Universal Naming Convention (UNC) of an equivalent feature. Explain the purpose of printer port capturing, and identify properly formed capture commands, given a scenario.

II.2.7 Given a scenario where equipment is moved or changed, decide when and how to verify and the functionality of the network and critical applications.

II.2.8 Given a scenario where equipment is being moved or changed, decide when and how to verify the functionality of the equipment.

II.2.9 Demonstrate an awareness of the need for obtaining relevant permissions prior to adding, deleting, or modifying users.

II.2.10 Identify the purpose and the function of the following networking elements:

- Profiles
- Rights
- Procedures/policies
- Administrative utilities
- Login accounts, groups, and passwords

II.3 Maintaining and supporting the network (6%)

II.3.1 Identify test documentation usually available regarding a vendor's patches, fixes, upgrades, and so on.

II.3.2 Given a network maintenance scenario, demonstrate an awareness of the following issues:

- The need for standard backup procedures and backup media storage practices

- The need for the periodic application of software patches and other fixes to the network

- The need to install antivirus software on the server and workstations, and the need to frequently update virus signature

II.4 Identifying, assessing, and responding to problems (6%)

II.4.1 Given an apparent network problem, determine the nature of the required action (such as information transfer vs. handholding vs. technical service).

II.4.2 Given a scenario involving several network problems, prioritize them based on the severity of each.

II.5 Troubleshooting the network (11%)

II.5.1 Identify the following steps as a systematic approach for identifying the extent of a network problem, and, given a problem scenario, select the appropriate next best step based on this approach:

1. Determine whether the problem exists across the network

2. Determine whether the problem is workstation, workgroup, LAN, or WAN

3. Determine whether the problem is consistent and replicable

4. Use standard troubleshooting methods

II.5.2 Identify the following steps a systematic approach for troubleshooting network problems, and, given a problem scenario, select the appropriate next step based on this approach:

1. Identify the exact issue

2. Recreate the problem

3. Isolate the cause

4. Formulate a correction

5. Implement the correction

6. Test

7. Document the problem and the solution

8. Give feedback

II.5.3 Identify the following steps as a systematic approach to determining whether a problem is attributed to the operator or the system, and, given a problem scenario, select the appropriate next step based on this approach:

1. Have a second operator perform the same task on an equivalent workstation

2. Have a second operator perform the same task on the original operator's workstation

3. See whether operators are following standard operating procedure

II.5.4 Given a network troubleshooting scenario, demonstrate an awareness of the need to check for physical and logical trouble indicators, including:

o Link lights

o Power lights

o Error displays

o Error logs and displays

o Performance monitors

II.5.5 Identify common network troubleshooting resources, including:

o Knowledge bases on the World Wide Web

o Telephone technical support

o Vendor CDs

II.5.6 Given a network problem scenario that includes symptoms, determine the most likely cause or causes based on the information available. Select the most appropriate course of action based on this inference. Issues that may be covered include:

- Recognizing abnormal physical conditions
- Isolating and correcting problems in cases where there is a fault in the physical media (patch cable)
- Checking the status of servers
- Checking for configuration problems with DNS, WINS, and HOST files
- Checking for viruses
- Checking the validity of the account name and password
- Rechecking operator logon procedures
- Selecting and running appropriate diagnostics

II.5.7 Specify the tools that are commonly used to resolve network equipment problems. Identify the purpose and function of common network tools, including:

- Crossover cables
- Hardware loopbacks
- Tone generators
- Tone locators (fox and hound)

II.5.8 Given a network problem scenario, select the appropriate tools to help resolve the problem. Methods include:

- Identifying the problem as hardware or software
- Using the Internet or vendor supplied support systems
- Referring to the vendor's published knowledge base and/or support CDs
- Referencing third-party books, white papers, and Web sites

Exam Preparation Tips

This appendix contains some useful tips and pointers to help you prepare for the Network+ Certification exam. Read these pages carefully before you schedule your exam, and review this appendix again just before you take the test. Pay special attention to the exam blueprint in Appendix C and make sure you understand all of the objectives covered on the exam.

Based on the A+ Certification program's success, the Computer Technologies Industry Association (CompTIA) developed Network+ certification. This program targets individuals with the desire to gain formal recognition for their abilities to understand and incorporate the entry-level skills of a network engineer. This non-vendor specific certification is a starting point for individuals with the knowledge and skills necessary to perform basic installation and troubleshooting of computer network components. While the Network+ candidate is not required to have A+ certification, he or she should have, at least, the equivalent in skills, along with 12 to 18 months of practical experience with personal computers and basic networking devices.

HOW THE NETWORK+ EXAM WAS DEVELOPED

In order to develop the exam objectives and formalize the final version of the exam, CompTIA leveraged relationships with many of the industry's leading vendors and recruited industry professionals, both from inside and outside of the organization, to develop the objectives and formalize the final exam. And many vendors offering their own certification programs have stated that they will likely wave their base test requirement to those who are Network+ certified. The following phases were part of the Network+ program development:

1. Identifying subject matter experts (SMEs) to develop test objectives

2. Conducting a blueprint survey to determine the number of test items needed for each objective

3. Writing exam questions

4. Reviewing the exam for technical accuracy, congruence, psychometrics, and grammar

5. Performing a beta test and analyzing it

6. Conducting a cut-score survey to determine the pass/fail rate

7. Completing a final review of the items

Exam Items and Scoring

The Network+ Certification exam questions are derived from an industry-wide job task analysis. The single exam consists of two distinct area groups: Knowledge of Networking Technology and Knowledge of Networking Practices. (This book mirrors the two distinct area groups in its organization.) At the time this book was published, CompTIA stated that there will be approximately 75 questions on the exam. These 75 questions are randomly selected from a much larger pool of questions, so if you take the test more than once, it is not likely that you will receive duplicate items. Each question and each section is given a weighted value (see Appendix C for the weight value chart). While the exact passing score has not yet been established, tests of this nature typically require you to answer 80 to 85 percent correctly in order to pass. If you do fail the exam, you are allowed to retake it as many times as necessary. However, if you study diligently, and take the practice exams presented in this book, you should be able to pass the first time.

The exam questions are a mix of multiple-score, multiple-choice, and (some) true/false. Multiple-score questions have more than one correct answer to a question. Multiple-choice, on the other hand, have a single correct answer.

The test is administered through the Sylvan Prometric Authorized Test Centers. You can schedule your test by calling Sylvan in the United States at 1-888-895-6116. When you call, please have the following available:

1. Your Social Security number. (If you do not have it on hand, or do not wish to use your Social Security number, Sylvan Prometric will provide an ID number.)

2. Your mailing address and telephone number.

3. Your employer or organization (optional).

4. The date(s) you wish to take the test. Depending on where you live, you may not be able to schedule the exam on your preferred date, so be prepared to provide a few alternate dates. The further in advance that you can schedule, the better chance you have of getting your first choice of times.

5. A method of payment (credit card or check). The final exam price has not yet been published, but it will probably be about $100.

Test-Taking Tips

Here are some tips that may be helpful as you prepare to take the Network+ Certification exam.

Before the exam

- Review the Exam Preparation Summary pages at the end of each chapter in this book.

- Answer the questions at the end of each chapter and on the Beachfront Quizzer CD supplied with this book. If you have trouble with questions, review the sections pertaining to the areas that you are not clear on.

- Pay special attention to the exam preparation pointers scattered throughout this book. These pointers help you focus on important exam-related topics.

- When possible, use the knowledge you learn while reading this book. If you have access to a computer lab at school or in your office, try duplicating the problems discussed and install some equipment to see firsthand how the hardware interacts. The IRS allows you to deduct certain expenses for continuing education pertaining to your employment. If you can, purchase a few PCs and some basic networking components and build a small network at home. You don't need the latest and greatest equipment, just about anything that runs will do. Remember: the exam measures real-world skills that you will not obtain simply by reading about them.

- Check out the Internet. There is more information available on the World Wide Web than in a library full of study guides. Review the Web search techniques discussed in Chapter 7 and the suggested Web sites listed in Appendix B.

- Don't study the entire night before the test. A good night's sleep is often better preparation than extra studying. Besides, if you prepare properly, you won't learn anything new by *cramming* the night before.

- Try to schedule your exam during your own *peak* time. In other words, if you're a morning person, avoid scheduling the exam at 3:00 p.m.

- Take the exam preparation process seriously. Remember, this exam is not designed to be easy – it is intended to recognize and certify *professionals* with specific skill sets.

On exam day

- Arrive 10 to 15 minutes early and don't forget your picture ID.

- Dress comfortably. The more comfortable you are, the more you are able to focus on the exam.

- If you carry a pager and/or a cellular telephone, leave them at home, or in your car. You will be asked to remove them before the test, and you don't want to accidentally leave them behind after you leave.

- Don't bring a note pad or other note-taking materials with you. The testing center provides you with such materials. Books, notes, and other such items are not permitted in the test area.

- Don't drink a lot of coffee or other beverages before the exam. The test is timed, and you don't want to waste precious time going back and forth to the restroom.

During the exam

- Answer the questions that you know first. Once you have these questions out of the way, go back to the beginning and answer the ones you're reasonably sure of. Mark any questions that you'd like to spend more time on. You will be able to return to these later.

- Remember that there are no *trick* questions. The correct answer is always among the choices listed. Don't try to read too much into the question; take the information as it is presented.

- Eliminate the most obvious incorrect answers first.

- Answer all of the questions before you end the exam. Unanswered questions are counted as incorrect.

- Read the questions carefully. At first glance, you may think you know the answer right away, but there may be a subtle shift in the way the question is phrased. Approaching the question from one viewpoint may lead you to the incorrect answer.

- Once you have completed the exam, you will receive immediate, online notification of your pass or fail status.

After the exam

- Take a deep breath.

- Make sure the testing administrator certifies your exam report, and take the report with you. Although the report is sent to CompTIA, you want to be sure you have it should you ever need to prove your results.

- If you don't pass, use the report to see where your weak points are. The exam report shows the percentage correct for each area. Go back to this book and spend a good deal of time reviewing these areas. Remember that you probably won't have the exact same questions on your next exam, but you will be tested in the same categories.

- If you did pass, congratulations! Job well done. CompTIA will send you your confirmation and certificate within a few weeks. Don't stop learning now though. Remember that this industry changes quickly. Your next certification test may be only months away.

What's on the CD-ROM

CD-ROM Contents

The CD-ROM included with this book contains the following materials:

- Adobe Acrobat Reader
- An electronic version of this book, *Network+ Certification Study System*, in .pdf format
- BeachFront Quizzer exam simulation software
- Microsoft Internet Explorer Version 5.0

Installing and Using the Software

The following sections describe each product and include instructions for installation and use.

Adobe Acrobat Reader

Adobe's Acrobat Reader is a helpful program that enables you to view the electronic version of this book in the same page format as the actual book.

▼ ▼ ▼

TO INSTALL AND RUN ADOBE'S ACROBAT READER, AND VIEW THE ELECTRONIC VERSION OF THIS BOOK, FOLLOW THESE STEPS:

1. Start Windows Explorer (if you're using Windows 95/98) or Windows NT Explorer (if you're using Windows NT), and then open the `Acrobat` folder on the CD-ROM.

2. In the `Acrobat` folder, double-click `ar32e30.exe` and follow the instructions presented onscreen for installing Adobe Acrobat Reader.

3. To view the electronic version of this book after you have installed Adobe's Acrobat Reader, start Windows Explorer (if you're using Windows 95/98) or Windows NT Explorer (if you're using Windows NT), and then open the `Books\Network+` folder on the CD-ROM.

4. In the `MCSE Network+` folder, double-click the chapter or appendix file you want to view. All documents in this folder end with a `.pdf` extension.

■ ■ ■

BeachFront Quizzer Exam Simulation Software

The version of BeachFront Quizzer software included on the CD gives you an opportunity to test your knowledge by taking simulated exams. The BeachFront Quizzer product has many valuable features, including:

- Study session
- Standard exam
- Adaptive exam
- New exam every time
- Historical analysis ·

If you want more simulation questions, you can purchase the full retail version of the BeachFront Quizzer software from BeachFront Quizzer. See the Beachfront Quizzer ad in the back of the book.

▼ ▼ ▼

TO INSTALL AND RUN BEACHFRONT QUIZZER, FOLLOW THESE STEPS:

1. View the contents of the BeachFront folder.

2. Execute `ExamName.exe`, whereas *ExamName* is the name of the exam you wish to practice.

3. Follow the directions for installation.

■ ■ ■

Microsoft Internet Explorer Version 5.0

This is a complete copy of Microsoft Internet Explorer. With Internet Explorer, you can browse the Internet if you have an Internet connection.

▼ ▼ ▼

TO INSTALL AND RUN MICROSOFT INTERNET EXPLORER, FOLLOW THESE STEPS:

1. Start Windows Explorer (if you're using Windows 95/98) or Windows NT Explorer (if you're using Windows NT), and then open the `\ie5` folder on the CD-ROM.

2. In the `\ie5 directory`, double-click `Setup.exe` and follow the instructions presented onscreen for installing Microsoft Internet Explorer.

3. To run Microsoft Internet Explorer, double-click the Internet Explorer icon on the desktop.

■ ■ ■

Index

Symbols and Numbers

A

continued

continued

continued

continued

IDG BOOKS WORLDWIDE, INC.
END-USER LICENSE AGREEMENT

<u>READ THIS</u>. You should carefully read these terms and conditions before opening the software packet(s) included with this book ("Book"). This is a license agreement ("Agreement") between you and IDG Books Worldwide, Inc. ("IDGB"). By opening the accompanying software packet(s), you acknowledge that you have read and accept the following terms and conditions. If you do not agree and do not want to be bound by such terms and conditions, promptly return the Book and the unopened software packet(s) to the place you obtained them for a full refund.

1. <u>License Grant</u>. IDGB grants to you (either an individual or entity) a nonexclusive license to use one copy of the enclosed software program(s) (collectively, the "Software") solely for your own personal or business purposes on a single computer (whether a standard computer or a workstation component of a multiuser network). The Software is in use on a computer when it is loaded into temporary memory (RAM) or installed into permanent memory (hard disk, CD-ROM, or other storage device). IDGB reserves all rights not expressly granted herein.

2. <u>Ownership</u>. IDGB is the owner of all right, title, and interest, including copyright, in and to the compilation of the Software recorded on the disk(s) or CD-ROM ("Software Media"). Copyright to the individual programs recorded on the Software Media is owned by the author or other authorized copyright owner of each program. Ownership of the Software and all proprietary rights relating thereto remain with IDGB and its licensers.

3. <u>Restrictions On Use and Transfer</u>.

   (a) You may only (i) make one copy of the Software for backup or archival purposes, or (ii) transfer the Software to a single hard disk, provided that you keep the original for backup or archival purposes. You may not (i) rent or lease the Software, (ii) copy or reproduce the Software through a LAN or other network system or through any computer subscriber system or bulletin-board system, or (iii) modify, adapt, or create derivative works based on the Software.

   (b) You may not reverse engineer, decompile, or disassemble the Software. You may transfer the Software and user documentation on a permanent basis, provided that the transferee agrees to accept the terms and conditions of this Agreement and you retain no copies. If the Software is an update or has been updated, any transfer must include the most recent update and all prior versions.

4. **Restrictions On Use of Individual Programs**. You must follow the individual requirements and restrictions detailed for each individual program in the "What's on the CD-ROM" appendix of this Book. These limitations are also contained in the individual license agreements recorded on the Software Media. These limitations may include a requirement that after using the program for a specified period of time, the user must pay a registration fee or discontinue use. By opening the Software packet(s), you will be agreeing to abide by the licenses and restrictions for these individual programs that are detailed in the "What's on the CD-ROM" appendix and on the Software Media. None of the material on this Software Media or listed in this Book may ever be redistributed, in original or modified form, for commercial purposes.

5. **Limited Warranty**.

(a) IDGB warrants that the Software and Software Media are free from defects in materials and workmanship under normal use for a period of sixty (60) days from the date of purchase of this Book. If IDGB receives notification within the warranty period of defects in materials or workmanship, IDGB will replace the defective Software Media.

(b) **IDGB AND THE AUTHORS OF THE BOOK DISCLAIM ALL OTHER WARRANTIES, EXPRESS OR IMPLIED, INCLUDING WITHOUT LIMITATION IMPLIED WARRANTIES OF MERCHANTABILITY AND FITNESS FOR A PARTICULAR PURPOSE, WITH RESPECT TO THE SOFTWARE, THE PROGRAMS, THE SOURCE CODE CONTAINED THEREIN, AND/OR THE TECHNIQUES DESCRIBED IN THIS BOOK. IDGB DOES NOT WARRANT THAT THE FUNCTIONS CONTAINED IN THE SOFTWARE WILL MEET YOUR REQUIREMENTS OR THAT THE OPERATION OF THE SOFTWARE WILL BE ERROR FREE.**

(c) This limited warranty gives you specific legal rights, and you may have other rights that vary from jurisdiction to jurisdiction.

6. **Remedies**.

(a) IDGB's entire liability and your exclusive remedy for defects in materials and workmanship shall be limited to replacement of the Software Media, which may be returned to IDGB with a copy of your receipt at the following address: Software Media Fulfillment Department, Attn.: *Network+ Certification Study System*, IDG Books Worldwide, Inc., 7260 Shadeland Station, Ste. 100, Indianapolis, IN 46256, or call 1-800-762-2974. Please allow three to four weeks for delivery. This Limited Warranty is void if failure of the Software Media has resulted from accident, abuse, or misapplication. Any replacement Software Media will be warranted for the remainder of the original warranty period or thirty (30) days, whichever is longer.

(b) In no event shall IDGB or the authors be liable for any damages whatsoever (including without limitation damages for loss of business profits, business interruption, loss of business information, or any other pecuniary loss) arising from the use of or inability to use the Book or the Software, even if IDGB has been advised of the possibility of such damages.

(c) Because some jurisdictions do not allow the exclusion or limitation of liability for consequential or incidental damages, the above limitation or exclusion may not apply to you.

7. <u>U.S. Government Restricted Rights</u>. Use, duplication, or disclosure of the Software by the U.S. Government is subject to restrictions stated in paragraph (c)(1)(ii) of the Rights in Technical Data and Computer Software clause of DFARS 252.227-7013, and in subparagraphs (a) through (d) of the Commercial Computer—Restricted Rights clause at FAR 52.227-19, and in similar clauses in the NASA FAR supplement, when applicable.

8. <u>General</u>. This Agreement constitutes the entire understanding of the parties and revokes and supersedes all prior agreements, oral or written, between them and may not be modified or amended except in a writing signed by both parties hereto that specifically refers to this Agreement. This Agreement shall take precedence over any other documents that may be in conflict herewith. If any one or more provisions contained in this Agreement are held by any court or tribunal to be invalid, illegal, or otherwise unenforceable, each and every other provision shall remain in full force and effect.

BFQ FEATURES:

Each database contains 200 to 1000 questions
Easy to installation
Easy to upgrade
Multiple choice questions
Performance based questions
Answers randomized
Questions randomized
Print one question
Print a category of questions
Cheat key or Flash Card option
Single module studies
Instant question feedback
Simulation exam studies
Adaptive exam studies
Instant exam feedback
Skills assessment
Statistical analysis
Historical analysis
Individual exam analysis
Resizable screen
Font selection
Explanations
Graphics
References
User Notes creation
Passing Guaranteed or your money back (With full version purchase)
Free version updates via e-mail
Links to Lab exercises
Links to Web resources
Links to Electronic book content

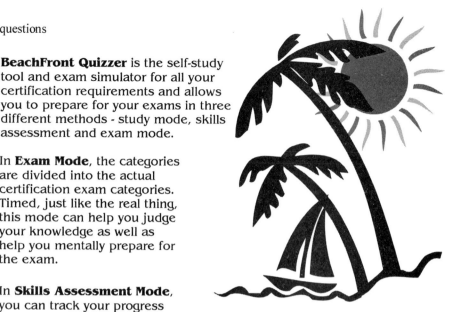

BeachFront Quizzer is the self-study tool and exam simulator for all your certification requirements and allows you to prepare for your exams in three different methods - study mode, skills assessment and exam mode.

In **Exam Mode**, the categories are divided into the actual certification exam categories. Timed, just like the real thing, this mode can help you judge your knowledge as well as help you mentally prepare for the exam.

In **Skills Assessment Mode**, you can track your progress by requesting questions that are basic, intermediate, advanced or a mix of all three.

In **Study Mode**, subject areas are divided into logical areas of preparation. You can choose areas on which to focus your efforts, or select questions from all areas. A new question appears automatically only if you answer the initial question correctly.

Understanding BeachFrontQuizzer:

Study Session

BeachFrontQuizzer tests your knowledge as you learn about various operating systems or applications through interactive quiz sessions. Study Session Questions are selected from a single database for each session, dependent on the subcategory selected and the number of times each question has been previously answered correctly. In this way, questions you have answered correctly are not repeated until you have answered all the new questions. Questions that you have missed previously will reappear in later sessions and keep coming back to haunt you until you get the question correct. In addition, you can track your progress by displaying the number of questions you have answered with the Historical Analysis option. You can reset the progress tracking by clicking on the Clear History button. Each time a question is presented the answers are randomized so you will memorize a pattern or letter that goes with the question. You will start to memorize the correct answer that goes with the question concept.

Standard and Adaptive Practice Exams

For advanced users, BeachFrontQuizzer also provides Standard and Adaptive simulated certification exams. Questions are chosen at random from the database. The Standard Exam presents a specific number of questions directly related to the real exam. The Adaptive Exam presents a Minimum of 15 Questions with a maximum number of questions ranging from 25 to 35 questions depending on the exam. After you finish the exam, BeachFrontQuizzer displays your score and the passing score required for the BFQ test. You may display the exam results of this specific exam from this menu. You may review each question, display the correct answer, identify a resource, link to an available electronic book and view an explanation for the answer.

"The FAST way to YOUR success!"

CD-ROM INSTALLATION INSTRUCTIONS

Each software item on the *Network+ Certification Study System* CD-ROM is located in its own folder. To install a particular piece of software, open its folder with My Computer or Internet Explorer. What you do next depends on what you find in the software's folder:

1. First, look for a ReadMe.txt file or a .doc or .htm document. If this is present, it should contain installation instructions and other useful information.

2. If the folder contains an executable (.exe) file, this is usually an installation program. Often it will be called Setup.exe or Install.exe, but in some cases the filename reflects an abbreviated version of the software's name and version number. Run the .exe file to start the installation process.

3. In the case of some simple software, the .exe file probably is the software — no real installation step is required. You can run the software from the CD to try it out. If you like it, copy it to your hard disk and create a Start menu shortcut for it.

The ReadMe.txt file in the CD-ROM's root directory may contain additional installation information, so be sure to check it.

For a listing of the software on the CD-ROM, see Appendix E.